YOU'RE NOT BROKE *YOU'RE * PRE-RICH **

YOU'RE NOT BROKE *YOU'RE* *** PRE-RICH ***

How to streamline your finances, stay in control of your bank balance & have more £££

EMILIE BELLET

Dedicated to you! May you find your financial independence 🤩.

An Hachette UK Company
www.hachette.co.uk

First published in Great Britain in 2019 by Cassell, a division of Octopus Publishing Group Ltd, Carmelite House, 50 Victoria Embankment, London EC4Y 0DZ
www.octopusbooks.co.uk

ISBN 978-1-78840-141-8

A CIP catalogue record for this book is available from the British Library.

Printed and bound in UK.

10 9 8 7 6 5 4 3 2 1

Disclaimer

Contents

INTRODUCTION

The Meeting

A few years ago, I booked a meeting with a financial adviser. Not really knowing what to expect I tried to gather my basic money information together, so I took a quick look at my bank balance – surprised by how little was in there – and tried to find the login details for my pension but couldn't get hold of them. I realized it would be the first real money conversation I had ever had. I was half-excited, half-wary of the unknown but I knew it was a necessary step on the road to adulthood. But it also had to be a quick one as I had work to finish.

I jumped on the Tube during my short lunch break and navigated my way to the building, trying not to be shoved and jabbed by someone on a phone wearing a suit. After a short wait, a very quick glance at the *Financial Times* and my Blackberry, I was invited to join the meeting by an assistant.

The room was an identikit of nearly every other office in the City, an expanse of white.

Good afternoon. Welcome, Mrs Bellet.
Thank you, good afternoon. Nice to meet you.

I tried to look relaxed but for some reason I didn't feel at ease at all. Perhaps this was always the case when you came face to face with a financial adviser for the first time, or perhaps it was just a feeling of not belonging? Although I, too, was wearing a suit...

The adviser started speaking:
You're here to talk about financial advice. Do you know how it works?
Looking at my blank face, he continued:
Oh, and where is your husband?

Where is Your Husband?

This question sent me into a fit of rage. Did this adviser not think that I was capable of managing my own finances? Maybe I had money of my own? Why on earth did I and my at-the-time *partner* (by the way) have to do this together? Was I not good enough to work with this adviser? Was I not good enough, full stop? Honestly, I can barely remember the rest of the meeting.

I was not born a feminist, but experiences like this can finally open your eyes to the real world and it shaped who I became.

I may not be Michelle Obama or Maya Angelou. But I'm enough. My name is Emilie Bellet, and I am the founder of a London-based start-up called Vestpod.

'Too Big to Fail' or How I Ended up Working in Finance

Looking back, I don't think I ever had a conversation about money when I was growing up, talking about money was considered taboo, even vulgar. In France you usually don't talk about money, even less than here in the UK. And I never received any formal financial education.

So, I *ended up* in finance rather than *deciding* to work in finance. Some people always know the path they will follow, but I didn't. I started doing an internship for a French bank before finishing my studies aged 23 when around 100 of us selected from top schools and universities all over Europe started a summer internship in a prestigious American bank. We arrived in Canary Wharf – London's financial district – for our induction week and were informed that our time would be a mix of training, placements, mentoring and networking to get a job by the end of the summer. My English was quite basic and definitely not good enough to follow a conversation in a loud pub but here I was: in the middle of 'the £££ show'.

I ended up working in private equity for Lehman Brothers – an investment activity where a fund (a pool of money) buys and manages companies that are not publicly traded. It was fascinating. I was working with smart people, analyzing businesses and transactions and meeting business owners. I also had the security of a well-paid job in London, allowing me to live fully, sometimes extravagantly, in the early years.

Over the years, I also got used to always being the only woman at the table, in meetings and at the pub. The financial world had been built by men and women just weren't part of it – yet.

I thought I had chosen a safe path for my career, an often challenging but stable route. But then the shock happened. What I thought was right and strong fell apart. On 15 September 2008, my employer filed for bankruptcy. This turned out to be the biggest bankruptcy in history and it became forever synonymous with the global financial crisis. It had a negative impact on huge numbers of people's lives and I was right in the middle of it all. I was 25 years old.

Being an insider made me aware of the huge financial literacy gap, the massive disconnect between banks and financial institutions and the public. Our generation, who lived through the Lehman bankruptcy and the financial crisis, believed we could trust the strong economic model that had been in place for hundreds of years, that it could never fail, indeed that it was invincible.

But we can't think like this anymore. We are responsible for our own future. We have to save to be able to fund a longer life than previous generations – possibly with fluctuating income, no job and no social benefit protection. There is massive pension deficit, and people won't have enough to retire on. How do we start to take responsibility for our money and safeguard our future in an age of financial enlightenment?

Banking: How it Works

Customers are either ignored or patronized by financial institutions. Banks continue to build more complex products to sell to uneducated consumers who struggle to follow the jargon. This, coupled with a lack of trust, makes customers feel completely lost. Financial advice is expensive and not inclusive. It's hard to find young advisers, especially women, who can give accessible advice to people like you and me. This gap has even been identified by the financial regulator (FCA), which is why recently we have seen so many apps for money management and investing, as the industry tries to reach a broader market. In the modern digital world, critical information has become submerged under a deluge of useless information. We now have too much choice, and all the alternatives make us feel overwhelmed, which leads to us either to make bad decisions or become incapable of any decision...

Now, more than ever, we need to get the conversation started. From peer-to-peer up the whole chain. My girlfriends are smart lawyers, financiers, product designers, founders, teachers, CEOs, strategists, marketing stars, freelancers and writers, but we all have one thing in common: we don't talk about money.

We know it's there, we know we have to start doing something about it, but we don't – time after time. You also don't know what you don't know. It's the elephant in the room, the last taboo. And this is because talking about money is a deeply personal matter which is often entangled with our emotional behaviour and feelings of self-worth. As a result, money has a negative image: we judge, we are judged and we compare ourselves to others.

But money also helps us to be financially independent and free, to avoid oppression, to have control over our lives, and to not be accountable to anyone. Money is also power – in your hands – waiting to be utilized. Not just for your own future but also to empower others. Money helps the world go round.

We live in an age where we have to learn to make our own choices. Going to school and university is not enough to thrive today. Thanks to the development of new technologies the world has opened up these private financial institutions of power, formerly in the hands of the few. Now millions of us can enter this sphere that we have been cut off from for so long. Today, we can learn anything and what we find out will set us free.

Financial education is key to addressing this wealth gap.

Becoming an Entrepreneur

Vestpod is my second start-up. The first one was a recruitment platform for developers. Start-ups were all the rage and after months of reflection I took the leap. I think people thought I was mad, but nonetheless I left a prestigious job in private equity because I wanted to build something meaningful and write my own future. Unfortunately, it didn't work out and I ended up having to close down the start-up and shortly after became pregnant with my first child. It was the first personal risk I had ever taken.

I started Vestpod as a blog with the help of two amazing writers: Veronica and Melissa. We prepared weekly newsletters talking about money issues and it immediately felt different from what we had seen before: fun, energetic and visual. The newsletter began to reach thousands of inboxes every week; Vestpod started to deliver workshops on personal finances and build a strong community of women who wanted to talk about money. And we, in turn, wanted to empower women financially.

I am not a financial adviser (and you may want to work with one, although perhaps not the one I met with), but I am passionate about finance and investing and I have been interviewing experts for a few years, in order to be a better money communicator. However, what has proven the most instructive and effective education has been meeting the women at Vestpod events and workshops, where we have shared our money challenges and fears, hopes and tears. Together, we're building something unique.

I haven't re-invented money management and personal finance but I have thoroughly researched and analysed everything I preach – and indeed have practised it myself. I like to be organized and rely on numbers but I also need chaos and flexibility. I never count every penny and, like everyone, I waste some of my money. So, whether you're a total finance newbie, or a more advanced money manager, I know there will be something in these concepts and conversations over the next 355 pages that will help you.

This is not a book about getting rich quickly – it's about embarking on a journey, building healthier habits, confirming knowledge and supporting each other. It's easy to get started on this adventure.

You're Not Broke You're Pre-Rich covers pretty much all of money management but it only touches the surface, as I want it to be broad, simple and full of topics that you can research further, armed with sufficient understanding to explore the financial landscape even more.

You can read this book in one go (or two) but you can also pick it up and find the specific £££ information you are looking for. Please, take it with you to meet your bank or your adviser, friends or partner. It is not exhaustive but it will certainly help you to build a strong foundation of financial concepts. It will boost your confidence and empower you financially.

The following chapters will give you the tools and guidance to start to optimize your financial life. It starts with you, with me. But tomorrow, where do we take it? To others, to the world, to all those who need this information and will continue to need it in the future.

I feel compelled to spread the word and I hope you will too, after finishing this book.

Remember: you're pre-rich!

Emilie xx

How to use this Book

The topic of money can be seen to be a bit boring and complicated. But it really doesn't have to be! We have designed these little smileys and key to help you to navigate the book easily – come back to these pages at any time to remind yourself what we are talking about.

£££ **Money. Money. Money.**

Happy Haha. This just makes us happy or smile.

Sad Grrr. This makes us sad or angry (i.e. statistics on the gender pay gap).

Warning Read this. It is important, always check it out (i.e. regulations change all the time).

Discovery Wow. Something you maybe did not know or that is worth discovering. We find these really cool (i.e. how to make money selling your old clothes).

Other resources Where can I find more information or learn more on this subject? (i.e. books, podcasts, websites).

Tips Money hacks and things that we have tried that should make your life easier.

Action Enough talking, start doing. This is your turn. These are blank spaces for you to fill in your goals, your numbers, your £££... (if you like!) and examples.

Apps What apps are we using?

Help Who can help us to do this: a financial adviser, a good website, a debt charity?

Conclusion 1 Each time you finish reading a chapter, you earn one beautiful gold knowledge coin. You have earned one coin learning about your money personality.

Conclusion 2 You understand where you are today with your money: two coins.

Conclusion 3 You have built a plan for your life and you know more or less how much it will cost you: three coins.

Conclusion 4 By understanding your spending habits and budgeting methods, you earn the fourth coin.

Conclusion 5 Asking for more £££? That means earning the fifth coin.

Conclusion 6 Looking at your bank balances allows you to get the sixth coin... getting wealthier!

Conclusion 7 We talk about investing here, so if you think you will learn new things you get the seventh coin.

Conclusion 8 How does the 'stock market' work? Are you ready to invest? You read you earn: plus eight coins in your wallet.

Conclusion 9 Do you want to get on the property ladder? By learning the tricks, you've earned your ninth coin!

1. The first chapter is all about discovering or re-imagining our **money story**. What is money for you? Do you talk about money? We will look at money studies to try to understand where money stands in our lives and how we can manage our relationship with it, learning that it is not net worth but self-worth we need when we start out.

2. The second chapter is about **your financial situation**. Where do you stand? How to know where you are today?

3. The third chapter is about **where you want to go**. What are your dreams? What does the journey look like? Because without a plan we find it hard to achieve our dreams.

4. The fourth chapter deals with getting a grip on your money. How much do you earn? How much do you spend? It provides **budgeting rules** and ideas to better manage your income and spending as well as cutting costs. This will help you feel in control of what's leaving your account every month and allow you to start building and accumulating your wealth.

5. In the fifth chapter, we will talk about **earning more** £££. Because money is out there, it's just a matter of getting it...

6. The sixth chapter is about **navigating your bank balance**, the jargon-busting chapter that will help you understand the best places to save and invest money. How is a pension different from an ISA? How do you choose a savings account? How do you care for your hard-earned saved money?

7–9. The final chapters are all about **investing**. And I wrote them with you in mind. We are not talking about the Wolf of Wall Street; investing is an essential, long-term strategy once you have mastered basic money management. We will look at how investing works and then what you can invest in, with chapters on the 'stock' market and property.

I am not a financial advisor! The content of this book is provided for information and educational purposes only and it does not constitute financial advice. You should consult with an independent financial advisor for specific guidance on your personal circumstances.

CHAPTER 1: WHAT IS MONEY?

* *

What you will learn in this chapter:
What does money mean to you?
Does it make you happy? How can you use it to make you happier?
How we can talk more freely and usefully about our finances?

* *

'IT'S NOT REALLY ABOUT THE MONEY – IT'S ABOUT THE FREEDOM'

Money: we all use it, earn it (or inherit it) or want more of it. When there is enough, it can help to make us happy but can also make us want more – which breeds unhappiness. When there is not enough it makes us feel sad or stressed. Some of us manage it well, some of us not so well. Some learnt about managing money when growing up, others by reading and some by navigating choppy financial waters all by themselves. Some may try to ignore it or forget about it, others may love it or be obsessed by it. How we feel about money and the role it plays in our lives changes over the course of our days, months and years.

Alongside love, health, time, relationships, politics and career, money plays one of the most important and personal roles in our lives. But it is the one currency that we do not have the words to talk about. How would you feel if someone asked you a question about your finances? Even worse, how would you feel if you were asked how much you owed or how much you managed to save each month, rather than depleting your bank account down to the last penny? Do you see what I mean?

EXERCISE

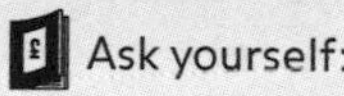

Ask yourself:

Do you like to spend money or to save money?
Did you have money growing up?
Do you trust yourself with your money?
Does it make you feel worthy?
Do you judge people by how much they make?

We have all been there: struggling to pay for stuff and being so used to having an overdraft that we can no longer cope without one. Research shows that majority of adults are stressed about money and debt. When did this start to happen? Why are we all so stressed out by not managing our money well? And why are none of us talking about it?

You're Not Broke You're Pre-Rich will empower you to take care of money, talk more openly about your feelings around money; because it will take care of you in return. This first chapter is 100% about emotions: it's just you and your money mindset.

After All, What is Money?

Your attitude toward money is the unseen currency that governs every part of your waking day: it is the reason you go to work, it is a motivator for whether or not you apply to go to university, it is related to how you shop and to what you do or do not buy, it helps to drive how hard you work in the hope of a promotion or a pay rise. Money is so central to our lives that it literally controls and governs us all, and because of its all-pervasive role, most of us spend most of our time trying very hard not to think about it; or even try to actively ignore it. Certainly, very few people are aware of their own emotional responses toward money. Why? Partly because they feel too busy to think about it. Partly because it seems too boring and difficult to think about. But the major reason we do not pay more attention toward our money is because – it terrifies us.

Ironically, understanding money gives us greater financial freedom. But to discover this we first need to take a step back from the merry-go-round of spending, borrowing and debt denial. In order to build a more intimate relationship with our money, we need to ask ourselves some tough questions. Together, we will cross-examine ourselves and analyse why money makes us feel so emotional and what we can do to build a better relationship with it.

Just before you run for the hills and think this all sounds too hard, it is *never* too late to start and *now* is the time! You already deserve a lot of praise and a proverbial round of applause or taking this massive step (and not closing this book when I told you it was going to get tough).

Ok, let's get to work... stay with me here.

Emotional money

A few years ago, while working in banking, I remember having lunch with a friend. Our conversation somehow turned to our salaries and she asked me point-blank how much I was earning. I freaked out and said I couldn't tell her. I am not sure whether this was because I felt I was earning too much (which I didn't feel I deserved, even though I was often working 15-hour days) or because I worried she would feel devalued if I told her my income.

Often, our negative relationship with money can seem hard to overcome . The problem is we feel so many complex and deep emotions around our finances: shame, embarrassment, greed, fear, pity, remorse, paranoia... as well as excitement, hope, relief, inspiration and desire. The next time you are feeling down about being in debt, or failing to save any money, for yet another month, ask yourself how you would talk to a friend if she/he came to you with the same problem? If your best friend called you up to say, 'I'm never going to save up enough for a deposit... I'm just rubbish with money. I don't understand how I've let myself down. I have always been hopeless with money.' What would you say? Probably something much more empathetic than the words you use to castigate yourself with. After all, you believe your friend can change his or her ways, and you are sure that they must not give up. You would encourage your friend to find out where she/he is going wrong with budgeting and to work out a plan to change it. Now try saying the same things to yourself.

The next time you find your heart sinking as you look at your depleted bank statement, think to yourself: *next time I will do better.*

But let us also examine the excuses we make, and find out what has stalled us so far on our money journey. Once again, it is all about emotions:

When money makes me feel good, I feel...

- *Proud:* I am making money, i.e. I am successful!
- *Excited:* I just got paid! I've won the lottery! (Ok ... maybe not.)

- *Relieved:* I deserved this bonus, which means I am good enough and I can pay off my overdraft.
- *Safe:* When I earn money, I feel safe and protected from losing all I have built around me.

When money makes me feel bad, I feel...

- *Jealous:* Remembering there will always be someone richer than me out there.
- *Anxiety and fear:* The deep-rooted fear of not having enough and of losing it all.
- *Stress:* Will I run out of money? Where has all my money gone?
- *Embarrassment:* Will my card actually work when I pay for this business lunch?
- *Regret:* I should never have bought that; I can't afford it and I don't deserve it.
- *Vulgar:* Is it acceptable to talk about it? Is my salary too much/too little?
- *Greedy:* Money is power and I want more and more and more of it.

When money makes me feel good and bad at the same time I feel...

- *Embarrassed:* At being successful and attracting attention, as well as feeling that I don't deserve it.
- *Like an imposter:* Comparing how much I earn with how good I think I am.

It's OK to feel *all* of these emotions, we just need to acknowledge what we feel and understand why we feel the way we do. Money is so deeply personal that we each have our own 'money script' that controls our financial beliefs and systems. Do any of these comments sound familiar?

- *I don't have a clue about personal finances.*
- *I don't have willpower.*
- *I'm terrible with numbers.*
- *I don't earn enough to save any money.*
- *I don't have enough left over to invest any money.*
- *I don't deserve to be earning this much.*

All these thoughts, expectations, emotions and feelings arise from our ingrained beliefs, and when they are negative they paralyse us, preventing us from making good, logical financial decisions. Ultimately, they prevent us from getting what we want.

Our money mindset has a direct effect on how we manage and deal with our finances. These beliefs are based on habits and systems that we have adopted over time. Some of them are rational and supported by logic, but others can be very irrational and supported by the emotional turbulence that surrounds money. It is important that we recognize our false beliefs and call them out, so that we can address and tackle them.

For example, you may have received a letter from HMRC stating that you owe a lot of money in taxes. You had totally miscalculated what you owed and you feel a sense of panic. Fortunately, you are able to pay your bill promptly, so you can file the letter and try to forget about it. But what you don't address is the spate of emotions you have experienced through this experience. Feelings of stress and anxiety can manifest as low self-worth, with thoughts of, 'I am not good with money', 'I don't know how to manage money.' Whatever our age and situation, this level of emotional wrangling can influence our internal dialogue. Instead we need to swap thoughts such as, 'I can't', 'don't know how', 'it's too hard' for a new mindset of, 'I can', 'I will' and 'I will get better and better'. This positive rewiring will help transform your fears into achievable goals.

You're Not Broke You're Pre-Rich focuses on establishing a *new mindset,* by seeing your money problems, not as failure but as challenges that you will overcome. I want to stop you reaching for negativity when something goes wrong, and start to believe instead that getting things wrong is a necessary stepping stone towards getting things (and keeping them) right. Altering your mindset in this way will help you to become more rational about money and less controlled by your emotions; this in turn will allow you to take control of your money opposed to being controlled by it.

EXERCISE

What are the things you tell yourself about money? What are your beliefs?

- ....
- ....
- ....
- ....

What's my money story?

Have you ever wondered why you handle money the way you do today? Where do your overspending habits come from? Why can't you resist the temptation of buying? It not as simple as whether you think of yourself as a saver or a spender, since truthfully, everyone is a bit of both. Our spending and saving patterns are determined by our habits, emotions and values, and what can really help us to reflect on our motives is to identify our *money personality*.

Our behaviour towards money is dictated by an inbuilt script or 'money algorithm', which has been written into our lives over time. This is the theory underpinning the concept of financial personality types, put forward by psychologists Brad Klontz and Ted Klontz in their research on money, beliefs and financial behaviours[1]. They studied people's attitudes toward spending, saving and investing money and, based on 72 commonly heard money 'scripts', identified four distinct groups with differing beliefs related to money: money worship (accumulating worth), money status (social differentiation), money vigilance (keeping money issues private) and money avoidance (avoiding money issues).

I think that these characteristics can be easily be applied to animals in the animal kingdom. This exercise is a very quick screening tool, which can help identify how you feel about money.

Animals	**LION**	**PEACOCK**	**ANT**	**HONEY BADGER**
	Money worship	Money status	Money vigilance	Money avoidance
Money Scripts	Do you idolize money? Do you see it as an almost mythical key to everlasting happiness?	Is money a status tool for success? Is money linked to your self-worth?	Does money make you uncomfort-able? Or is it a taboo subject?	Do you see money as negative? Are you against either you or others having more of it?
Top factor highlighted by the study authors	'More money will make me happier.'	'Most poor people do not deserve to have money.'	'You should not tell others how much you have or make.'	'I do not deserve a lot of money when other have less than me.'
In reality:	*I think money will make me happy and will solve my problems.* *I tend to overspend, and take risks.* *I do not pay my credit card in full at the end of the month.*	*I want to show off in front of my peers.* *I tend to overspend and lose control of spending.*	*I hide money under my mattress.* *I lie about the cost of certain things I buy.* *Money is a sensitive subject.*	*I don't want to manage my money.* *I am worried about credit cards and overspending.*

The findings of the Klontz study helps us to name and identify our beliefs around money and allows us to see whether they have any self-destructive side-effects or are influencing our use and abuse of money. Our beliefs have a knock-on effect on our ability to attain financial goals and independent financial security. According to the study, 'individuals who adhere to the avoidance, worship, and/or status groups are more likely to have lower levels of education, income, and net-worth. It is not possible to determine whether the money beliefs precede education and income attainment or whether the lower levels of education and income lead to certain beliefs about money. It is simply known that there is an association between them to be aware of [when working with clients around money].'

EXERCISE

So which animal do you identify with?

*Do you avoid opening letters from the bank? (Many people do.) – You are a **Honey badger***

*Do you strive to buy symbols of the success you so desperately want others to know about? – You are a **Lion***

*Do you worry about your overspending but don't seem to be able to afford your lifestyle without it? – You are a **Peacock***

*Do you try to live frugally and yet, never have any cash at the end of the month? – You are an **Ant***

Are there other elements or characteristics that you can spot within yourself?

....

....

....

The good news is that our financial personality type is not set in stone. As with any unhelpful learnt behaviour, we need to employ self-awareness and to recognize and accept the way we behave, in order to break the cycle. Rather than seeing these as inherent issues, let's just consider them systemic glitches in the way we are currently wired. A glitch can be fixed easily and efficiently with a little bit of fine-tuning.

The Klontz study focuses on just four money scripts, however in my experience there are as many money scripts as there are individuals. It can be a bit misleading to think you have only one profile. Maybe you can try to understand your own beliefs by starting with the four different profiles, and then build one that corresponds more accurately to your own money story. Perhaps you can think of another animal that better represents your beliefs around money?

Starting to recognize why you currently behave in the way that you do, and understanding that you need to change, will drive that change. If that isn't enough to get you started, remember that by looking after your future self you are protecting and preserving a decent financial future. It is the greatest investment you can make in yourself today. This is purely practical, not emotional.

With this in mind, really try to identify your personality type and consider what aspect of your 'script' is stopping you from achieving your goals. It is so much easier to make changes once we realize our mishandling of money is due to a glitch in our internal programming rather than being an ingrained fault in us as people.

Where do our £££ glitches come from?

I don't know about you, but I never received any kind of financial education.

We often believe that managing money is complicated, that it requires an understanding of numbers, spreadsheets and complex calculations. But managing money is not rocket science. It is not technical (at least not when you first get started), and it is something we all have the capacity to understand and manage.

So how do we learn about money? According to research by the Money Advice Service (MAS)[2] and behaviour experts at Cambridge University,[3] our money habits are already set by the age of seven. I know that sounds alarming, but children absorb their parents' habits both consciously and unconsciously. By seven, you had grasped how to recognize the value of money and count it out but you were also capable of more 'complex functions such as planning ahead, delaying a decision until later and understanding that some choices are irreversible'.

EXERCISE

Do you remember some of your early memories with money: did you receive pocket money to manage? Do you remember your parents checking their bank statements and cross-checking them? Do you remember whether they negotiated the price when buying something expensive, such as a car? Was money always short, or was it never really talked about? Did they sacrifice family time to amass wealth? Did they hide cash under the mattress? Was spending or saving associated with their self-worth?

Of course, our parents learnt about money from their parents too, so we probably inherit generations of money knowledge and behaviours from an ancestral line of (mostly) unqualified people.

All the attitudes witnessed and decisions made on our behalf when we were young are now etched into our own money scripts. They are still the dominant forces to be reckoned with in our adult minds: every time a letter from the bank drops on to the doormat or we ignore the nagging sense that we are about to tip into overdraft.

Once we have accepted that we are not beholden to our feelings about money, we become freer to change the script without blaming ourselves or judging our habits too harshly. It is just like the other areas of life that we have to adjust as we get older and become a little wiser...such as eating more healthily or taking up more exercise. It may take a good few years – decades sometimes – of adult living before we can identify the habits that are no longer working for us or that do not help us achieve the life we want.

Take an honest look at what money means to you. Identify where the values came from and how they are keeping you from reaching your financial goals; and change the script until it sounds like the person you want to become.

EXERCISE

What does money mean to you? What are the things that could have impacted your relationship with money?

....

....

....

....

Apply the growth mindset to your finances

No attitude or behaviour is set in stone. Our bad financial habits may be rooted in our childhood and the money culture we were raised in, but that doesn't mean things can't be changed if you want to change them enough. Having a healthy and controlled approach to spending is something that you can build, through greater financial education and a more balanced personal outlook.

Stanford University Professor Carol Dweck specializes in the psychology of motivation, and has identified two different ways that people think: the growth mindset and the fixed mindset[4]. With a fixed mindset, we see our abilities and characteristics as set in stone. In times of stress our inner voice operates in a rigid and judgemental way: 'I'm bad with money', 'I'm so forgetful' or 'I have no willpower when it comes to spending / food / exercise.' This means that when our attempts at self-improvement go wrong, we give up. In contrast, a growth mindset sees problems as an interesting challenge and an opportunity to learn and grow, rather than a sign of failure. A growth mindset attaches no fixed negatives to getting something wrong, because it believes in the ability to constantly evolve and learn (which is a pretty cool and inspiring state to be in, rather than imprisoning yourself with your failures).

None of us are definitively 'fixed' or 'growth': we're all a combination of both. As an entrepreneur, I have developed a growth mindset over time, and I am sometimes amazed, when I look back, at how fixed my attitude was a few years ago. I still need to consciously adjust my mindset when I feel daunted by something that initially seems impossible.

For example, at work you are asked to prepare and deliver a presentation for the whole company. You have never done this before. Of course, your initial reaction would be: *I am not capable of doing this, I will say no. I am not qualified enough, why me? What if I fail? What if people don't like it and judge me?* You are looking at all the negative outcomes and obstacles. But are these real? Could you instead try asking yourself: *What are the benefits of doing this presentation? What can I learn? Where can I find the resources? Why don't I just try? Perhaps the outcome will be really positive? When I am asked to do something new, I always have this first negative reaction, but what I am trying to do is turn it into a positive... as quickly as I can!* The same growth mindset can be applied to dealing with our finances.

A big goal for most of us is to save for retirement. But a lot of people don't start, why? Because the goal can seem so big that it feels overwhelming. A glance at one of the retirement calculators can be enough to put us off ever starting. But if we break the long-term goal down into smaller goals – a specific amount this month, a plan for next year and so on – and tackle it with a 'can do' mindset, anything is achievable. If I can do it, you can too. Ultimately, understanding these two types of 'self-talk' really helped me to work towards my goals. And I hope it will help you too.

Next time things go wrong or have not turned out quite as intended (you know, the usual situation: you haven't checked your balance for a whole month and are then *surprised* to see how little money you have left) choose to approach the problem like a money detective: not as a judge or your very own worst personal critic, but as a forensic investigator who just needs to find out what, why, how and when things went awry. Was there an emotional trigger that made you spend all that money on clothes or a new piece of tech? Maybe you were nervous about not looking cool enough at a particular event? Maybe you got into an anxious tailspin about the state of your health and threw away half of your weekly budget on some mad food supplement? Once you know what you are dealing with, you can set a goal and make a plan to change the behaviour.

You can apply the same 'can-do' attitude to your personal finances: When you begin to cross examine all those doubts about your abilities, you will start to see how dull and restrictive they are. Next time you find yourself saying 'I'll never get out of debt!', remember that talking to yourself in a negative way will reinforce the frame of mind that is preventing you from making positive changes to your money habits. Rather than being short-sighted or hot-tempered with ourselves: we need to remind ourselves that we are continuing to learn! Taking lessons from the moments when we fail helps us to get better at everything we do.

Self-worth should not be dependent on your income

Your current amount of self-worth is important to take into consideration because it has an impact on how you manage your money. Because, if you don't believe in yourself, you may not believe you can earn more, or save more.

I closed my first start-up a few years ago and had my first child a year later. I went from earning a salary to earning zero. To my surprise this had a real impact on my self-worth; I felt literally without value. Too often, we measure success solely by whether or not we are employable. In our capitalist society characterized by individualism, when unemployment strikes and we lose our jobs, we blame ourselves. Researchers suggest that when we are unemployed we are at often higher risk of depression and despair.[5] The longer the period of unemployment, the more despairing we feel, with concerns that we may not be able to earn enough to protect and provide for our family, which increases feelings of guilt and worthlessness. An article in *Harvard Business Review*[6] shows that unemployment has the same effect on the confidence and the self-worth of a younger generation. The authors also looked at the negative impact of parental financial support on confidence: that is, the more assistance a person has, the less worthy they feel.

Do you assess people by how much they make? One of the ways that we value ourselves is through our ability to contribute to the economy. We constantly compare ourselves to others, looking for evidence of our status and for recognition of our perceived success. We feel we are being judged by how much money we earn, how much we spend, how we dress, what car we drive, what holidays we take and so on. This is exacerbated by the role of social media, which encourages us to share our achievements publicly. Many feel a heightened pressure to earn more, in order to spend more, in order to further validate their online status. Who has never bought something to feel more valued by others or to impress? Our relationship with our income is complex: while money is not a measure of self-worth, we perceive ourselves to still be a part of a social tribe and we are still 'hard wired to believe in hierarchy'.[7] Our need for status is difficult to ignore.

According to a study by Lora Park, an Associate Professor of Psychology at the State University of New York at Buffalo, the pursuit of wealth can have an adverse effect on mental health, promoting stress and anxiety rather than making us feel better or increasing our sense of self-worth as we might expect. Again, the issue here relates to social tribe.

How do I make the change?

Our instinct to judge and be judged is central to our belief systems as a way of ordering who is important and who isn't. This pursuit of money is dangerous and self-destructive. I want to let you know that your financial worth is NOT your self-worth. The good news is, there's a lot we can do to change our unhelpful subconscious pre-programmed settings:

1. **Identify negative thoughts:** When you receive an unexpected bill or fail to get a pay-rise, how do you react? Try to engage with the rising emotion before it becomes an active feeling: how does it make you feel or think? Does it feel like another example of failure, or further evidence of an uncaring universe? OR is it an opportunity to take stock, to plan to move forward, to make the universe work for you, and to see this an opportunity for a new approach to your life?
2. **Get educated:** Becoming money literate really helps, as it allows you to feel equipped with knowledge and ready to cope with your own crises. Whether via books, blogs, friends, TED talks, financial seminars or by taking professional advice, you are going to feel so much more empowered if you know you are doing all you can to learn about new ways of saving and spending that will work for you. Knowledge is power and power is freedom.
3. **Change your money language:** Stop thinking you don't have enough. Money in reality is abundant but you have to find smart ways to get hold of it.
4. **Be kind to yourself:** We all make mistakes and we all need to get over them to in order to move on.
5. **Stop the comparison trap:** No matter how successful you become, in whatever given field, there will always be someone who has a bigger house, more extravagant holidays and greater financial security than you. So, when your thoughts wander to the Joneses (or even the Kardashians!) with their easy life, counteract them by dwelling for a minute on all the great things that make you feel wholly unique from them.
6. **Make a plan:** Deciding on what you want and then creating a plan to achieve it results in such a good feeling, as it underpins your desire and roots it in realism. Create small, formative steps towards making the big dream achievable through small incremental manifestations.

There are lots of resources out there (and in this book) to get you started with your financial plan. If you *know* you're going to splurge when you are unhappy or under pressure, take your reactions into account when you budget, to allow for it. Or indeed find ways of satisfying your cravings with other stimulating activities that actually resolve two issues you face rather than fixating on one. Once your personal plan is in place, even your unexpected bills can be accounted for and you'll feel more in control of yourself, your finances and your life. Plus, dare I say it, you will probably have a little extra money every month to invest in yourself and your future because your budget allows for it.

This table is your path from a broke to a pre-rich mindset. *Ker-ching!* 

Stop saying 'I am broke'	Start saying 'I am pre-rich'
I can't afford it.	I can afford it by doing...
I don't have money. I am broke.	I chose to invest it in... I am pre-rich...
How much can I lose in the 'stock' market?	How much can I spare to explore the markets? (View the money invested as something you have bought; that is, you may never see this cash back, though it has greater potential value in the long term.)
How will I pay my bills?	This is my budget and there are even little savings for my goals...
It's on sale. I will buy it. Sample sale day.	It's on sale, but do I really need it? Even at this price, is it really good value for money?
I need this now...	What is the value of this purchase tomorrow / what do I need to sacrifice for this today?
I'll never be able to afford: ...to buy a house. ...to rent my own place / rent where I actually want to live. ...to go freelance. ...to travel to my dream destination.	I am making my money work for me in order to achieve.... With goals, careful planning and investing I can afford anything I want.
This is not my fault because I don't / I never... I am not responsible for this, I can't fix it...	I can make it work, wherever I'm starting from... Let's learn from this and fix it...

EXERCISE

What about you: what can you change?

Fixed mindset	Growth mindset

How do we make sure going forward money will not kill your self-worth?

In our society, we tend to consider wealth as the money we make and the things we can buy. But unfortunately, financial success alone does not provide happiness. Wealth is personal, and we should all have our own definition of what being wealthy is. Wealth for me is a support....

For example, I invite you to read Tony Robbins's books or watch his videos online. He is a celebrity life coach and bestselling author, but he wasn't born with money. Tony talks about wealth as the ability to live the life you truly want on your own terms, dream big and fulfil your life ambitions. Money helps you in this process but is not the end goal.

EXERCISE

Can you invite yourself to think for a minute about what represents 'wealth' to you?

....

....

....

....

....

Creating an identity defined solely by financial pursuits is dangerous and damaging to the psyche. Money is a great equalizer but should never become our tormentor. It will never be worth less than anyone else's, nor will it be worth more.

Let's Break the Money Taboo

When is the last time you talked about money? And when was the first time? I started talking about money relatively late in life, and only when I started building my money start-up Vestpod.

The reality is that we are not yet willing to talk about money. When researchers at University College London conducted a survey into sexual attitudes and lifestyle,[8] they found out that people were more inclined to answer questions about their intimate lives (including 'how many sexual partners they've had, whether they've had an affair, and whether they've ever contracted a sexually-transmitted disease'[9]) rather than questions about their household income.

I have since become fascinated by Refinery29's '*Money Diaries*' offering where strangers write about their anonymous spending habits and money secrets.

Why is money such a taboo?

Do we really want to tell our peers and colleagues or even our friends that we have been struggling to repay our credit card debt, or that we are addicted to shopping, or that we have no clue how much is going in and out of our bank account each month; or that we are always comparing ourselves to others (Hello Instagram...)? Well, no, we really don't. We don't want to expose our weaknesses or reveal our insecurities and vices.

There can be deeper psychological issues at work too, related to self-worth and handling responsibility. When it comes to valuing ourselves, it can be harder than it should be to stand up and say (to your boss, to your partner, and even yourself) – *I'm worth more than that.*

Most women and men have been raised not to talk about money, and the world of finance, traditionally strongly male-dominated, has made it difficult, nay impossible, for the general public (especially women) to understand its models of government. The jargon-fuelled language fuels a sense of disempowerment. Debunking this jargon, however, is incredibly important if we're ever going to break the historical taboos. Women need to be invited to the table and be educated with technical words and phrases.

Let's start the conversation...

Talking about money is liberating. Breaking the silence and oppression around anything (let alone something as personal and globally important as money) will set you free. Once you can talk about your finances freely, you can start to enter into practical and non-emotional conversations about your own worth and value.

While the financial markets have become increasingly more sophisticated, households have been forced to take bigger risks and assume greater responsibilities. There has never been a greater need for financial literacy. Our level of financial understanding plays a crucial role in equalizing the wealth playing field and reducing the divisive impact of money. Having sound financial knowledge helps us to make better-informed decisions, save more for retirement, manage investments carefully, and better manage the household finances; all of which improves our safety and provides more options. On the other hand, those who are financially ill-informed rarely make efficient choices and are likely to incur more debt and save less; all of which can have disastrous consequences for life and health.

There needs to be greater focus on providing access to better financial education for all, including in schools and universities. Financial literacy training should be provided in the workplace, and to the ever-increasing number of self-employed people too.

We are in desperate need of education and a good confidence boost; we need to engage with the subject of money – voluntarily. Money has the power to change our lives; it can unlock personal potential because it has power, and influences so many aspects of our society. Once you are in charge of your finances, you can decide to be better with money.

Breaking the money taboo starts on the micro-level by talking with friends, family, strangers or finance professionals. There is no right or wrong way to have these conversations; you just need to start. Slowly your financial awareness will start to click in, and this greater understanding will allow you to have easier macro-level conversations with your employer or others: to negotiate a proper salary, understand how your pension works, negotiate with your bank for a better type of card or better saving rates, or with your lender for a mortgage. Once we finally and totally own and control the world of money that spins around us, we will also save money!

Money talk with your partner

Talk about emotions? OK. Talk about money? *Sorry... what?!* Talking about money in relationships is the equivalent of facing the final frontier. The issue could be something as glaringly obvious as one partner having a massive student debt, or something more subtle, such as the financial culture each partner grew up in. If you need to brace yourself for these necessary conversations, remind yourself that to develop equality within a relationship, you each need to know what the other is bringing to the table; and yes that includes your salaries, debt and other £££ secrets.

According to a research by the Money Advice Service,[10] many people keep secrets from their partners: one in ten married UK adults has an 'escape fund' in case they want to leave; 13% have a 'secret stash of cash' that their spouse doesn't know about. Even more shocking is that almost three in every ten adults in the UK have had a partner who they later found out was in serious debt. Why do we not communicate? Does this show a lack of trust? Shame, lack of self-worth, the fear of what a partner might say or do? Perhaps a past relationship did not end well because of the same issue, or someone advised you not to say anything. We need to understand why we keep this secret, or what we feel we would lose if were to reveal it.

Ultimately, relationships thrive on trust, and trust is heightened by total transparency. Are you ready to expose all your money matters to your partner? A study from Utah State University[11] concluded that if a couple argues about money more than once a week, they are 30% more likely to split up – which is a pretty scary statistic.

You and your partner will have different money mindsets and if you haven't done the exercise above already, (see page 22) or tackled where you fit on the fulfilment curve, then now is the time for both of you to do this together. There is no point engaging in the conversation if you don't know where you stand. Be objective and try to understand both of your behaviours and mindsets instead of casting judgement.

EXERCISE

A good way to get started is to frankly discuss household or other common expenses. Since you're spending lots of time together, could you decide who pays what, or alternate and prepare the accounts at the end of the month to see where your collective money has gone.

While money conversations with partners are not necessarily mandatory when we're still legally single, they do become important when we get married because they impact grander decisions: do you want to buy a house, have kids, change jobs, chose to pay for your children's education – like it or not, you're in this together. Even if you decide to keep your finances separate you have to understand how it works for the household, for your protection (does your partner have debts?) and for your choices (will we be able to live on one salary for the other to start a business, for example).

You need to discuss openly how you both spend money, what seems expensive to you both and how much money you want to earn. This can enable the trickier conversation surrounding how much your partner earns. According to a study by Fidelity,[12] 43% of couples failed to identify how much their partner earned, and 10% of those were off 'by $25,000 or more'.

Share knowledge: Knowing each other's salaries is key if you are to take shared financial decisions. Can you afford to buy a house or a car? Can you risk investing some money? Can you afford a holiday? Ignoring this information leaves you both in the dark and becomes difficult to be financially aligned. You want to work together towards common goals.

Schedule time to talk: You can also schedule a regular conversation to talk about money matters: find a time and place where you can be undisturbed for an hour – perhaps in a neutral space – then sit down together to 'do the books'. This offers time for you to raise concerns and brainstorm future financial plans, which could involve your pensions and your property. These are topics you would never choose to bring up over dinner, after a hard day at work – and nor should you, because you'd probably be starting from a place of stress and exhaustion. It becomes much easier to discuss these matters calmly at a specific, designated time.

Create a budget: I will say this many times during the book. It may seem obvious, but setting a budget really does take the stress out of your personal finance, and if you are setting the budget as a couple, you are sharing the load and the responsibility (and guilt if you break it.)

Ask questions – and really listen to the answers: If you feel annoyed or perplexed by your partner's spending habits, don't attack them. Try to understand where they have stemmed from. Ask them how money was talked about in their family growing up. Find out what their hopes are regarding property, retirement and their career. Perhaps you could each determine your money animal (see page 23) and discuss which of that animal's characteristics you identify with? This could help you, for example, to recognize the similarities and differences in your approaches to spending and saving. The over-arching goal is to feel as though you're in this together: You love each other, right? So, you needn't feel ashamed or apportion blame every time you are overdrawn – and bear in mind that a hidden overdraft or debt, if discovered, could highlight issues around trust, lead to one partner starting to 'parent' the other or put so much pressure on the relationship that it ends in separation. Keep the channels of communication open and your finances will be healthier for it.

Money talk with friends

Friendship groups can be surprisingly riddled with money fear and shame. Sure, we have fun together, but are we prepared to admit when we can't afford to go on a night out, or on a hen do, or to buy a new outfit for that birthday supper? Are we willing to admit that we earn a lot more money than they do; or a lot less?

For the sake of friendship, we all need to open up a bit about our budget woes or saving worries. One of us needs to enable the others to feel as though it is safe to speak real money truths. If they are true friends, not only will they sympathise but they will probably start to discuss the problems that they are facing too. Be honest and declare your salary and your outgoings, it will also help you to see if you are managing your money well and may help you work out whether it is worth finding somewhere cheaper to rent or to buy your food shopping. Whatever you discover by speaking frankly, you will discover a greater sense of what money means to your friends.

START A DISCUSSION!

Here are some questions I like to use to start a money discussion. Let's keep it casual and have coffee or a glass (or two) of wine.

- **How do you feel about money right now?**
- **Anything weighing on your mind/ affecting your outlook?**
- **How was money growing up? Did you have a lot/not a lot?**
- **Did you have any pocket money growing up?**
- **Did you use to talk about money with your parents?**
- **Why should we have this conversation?**
- **What is money for you? A means, a goal, something stressful, something cool?!**
- **What's is my/your challenge when it comes to money?**
- **How much money do you need to live on?**
- **What are your goals when it comes to life and how do they translate in £-terms?**

Money talk at work

A few years ago, while I was working long hours one weekend at the office, I found a list of all the team's salaries lying on top of the printer. Exciting, awkward, powerful? A bit of all three. It gave me knowledge and allowed me to discover who was paid the same, more or less than I was. I could then find allies and start an open conversation about our collective salaries. (*Lesson:* Hang out by the printer, it can pay off.) 🤩

Had that not happened, I don't think I would ever have sat down with co-workers after work to discuss how much they had earned in the preceding month. Finding a neutral space where everyone can compare salaries (unemotionally, mind) could help all of you to get the remuneration you deserve. Sure, not every office culture can support this, but if you suspect you are being underpaid in comparison to a colleague with the same title, you owe it to yourself to open up. You need to find out if you are being paid fairly. And only you and your employer can figure this out and fix it.

PayScale[13] is a US company that specializes in cloud compensation data and software for businesses and individuals. When conducting a survey of more than 500,000 people they found out that employee satisfaction is driven largely by feeling that the wage system is fair and transparent at their organization. Due to recent gender pay gap rules enforced by the government, we are now in a better place to ask questions and call out any unfair treatment. All companies could and should disclose their pay bands and if yours doesn't, start the conversation by asking 'why not?'

→ Head over to Chapter 5 for some inspiration on earning more and salary negotiation!

Is Money the Key to Happiness?

Do you think money can bring happiness? Would you pursue money as a goal to increase happiness?

Money vs. happiness

This is the million-dollar question that has been debated since the dawn of time, well at least since money was invented – some say as long ago as 5,000BCE. In our modern society, we have been led to think that if we work hard we will earn more money and that that will make life easier.

According to Abraham Maslow, a psychologist who conducted studies on the sources of happiness in the 40s and 50s, there is a hierarchy of needs that must be 'tended' for true happiness to be achieved.[14] At the base of the Maslow pyramid are our most fundamental needs (food, water, sleep); next are our psychological needs (safety and security, love and belonging – including friendship, family, sexual intimacy); then self-esteem (confidence respect for/by others); and finally self-actualization or the realization of one's fullest potential (morality, creativity, problem solving etc.). Maslow maintained that not until our basic physiological needs have been met can we attend to our psychological needs, and not until we feel safe and secure can we reach our full potential. This summary is a simplification and of course the steps to happiness differ according to personal needs and motivations. However, the levels are much more easily achieved when one has money; it is harder to achieve self-actualization if you are struggling to make ends meet.

These days, we talk about financial well-being as being part of our overall well-being. Which is better for you, being poor or being rich? Many studies have been conducted and it seems that rich people live a better life and are able to do more things, thanks to the choices that money affords them. At the same time, the more money you have, the more money you are likely to want, and this pursuit of money has an impact on our well-being and how we feel. When you have more money you usually have a more costly lifestyle too, so unless you manage to maintain this level of money this can still be a source of stress. As the song says, 'Mo Money / Mo Problems'.[15]

Many economists have long explored the correlation between happiness and economic indicators, with varying results. Certain trends have been identified however: richer countries are happier than poorer countries, but growing national wealth is not always accompanied by growing national happiness. This is called the Easterlin paradox (formulated in 1974) and has been much discussed and argued much since then. In 2010 it was used to showcase that, 'at a point in time both among and within nations, happiness varies directly with income but over time (10 years or more) happiness does not increase when a country's income increases.'[16]

According to the United Nations' World Happiness Report 2018,[17] Finland is currently top of the world for happiness, followed by Norway, Denmark, Iceland, Switzerland and the Netherlands. And some of the world's richest nations, the UK and US, came in at 19th and 18th places respectively. Happiness is measured by subjective well-being. All the top countries tend to have high values for six key variables that have been found to support well-being: income, healthy life expectancy, social support, freedom, trust and generosity.

Spending money on experiences vs. material goods

Ah that, sweet, sudden chemically induced dopamine rush that we experience when we buy *things*. But why does shopping make us feel so good? The answer is: dopamine. In 1957, Dr Aivid Carlsson[18] discovered that dopamine functions as one of the brain's neurotransmitters. It helps to regulate 'movement, attention, learning, and emotional responses.'[19] When we encounter something new and exciting, dopamine increases and make us want this thing!

That is why, when you go shopping and get the unexpected surprise that the sales are on and everything is 50% off, you feel good about it. You want to fulfil this instant need for gratification, which is just within reach, and so you shop. This chemical response is called a *shopper's high*[20] and because it makes us feel so darn good we want to do the same thing again and again – and again. This, in turn, impacts on how you feel after the splurge: you experience shame, guilt and even remorse. But rather than reflecting on this feeling you repeat the behaviour to feel better.

So, buying things can make us happy in the short term, but the pleasure doesn't last and has negative consequences. A study by Cambridge University discovered that money really can buy happiness, but only when the spending fits our personality.[21] However, Thomas Gilovich, a psychology professor at Cornell University who has been studying the question of money and happiness for over three decades, has been at pains to point out that such a rush is short-lived and in order to achieve longer-term happiness, we should spend money on experiences rather than things[22] (such as a concert rather than shoes, and trips rather than clothes).

Ryan Howell, Associate Professor of Psychology at San Francisco State University,[23] counters this point by asserting that even when we know that buying life experiences will make us happier in the long-run, we continue to spend money on material goods because we think they are 'better value'. He is describing why we feel we are getting less financial value from life experiences than from stuff we could buy.

Certainly, the constant and ever-more sophisticated advertising that we consume daily continues to play with our emotions by encouraging us to buy things that we don't need. However, pre-rich people, it is important to remember that happiness isn't just one fleeting moment of satisfaction – it is something that needs to be measured and sustained over time, and that in the pre-rich mindset, it is our experiences, not our possessions, that create greater longer-term happiness.

We need to align how we spend money with our values

The following exercise is designed to help you to align your values with the way you spend money. When I first completed this it really helped me to understand how spending money actually brought me happiness.

EXERCISE

Here is a short list of values. Circle a few that speak to you.

What do you value in life? Is it your family, the freedom to travel, helping others, being freelance?

Achievement	Environment	Honesty	Money	Responsibility
Adventure	Equality	Humor	Openness	Security
Autonomy	Empowering	Influence	Optimism	Self-Respect
Balance	Fairness	Integrity	Patriotism	Spirituality
Compassion	Faith	Kindness	Peace	Stability
Challenge	Fame	Knowledge	Popularity	Success
Community	Family	Leadership	Privacy	Status
Cooperation	Friendships	Learning	Recognition	Wealth
Creativity	Growth	Love	Religion	Wisdom
Curiosity	Happiness	Loyalty	Reputation	Work
Determination	Health	Meaningful work	Respect	
Education				

Now can you narrow down the list to your top three, or add your own values?

Write them down:

....

....

....

Our values today may (or may not) be different tomorrow. You may value travel and hard work today but move towards family and equality tomorrow. They will change as you change but it is essential to hold them consciously at the forefront of your mind. So, let us all write these values down today in order to establish what presently makes us happier, but ensure that we come back to the list regularly (every year at least) and reflect upon them.

Put a reminder in your diary to review your principal values and expectations this time next year as well.

EXERCISE

What about you:

What is the most recent thing you spent money on?

....

How do you feel about it? 🤩 *or* 😞

Was this aligned with your values? 🤩 *or* 😞

What is the biggest financial decision you have ever made?

....

How do you feel about it? 🤩 *or* 😞

Was this aligned with your values? 🤩 *or* 😞

'HAPPIEST PEOPLE EARN $75,000' (ABOUT £60,000)

Can we really put a figure on happiness? According to a study by Nobel Laureate Angus Deaton and Daniel Kahneman of Princeton University's Woodrow Wilson School,[24] there is no significant correlation between income and happiness once households earn more than $75,000 (£60,000). While this study has been much discussed, it is important to note it is US focussed and that this number may be higher or lower in other societies. In the study, the authors are explicitly talking about happiness and not life satisfaction, and money seems to have a better impact on the latter. Earning a lot tends to promote higher levels of life satisfaction, but the authors make the distinction between being satisfied with life and actually being happy. After all, being happy is not a consequence of how much you earn. Earning too little, however, is usually linked to a lower level of happiness and to having negative feelings about your life.

How much money is enough?

Bear with me while I discuss your 'fulfilment curve'! Presented by Joe Dominguez and Vicki Robin in their book *Your money or your Life*,[25] there is a sweet spot for everything and that sweet spot decreases the maximum fulfilment you will ever get from anything. You can use this tool to examine how spending more (when you are buying stuff) can impact on how you feel i.e. your fulfilment levels, and equally the tipping point at which spending more starts to make you less happy. (This is another term for overspending.)

There are four points presented by the authors, and these range from not spending a lot of money (or not being able to spend money) to spending a lot. These indicators are known as: 'survival', 'comfort','luxury' and 'enough'. Using these four points, the authors show a direct correlation between the money that you have spent and the enjoyment (or fulfilment) that you will feel from your spending.

Survival: The stage when we are struggling with money and we don't have enough to live on and pay our bills. This is a super difficult situation to be in and your happiness is affected by the situation.

Comfort: The point when we manage to earn and pay our bills but also start saving a little bit of money. Fulfilment is still going up. Things we spend money on contribute to our needs and bring us comfort. This state feels superior to the last.

Luxury: The stage when we earn a good amount of money, can save and invest money but also think about extras and luxuries we could afford. This state feels superior to the last.

Enough: This is the perfect level of wealth and spending, where fulfilment is at its zenith. Spending more will not bring us extra happiness at this point.

This works up to a certain point, when spending too much money is no longer helping. So here I am adding a last point, that I would have to call 'Too Much £££'. Our disposable income has increased but our needs have now increased to match our income: schools, high fixed costs, a big house, mortgage and savings. Now the money we earn is not enough to cover everything. This leads to a decrease in our level of fulfilment.

The fulfilment curve is useful for understanding the evolution of our relationship with money, from our purchases for necessities to being able to afford greater purchases. As life becomes more complicated and expensive, we spend money differently and the fulfilment from these evolves as our life and needs change.

We are always chasing more: more money, more income, but for what? This fulfilment curve proves that we can be fulfilled by less money than we strive for. We need to become aware of what we really need money for and to question how it fits with our values? The fulfilment curve will be different for all of us; what is 'enough' for me may not be the same as 'enough' for you. You need to find your sweet spot. Understanding this can be incredibly liberating and preventative, as awareness enables you to stop sacrificing time to pursue financial gain.

EXERCISE

Where are you today on the fulfilment curve?

Survival

Comfort

Luxury

Enough

Too much £££

Think about 3 things that make you more fulfilled/happier? This can be spending less on high street shop clothes, putting money towards a charity, cutting down on fast-food sandwich lunches and branded coffees in order to spend money on a nice dinner...

....

....

....

The power of giving

We are often taught that ruthlessness and a self-centred approach are needed to get ahead in life. But giving money away is proven to actually make us feel good 😎. Try to think back to the last time you gave something away – perhaps a donation, or a gift to someone in need. How did it make you feel? This is called *pro-social spending* and it probably makes you feel pretty good.

Scientists are finding that the brain is hardwired for generosity and a study by professors Elizabeth Dunn, Lara Aknin and Michael Norton[26] highlights a direct correlation between giving and feeling happy. In fact, when making a donation the dopamine levels in your brain, which relate to the body's reward system, increase in much the same was as they do when you are eating chocolate: yes, you read that right, chocolate. So, generosityis not just a virtuous trait, it also is proven to make us feel good (and arguably it is much healthier than bingeing on chocolate...)

Being altruistic also promotes social recognition and connection: sociologists Brent Simpson and Robb Willer[27] have suggested that your generosity is likely to be rewarded by others down the line – a little thing we like to call *good karma*.

Well Done! You have earnt (£) coin!

The principles I have set out above lay the absolutely crucial foundations for our ongoing handling and understanding of money. In the end, personal finance is all about controlling your emotions and building a kick-ass money mindset. Your experiences, successes and failures will help you to recalibrate your relationship with money and understand its value and power in your life.

Talking about money will help you strengthen this relationship and make you more confident. Remember, 'I am not broke, I am pre-rich'. You are worth the effort of making this happen.

The chapters following will offer a motivational and practical money education. Are you ready? Let's do this 🤩.

Money Talk
with Alice Zagury

Job: CEO and co-founder of The Family

Fun fact: A doer with a creative mind, Alice cares for entrepreneurs and dedicates all her energy to helping them succeed. She has been supporting over 500 start-ups all over Europe, providing them with education, tools and access to capital.

Money motto: *'Money flows, money comes and goes, just get your dose!'*

What makes you happy?
I'm truly happy when my brain, heart and gut are aligned: when what I do follows what I love, and that I can feel it. So talking about money, as an entrepreneur...what I enjoy the most is to create something people are thrilled to buy, and that the benefits have a trickle-down effect on my team and me.

What is your most treasured possession?
Materially, I would say my company, The Family. But I try to demerge from thinking that it's a 'possession', because I don't want to end like Gollum – 'My precious!'

What is the best money advice you have ever received?
What you save is a gift to your future. What you spend is a gift to your present time. So what you generate depends on how much you believe in your future, and how much you value your present time.

What is your biggest money failure/mistake?
Not taking care of it, as if it wasn't something important, and ending up each month in the red.

Who is your go-to person to talk about money?
My therapist. Oopsy, is that a problem?

What is your top money hack?
Give me one, because I need it! My money hack is weak: work so much that you don't even think of spending your money. In business, I would say, increase your price as long as you get happy clients.

What is your greatest money achievement?
Getting free, a little bit more every day! Recently, I was very proud of getting rid of the fear of expressing my 'creative self'. I decided to draw a comic telling the story of my company. It's been a huge pleasure for me, as well as a great feeling of accomplishment.

What is your personal mission?
I'm still searching for it, but I think it's something that has to deal with the 'truth'. I know there isn't '*one*' truth, but there are some invisible laws and I enjoy discovering them. I'm always wondering 'Why?', asking questions and trying to get as many points of view as possible. I like going from one group of people to another and creating my own comprehension of the world.

Who is someone you admire most in life?
Michelle Obama. I just finished her book *Becoming* and I've been learning a lot, especially on the duty of the majority to include the minorities.

What is your favourite book?
I felt smarter thanks to *Factfulness* by Hans Rosling. Every human being should read that book at school. It simply gives orders of magnitudes that facilitate comprehension of the world.

What is money for you?
One of the sources of freedom, after love and health.

What do you invest in, in a broad sense: financial but also well-being, etc.?
I'm starting only right now to invest in classic financial products... Let's see.

CHAPTER 2: GET REAL WITH YOUR MONEY

* *

What you will learn in this chapter:
How can you do a financial check-up?
If you have debt, how can you deal with it?
Who can help you in this journey?

* *

'I AM SO TIRED OF NOT BEING A BILLIONAIRE.'

'I am lost. Where do I need to look to understand my finances: at my bank balance, my income, my credit score, my spending or my budget?'

Do these comments sound familiar? Like many others, I thought for many years that my worth was measured by my salary and that what I could afford to buy was linked directly to that too. How wrong this conception is: wealth is so much more than your salary. In this chapter we will take a look at the big picture and you will start to get really intimate with your money!

Having read Chapter 1, you now have a clearer idea of your money mindset and what you need to do to feel better about your money. Now it's time to start dealing with personal finances. We all want to get richer and improve our financial situation, and for this to happen we need to become financially aware. This means getting to grip with where we stand financially... today.

Doing the groundwork is important, because it is vitally important to think about the reality of your situation and to understand how you can build and accrue greater wealth over time. This is no time for generalities, approximations and estimates – you need to look at the hard facts and figures. Don't worry, this needn't be overwhelming – because once you can see the reality and understand the factors that create these figures, there can be no more frightening debts, bills or standing orders lurking in the fringes of our bank balances waiting to wreak havoc on our finances. It's time to count out (almost) every last penny and understand, truly, what you are worth.

We're going to start with a financial health check-up, so arm yourself with a notebook, or Excel file, and let's get started.

Don't forget that you can always arrange to meet a financial adviser to get help on any of these topics. The following does not constitute financial advice – it's just a set of useful tools to help you to understand where you stand with your money.

Financial Health Check-up

This section will discuss how we can measure and build wealth. It will outline how to achieve the very realistic transition from being broke to being pre-rich – which starts with understanding where you stand today. So, let's look how to perform your own financial health check.

Are you financially fit?

I used to focus solely on my income as a measure of my wealth: if I was earning a lot, I must be rich and if I wasn't then I must be poor. But earning is only one parameter for measuring wealth. If you don't save any money and instead spend it all each month, then you will have to keep earning more money to live. This is often referred to as living 'pay cheque to pay cheque'. Social media depicts being rich as associated with high fashion, fast living, swanky cars, travelling business class, new kicks and threads, and buy, buy, buying material goods. Enough to say that it encourages us – nay brainwashes us – to spend a lot of our money.

Once properly understood, the concept of wealth will change the way you perceive and think about money for good. I learnt that the difference between being broke and being rich is not related to how much you earn but to how much you keep – and therefore how much wealth you can build. This measure of wealth we will call your *net worth*. Hold on, don't go – the concept really is very simple. Remember 'knowledge is power' when it comes to money!

Evaluating your net worth is a precise and easy way to monitor and check your financial health...It has nothing to do with your self-worth. It is a phrase that we hear all the time – often in relation to what celebrities earn when they are being written about in the media. What exactly does it mean, and why is it so important for you?

Essentially, your net worth is a snapshot of your financial state of affairs and therefore your economic position. It normally refers to what you own (known as assets) minus what you owe (known as your liabilities). It will tell you how much money you would have left if you were to sell all your assets and repay all your debts 'today'.

Your net worth will vary over time, because your assets and liabilities will fluctuate (for example, as you earn interest on your savings or repay debts). Monitoring your net worth is a simple, necessary step towards gaining greater financial independence. Doing this is also extremely empowering because it encourages you to take full control of your bank balance, financial health and ultimately your life. Understanding the numbers on your bank account statement helps you to become more rational with money. It also allows you to keep track of cashflow, set goals and focus on how your personal wealth is evolving.

We earn money and we spend money – this is called cash flow. If there is a surplus at the end of the month, we hopefully try to save it and when there is a deficit, we usually borrow it. (Credit card debt anyone?)

How to calculate your net worth

Your net worth is quick and easy to calculate and it really is such a necessary step towards gaining financial independence. Because it is a simple number, it is easy to track.

Net worth equals what you own (your assets) minus what you owe (your liabilities): *Net worth = Assets – Liabilities*

What are assets?

Your assets are items of value that you own:

- *Cash on hand*
- *Real estate: house, flat*
- *Bank account balance: current account*
- *Savings*
- *Shares, investments and insurance*

- *Car*
- *Pensions and retirement savings*
- *The value of your business or a start-up*
- *Other assets: car, jewellery, furniture, anything of value that you own*

The value of your assets has to be accounted for at the current 'market value' (that means: how much you would get if you had to sell that asset today at current price) rather than the bought value (the price you paid for the asset).

What are liabilities?
Your liabilities are your debts, or the money that you owe:

- *Mortgages*
- *Credit card debt*
- *Student debt*
- *Other personal loans*
- *Car loans*
- *Other liabilities*

You may have noticed the absence of earnings and outgoings in the chapter and the net worth calculation. In this exercise, we are only looking at the balances of your accounts on a given day, not at the cash flow (such as paying for groceries, rent and the cost of living). This table is a picture of your financial position today. If last month you were left with extra cash after paying your expenses, it can be used to repay some debt or be saved, and this will have a positive impact on your net worth. If you struggled last month and ended in red, you will have a negative impact on your net worth. We will look into cash flow when we talk about budgeting in Chapter 4.

Let's look at a real example, to show how this works.

Amanda is 28, she is living in London and works in a tech start-up. She rents her flat, has some savings but also some student debt.

This is a simple example of how to calculate her net worth. (Negative amounts are shown in brackets).

Amanda's assets	£££	Amanda's liabilities	£££
House, flat	0	Mortgage	0
Bank accounts balance	500	Credit card debt	(5,000)
Emergency savings account	1,000	Student debt	(20,000)
Pension	3,000	Other personal loans	0
Car	0	Car loans	0
Other assets	0	Other liabilities	0
Total assets	**4,500**	**Total liabilities**	**(25,000)**
Amanda's net worth is 4,500 – 25,000 = (20,500)			

You will be able to calculate your own at the end of this chapter.

As you can see, Amanda's net worth is £20,500 negative because her assets are valued at less than her liabilities, and this is largely due to her student debt – which, as we'll see later in this chapter, is considered to be *good* debt. What is more problematic is her credit card balance because, if she is not able to repay the balance in full at the end of the month, it will cost her a lot of money in interest payments. Amanda has some savings in cash deposits of £1,000 and approx. £500 in her bank account. When she can save more, she should maybe try to build up her emergency savings net to about 3–6 months of living expenses in case she receives an unexpected bill or loses her job, because she doesn't want to take on more debt.

What will make the difference for Amanda, when growing her net worth, is how much she earns and manages to stash away in savings and debt repayment. While net worth does not show income and spending, they are of course intricately linked.

Net worth is very individual: some people might have a low net worth even though they earn a lot of money; others might have a high net worth even if they don't earn big salaries.

Back to Amanda, this month she is on track to get a £2,000 yearly bonus. She can use it to repay some of her expensive credit card debt and reduce the balance to £3,000. That has a direct impact on her net worth, increasing it to £3,000; it is still negative but is moving in the right direction. The money she manages to save every month will have the same impact...

When referring back to our animals in Chapter 1, we could say that Amanda is an ant with money – she manages to save some, but at the same time her caution is leading her to overspend on credit card interest, because she wants to keep some savings in the bank.

Don't panic if your net worth is negative. There are plenty of financially healthy reasons for having a minus total: perhaps you have a student loan, or have only just started working. Understanding your current situation is a good place to start, so you can see what can be improved. As soon as you start to save money or repay a loan, you will also start upping your net worth. This is the first step towards building wealth. To achieve this, you first need to find a way to improve your worth. This means breaking down your spending and saving by category, in order to understand where each +/- value comes from.

➔ See Chapter 3 for some budgeting tips.

Building up your wealth

In theory, increasing your net worth is simple: you use your income (the money you make, for example from your job or investments) to increase valuable assets while reducing (paying off) your liabilities. Once your assets are worth more than your liabilities, you have positive net worth.

If you want to accumulate wealth, you have to focus on acquiring assets that will appreciate (increase in value) over time rather than creating further debt. Your goal is to have fewer liabilities (such as credit card debt) that cost you money (such as interest) and not to invest in items that will depreciate (lose value).

As mentioned above, your salary is only one way to build net worth (you might have another source of income from some side-hustles, for example). The big difference when you start trying to build wealth is that you start to generate money from other sources: your 'assets' (the things you own). The goal, over time, is that these should generate more and more money and allow you to work less and less (and retire one day). True wealth is achieved by acquiring assets that will increase in value and generate money for you.

For example, you may decide to buy a property and, if the price goes up in value over time, it should help you to build your wealth. On the flipside, a new car is rarely an asset that will increase in value over time, so it is not creating wealth. Other assets that help to build wealth are ones which produce income, such as personal savings, your retirement contributions, and other investments that generate interest, as these usually increase in value and may generate income. So, by acquiring assets and making them work for you, you can generate more money that just your salary or take-home pay.

Of course your liabilities will also increase because you are paying interest on them. Any outgoings that you are repaying over time, such as credit card debt, loans or a mortgage, will impact your ability to save and build assets.

Calculate your net worth

EXERCISE

Net worth is what you have (assets) minus what you owe (liabilities).

What are your assets today on ____________ (date)?:

Type of asset	Where?	Value £
Total assets =		**£**

What are your debts on ____________ (date)?:

Type of liability (debt)	Where?	Value £
Total liabilities =		**£**

NET WORTH = ASSETS (–) LIABILITIES

My net worth is £. . . . . (–) £. . . . . = £. . . . .
on ____________(date).

How often should I look at my net worth?

Some people look at their net worth on a weekly basis, but I think it is useful to calculate it monthly or quarterly. Your objective is to see it increase in value, from one period to another, so you know which direction it is going in. Remember this is for YOU only – you don't need to show it to anyone.

If you want to see how some other people measure their wealth, you can find a selection on the Rockstar financial directory.[28] Thousands of financial bloggers in the USA have been publishing their monthly net worth online, for years. Every month, they reveal their spending and saving secrets to show how they are working on increasing their net worth. These testimonials can be extremely motivating because you can see how many who start out with negative net worth change their net worth to positive as their balance increases over time. Indeed, one of them has been publishing his net worth monthly for 10 years and has managed to multiply his worth ten-fold during that time.

Where do I start?

As a reminder: the main principle behind growing your net worth is to increase your assets and decrease your liabilities. This is a very broad guideline and we will look into the different ways you can do this in future chapters. For now, here are a few ways you can begin to affect your score:

- **Build an emergency saving net:** Because if something unexpected happens, such as your boiler breaking down, you can dip into your emergency fund rather than take on debt (such as credit card debt) to pay for it.
- **Pay off some of your debts:** Focus on repaying the expensive debts first, i.e. those that are generating the highest interest rates, such as credit cards.
- **Top up your pension:** If you are not already contributing to your employer's pension or a personal pension plan, you should take specialist advice and start now.
- **Reduce your spending:** Calculating your net worth can help identify where you spend too much money and enable you to cut out bad habits.

- **Save some money:** Open an ISA or a cash savings account if you don't have one already.
- **Grow your savings:** Keep an eye on your savings and potentially start investing –provided you have taken advice and you understand the risks.
- **Talk to a professional:** Speak to a financial adviser about your needs.

Be patient. Building net worth is a long process and does not happen overnight. But the big advantage of tracking your net worth is that it gives you an accurate and real picture of where you are financially. When it comes to managing money and saving money, patience is key. There will be ups and downs and unexpected things can happen in your personal life (losing a job, moving to a new house, paying more rent, getting divorced) but this commitment to grow your net worth should remain. You need to be convinced that you can grow this number. It's empowering and one of the most fulfilling tasks you will ever undertake. Being able to measure your progress should help you to build your confidence around money management and strengthening self-worth.

DO YOU KNOW PEOPLE'S WEALTH IN THE UK?

According to the Office of National Statistics (ONS)[29], the median household net wealth in the UK rose by 15% to £259,400 from July 2014 to July 2016, mainly due to the increased value of pensions and property. This is no surprise, but the statistics also show that the wealth is not equally distributed, with the top 10% of households being five times richer than the bottom half of all households.

Use a dashboard app to access your bank account online. These apps enable you to view all of your financial accounts online and in one place. A good one will order your transactions by category, so you get an even clearer understanding of exactly where your money comes from and how you spend it. The Vestpod community has been using MoneyDashboard, Yolt, Moneyhub, Bud, Bean and Emma in the UK, and Mint in the US. Check whether your existing bank is also offering this type of service. New banks such as Monzo, Revolut and Starling are amongst the Vestpod favourites. Check out our Little Black Book of resources on pages 362–5.

Are you creditworthy?

There is another 'number' widely used in personal finance: your credit score. While the net worth is your own personal number to measure your wealth, the credit score corresponds to your financial footprint and it measures how responsible you are with your money. Did you know that *we all need to have a credit score*? Most adults have one but most of us have never checked it.

Your credit score is based on your credit history and how good you have been at repaying your debts. So – newsflash – credit is actually a good thing, provided you handle it with care, because it eases your cashflow and allows you to have access to money to pay for things you need, before the money is available. The way you use credit also gives financial institutions an indication of your financial health. Looking into your actions, transactions and pattern of repayment is quite revealing. The credit bureaux determine their scores based on the financial footprint you have left behind. If you don't use a credit card, it becomes harder to measure your creditworthiness.

Why your credit score matters

Why would anyone want to check my credit score, you may be thinking. Lenders want to understand whether you are creditworthy and financially fit enough to be lent money. Your credit score plays a key role in determining how much they will lend you and how much interest to charge. The better your credit score, the better your chances of getting a good deal with lower interest. Your credit score informs lenders of how robust and reliable you are. They then use this intelligence to try to predict your behaviour in the future, to safeguard themselves against your potential risk.

You may think that you would never want to borrow any money, but most people find that they need access to credit at some point in life. Your individual credit score has broader implications for many areas of your personal finances: from setting up a credit card to taking out a business loan, a mobile phone contract, car insurance, opening a bank account or securing a mortgage. If you are thinking about applying for a mortgage to buy a house and you have a strong credit score and report, lenders will see you as reliable and the chances of you getting a loan are much higher. Added to which, if they see you as a reliable potential customer, they may also offer you a better mortgage rate too (that will cost you less money), helping reduce your monthly payments. Having a high credit score and being creditworthy helps to reduce the cost of your financial life. In contrast, having a low credit score impacts the probability of you being offered a loan and will mean that financial institutions are more likely to charge you a higher rate of interest.

The credit score system really applies to everybody. British pop singer Lily Allen has openly discussed her struggles with money and credit in her book *My Thoughts Exactly*[30]. While being number one in the charts and earning a lot of money, she didn't pay her parking fines and a few years later she felt the painful sting of this disregard when she looked into buying a house. Although she could afford the deposit, she needed a mortgage. That proved incredibly difficult to get, because of her credit history. Lesson learnt: pay your debts even when they seem small and irritating.

Lenders love stability and hate surprises. They also love to see your data so they can make as informed a decision as possible. The more visible you are, the more detail they can gauge about your financial stability and personality type. This can be infuriating if you are young or have never been in debt or never used a credit card, because having no or little credit history can impact negatively your score. You are an unknown, and uncertainty makes you less of a certainty and therefore unpredictable.

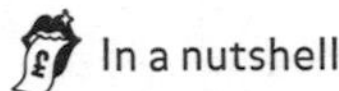
In a nutshell:

High credit score = Likely lower rate of interest charged on your loan, with the opportunity to borrow a higher amount of money.

Low credit score = Likely higher rate of interest charged on your loan, with the opportunity to borrow less money, and the danger that a bank will not lend to you at all.

It is incredibly important to have a consistently good credit record as this will result in a strong credit score from a reputable credit agency which will in turn mean you will be rated well by lenders.

How do I get my credit score?

Finding out your exact credit score is simple and quick. You can use an online credit bureau such as Experian, Equifax or Callcredit to do this. Try to use a free service[31] and don't waste your money on a full report as the basic service is very good. You can register for emails that prompt you to review annually.

Different credit bureaux may sometimes provide you with a slightly differently score so it is useful and good practice to compare your score with the other providers. Once you have entered basic information on these platforms, you will be able to see your credit report.

You can always ask to have a copy for free – this is your legal right, as they hold lots of information on you.

Let's examine your report:

- **Your personal information:** Name, address, date of birth, have you registered on the electoral roll (this too can impact your score).
- **Your credit score:** This is your financial footprint.
- **Your debts:** Short-term as well as long-term: credit cards, payday loans, student loans, car loans, mortgages, personal loans, and so on.
- **The search history:** Each time you ask for credit (that is, you want to borrow money or open a new bank account) the lenders will check your

credit score. Lenders can see, from this section of the report, who has checked what, where and when.

- **Your financial connections:** Are you married and do you have a mortgage? Make sure you are associated only with people with a good credit history, otherwise their history could also impact yours. Check your address through an online credit bureau to verify that your information is up to date. It's often said that a previous home-owner or tenant's credit rating at the same address can affect your credit score, but no checks are done on you. However, if you shared a bank account or mortgage with them, their credit rating may impact yours.
- **A report by Cifas:** This is the UK's Fraud Prevention Service and will highlight whether you have been a victim of fraud.

EXERCISE

After checking your credit report, write your credit score here. And don't worry you can check your own score as often as you want, it won't impact your rating!

My credit score is .... on ____________ (date).

How can I improve my credit score?

Are you blushing at the memory of a credit card bill you didn't pay off on time, or that standing order for a gym membership that you cancelled (no judgement), without telling them of your intentions? Don't worry, there are simple ways to give your credit score a much-needed boost.

Your score is drawn mostly from evidence of how you have managed to make payments historically, the amount of debt you have outstanding and the way you use your credit (credit card, mortgage, bills and so on).

Credit history is built over a long period of time, and while there is no quick-fix trick for improving your credit rating, you can definitely make a start.

- **Repayment history:** Lenders try to predict your future behaviour, so they look for clues as to your spending, saving and overspending habits. They examine how good you have been at making prompt and regular payments on different types of debt, whether loans, bills or overdrafts. So, you need to make sure that you pay your bills on time from now on (and that includes parking tickets – no cheating). Paying off your credit card balance in full every month is key but, if you really can't, at least make sure you repay the minimum balance. Making late payments can impact negatively your score.
- **Credit utilization ratio:** This is the difference between how much credit you are allowed, and how much you are using. For example, if you have a credit limit of £2,000 on your credit card, but are using only £200 of credit, you would have a low utilization ratio. If you start maxing out all your credit cards, you will have a high utilization ratio – and will also be seen as someone who appears unable to manage debt carefully, and so may be unreliable. For you to look good, you need to maintain a low(er) utilization ratio, usually around 30%. So, if you have a credit limit of £2,000, make sure you don't have an outstanding balance of more than £600 on the card that you should repay in full at the end of the month, otherwise you will be charged. This calculation should be employed across the board.
- **Outstanding debt:** How much debt do you have? If you have lot of outstanding debt it can be difficult for banks to lend you more money as they will be concerned about your capacity to repay.
- **Repeat applications:** Don't make repeated applications for new loans and credit cards, as lenders may see you as impulsive or financially unstable.
- **Make sure you are registered on the electoral roll:** This is a simple and reliable way for lenders to verify that you are who you say you are and to protect against fraud – so it's important.
- **Check your statements:** Make sure you check each entry on your account for any errors or inconsistencies, fraud or anything else.
- **Use your credit card:** And finally, it may sound counter-intuitive but keep using that credit card (or go out and get one) – but make sure that you make payments regularly and do not exceed the 30% rule. The steadier your payment history, the easier it is for credit agencies to process your application.

- **Stop making cash withdrawals with your credit card:** Be aware that credit cards should not be used to withdraw cash for two reasons: first, doing so can be recorded on your credit file; second, most providers will charge you a cash advance fee as well as daily interest (until you pay off the balance). Could you use a debit card instead?

EXERCISE

Based on these tips, could you find a few ways to help build up your score?

....

....

....

CREDIT CARD TEMPTATION: DOES MORE CREDIT EQUAL A BETTER CREDIT RATING?

More credit! More miles! More money-off vouchers! **How often have you received a letter to say: 'Congratulations, we have increased your limit and you can now borrow up to £2,000 on your card.' You may also be offered air miles, online shopping vouchers and other incentive add-ons with your card. Even though your income has not increased, and your debt has not decreased, the amount you can borrow on your credit card has mysteriously gone up. You do not have to accept this increase, and nor do you have to use it or use the vouchers. These are all designed to tempt you to use more credit and to spend more. This will not increase your credit rating – especially if you have already brimmed your previous credit limit.**

Don't Let Debt Scare You

If your debts are higher than your assets you will have worked out that your net worth is negative. Do not worry, debt doesn't have to be scary. Understanding your money and getting to grips with the situation is what this book is all about.

According to a report by the NAO (National Audit Office) and the Money Advice Service, more than 8 million people in the UK are said to have problem debt, i.e. they are over-indebted and can't repay their debts or bills. The other concerning statistic is that 22% of adults have less than £100 in savings, making them at risk if anything unexpected, such as an emergency or unemployment, happens.[32]

The average UK household debt (including mortgages) was £58,540 in June 2018, according to The Money Charity.[33] More than six million people in Britain believe that they will never be debt-free, according to a research by the Royal Society for Public Health (RSPH) and that, 'consumer credit debt is concentrated in just over half of the population, with the average amount owed by these borrowers standing at around £8,000 [not including mortgage debt].'[34]

Debt: the good, the bad and the ugly

The first thing to know is that if you are in debt, you are not on your own. Most of us carry debt of some kind. The second thing to remember is that being in debt is not necessary a bad thing.

The term debt is used very broadly but essentially it means owing money to someone. There is good and bad debt and we all need to be able to understand the difference:

- **Good debt:** Is money you borrow for things that increase in value over time (student loans, mortgages). It usually bears a low(er) interest rate.

- **Bad debt:** Is money you borrow for things that lose value with time (impulse shopping on a credit card; payday loans). This debt usually bears a high(er) interest rate.
- **Ugly debt:** Is not an official term, but it is real enough. It relates to over-indebtedness, or problem debt, which develops when someone becomes unable to pay their debts or other household bills.

To simplify your goal, when managing or incurring debt, you should focus on reducing bad debts and monitoring your good debt. Bad debt is the type that keeps you awake at night; good debt shouldn't.

Good debt	Bad debt	Ugly debt
• Student loans • Mortgages • Business loans: investing in your business for example	• Credit card debt that you can't afford to repay • Payday loans • Money borrowed to pay for things you should have paid from your income or salary and are in a difficult position to repay • Bills unpaid	• Debt spiral • Debt management • Can't keep up with payments

There are two main types of loan: *secured* and *unsecured* and understanding the differences between these two terms is crucial.

When your debt is secured: It means that you borrowed money against something, such as your house. If things go wrong and you can't pay back the debt, the bank still needs the money back so they may want to take the house (this is obviously a worst-case scenario). If you are a home-owner, it gives the lender some guarantee.

When your debt is unsecured: It means that you have borrowed money to spend on something that the lender can't take back: such as clothes, a holiday, or something the bank is not interested in. These kinds of debts are often on a credit card.

Borrowing money can be very helpful to progress and get the things you want in life: to educate yourself, to buy property or to pay for important things when you need them. If you are fully aware of how much you have, how much interest you pay on your debt and when you have to repay it by – then you are in the clear.

However, when borrowing gets out of hand, you can end up bearing a seemingly impossible burden. The level of interest can mount up fast and become very expensive, gradually you find you can no longer pay the ever-increasing charges. At this point your debt becomes detrimental to your well-being and can lead to mental health issues, such as losing sleep, problems in relationships, absenteeism and lost productivity at work.

Whether you are comfortable with your debt or are seriously worried about it, you need to find a way to be in control of it (see page 80).

What are the most common types of debt?

Credit card debt

How do credit cards work? A credit card gives you access to credit, which you can use to buy something you cannot afford or to ease cashflow. The crucial thing to understand is that the company that lends you the money does so because it makes good business sense to do so. When you use your credit card you are effectively borrowing money, which you will pay interest on if you don't pay off your balance in full at the end of each month.

A credit card agreement allows you choose how much to repay every month – which can be extremely dangerous. A minimum repayment has to be made each month in order to avoid a late payment charge: this is usually set at between 1% and 3% of your outstanding balance. This is not great news because it is quite low and does not encourage you to repay your debt in full. If you do not pay off the full amount you will keep being charged an increasing level of interest, which is added to the total balance.

The following calculation is for illustration purposes and only gives you an estimate of interest and how long it could take you to repay your credit card debt...

You have an outstanding balance of £3,000 on your credit card and the interest is being charged at a rate of 18% APR (Annual Percentage Rate). The minimum repayment is the greater of 3% or £5 and your minimum repayment this month is £3,000 x 3% which equals £90.

The interest payable is £3,000 x 18% divided by 12 months, which equals £45. So £45 of the £90 payable is going towards paying off your debt, and the other £45 is going to the card company as profit.

After this payment, your debt balance is £3,000 – £45 = £2,955. Meanwhile, interest continues to accrue (build up) on the remaining balance.

By paying only the minimum on the card (and never using it to buy anything again, assuming there are no other late payment fees and interest rates stay the same) it may take more than 19 years to clear this debt and cost you almost £2,900 in interest... (this is just a simplified illustration, but it gives you an idea!).

Credit card debt becomes bad debt only if it is not repaid in full at the end of each month. This is why our relationship with credit cards gets complicated, because while they are a great tool to help build up a positive credit score, there is always that moment at the end of the month when you have to take a deep breath and pay back what you owe. Because yes, you have to repay your credit card balance monthly, otherwise it will be very expensive, and you could lose control of your repayments. Typical rates on credit cards can be around 18% APR – and this is why credit card costs snowball. The less you repay one month, the less you are able to repay the following month, and things can go badly wrong very quickly.

The bury-your-head-in-the-sand strategy of ignoring the balance never works, and as it hits the income available in your current account it can become really painful. Making low repayments will also have a big impact on your credit score. The key to using a credit card is to use it only as a means to build your credit score and to ensure that you set up a direct debit so you don't miss the deadline for payment. You can usually set it up to pay the minimum amount, the outstanding balance (recommended!) or a fixed amount each month.

If you can't clear the whole balance straight away, try to pay back as much as you can, as soon as you can. Paying back only the minimum amount each month is expensive and it will take you longer to pay back the debt. Credit card companies make their money from the interest you pay on the debt, so they will increase your credit allowance, increase cash savings, add rewards and perhaps do some promos. It is not that they are being nice to you when they reach out with these offers, they are simply trying to get you to spend more money, in order that they can gain more from you in the long term.

SAY A BIG NO TO PAYDAY LOANS

A payday loan is a short-term loan. The idea is that you can apply to be lent money quickly, for an emergency, and are then supposed to repay the debt on payday (even if this ranges from a few weeks to a few months). As the money is made available quickly and most people are eligible, it is a very expensive way of borrowing because of the high interest rates, especially if you don't repay the debt within the fixed term of the agreement.

According to Money Advice Service, the average annual percentage rate of interest has been as high as 1,500% APR on one of these loans. The cost of payday loans has now been capped by law, under rules made by the Financial Conduct Authority (FCA). Since 2015 lenders can no longer charge more than 0.8% of the amount borrowed and a maximum 100% of the loan in charges and fees. The hope is that this type of loan will be banned completely.

It's very easy to obtain a payday loan and this accessibility has allowed people to make use of them without fully understanding what they are getting themselves into. They appear to be a quick-fix solution but instead can only worsen an already vulnerable financial situation.

Two other examples of types of credit that are similar to credit cards are:

- **Store-card:** If you have been doing some shopping recently, you may have been offered one of these. They essentially work like credit cards but for a specific shop (Amazon or New Look, for example) and they allow you to pay for your purchases later. Normally they have a high APR and they also offer discounts and rewards.
- **Charge cards:** With a charge card, such as Amex, you pay a yearly subscription instead of interest. You must repay your balance in full each month otherwise you have to pay late charges. The application process

is usually selective and, because of the short-term nature of repayment, charge cards are reserved for people who earn a minimum salary or intend to use them for business purposes. Spending limits are usually high and you can also earn rewards, perks and sometimes cash back.

Overdrafts

If you apply to the bank to borrow money that is not in your account, the bank is lending you money and you are falling into what is called an overdraft. Some bank accounts come with an authorized overdraft limit, but not all, so when you choose to open an account (see Chapter 7), make sure you check the overdraft limit and the interest charged.

As with credit cards, an overdraft should be used as a one-off loan, because it can be expensive and banks will charge you high fees for the service. Make sure you read the small print in the agreement.

Interestingly, according to the FCA and Money Advice Service, 'you are 24% less likely to suffer unarranged overdraft charges if you use a mobile banking app and a text alert service.'

YOU CAN TALK TO YOUR BANK TOO

If you have problems with your credit card debt and/or an overdraft, get in touch with your bank. The bank will contact you only as a last resort, but if you make the first move and ask to discuss your account, they may suggest altering your overdraft limit, waive some of the fees on your account, or help you to find a financial product that works better for you.

Mortgages

A mortgage is a debt that is arranged via a lender (usually a bank or a building society) to buy a property. This debt is secured because, if for any reason something goes wrong, the banks can take back your home to repay what you owe. When you borrow money to buy your first property you will usually arrange to pay it back over a long time-frame, typically about 25 years. In the past, owning a property has been a major objective in life, both financially and psychologically – but things are changing. Millennials are no longer buying as much property as previous generations due to the unrealistic costs involved combined with a gradual shift in our value systems.

Will you be able to sleep at night when you have a mortgage debt over your head? The answer is usually yes. By this stage, you will have been well-advised by an adviser and will have checked that you can afford the monthly payments.

A word to the wise: If you later find that you are struggling to pay your monthly mortgage costs and you begin to miss payments, the amount of interest that you owe to the bank will increase – a lot. This can be the beginning of a difficult situation, as the bank could potentially take you to court and even repossess your house. However, those who have got into difficulty are often amazed at how helpful their lender can be. In order to prevent the worst from happening, make sure you speak to your bank or building society as soon as problems start. Build a plan to catch up with the payments and if you need help doing this, get further debt advice.[35]

→ If the question of buying versus renting is in your head, go to Chapter 9. It will help you to figure out what you can afford, how to get a mortgage, find a broker, buying costs involved, and so on.

Student loans

You graduated from university, and your degree has enabled you to start your professional journey. However, you are left with a hefty debt (sometimes up to or over £50,000 according to the Institute for Fiscal Studies[36]). Don't stress or panic. Student loans are less of a loan and act more like tax, because you only repay them if you have enough money (income) to do so.[37] Of course, the repayments will impact on your available income and can make saving for other financial goals harder, but it has enabled you to pay for your studies and you should see it as an investment in your future.

Student debt grows with interest over time and, as soon as you start earning enough money, a percentage (9%) of your income will be deducted via your employer's payroll and paid to the Student Loans Company. This will continue until your loan has been paid off.

If you are self-employed, the amount you have to pay will be calculated in your self-assessment tax return (I recommend that you work on this with an accountant) alongside your taxes and National Insurance contributions. HMRC will then liaise with the Student Loan Company to inform them of your repayment.

You can also decide to pay more towards your student debt to repay it faster, but keep in mind that you could be using your surplus to go into other pockets, such as saving for your pension fund, or a home deposit, or any other financial goal you may have. If you stop earning, the repayments will stop until you start work again.

Remember that after thirty years (from the time you begin repayment) the debt will be erased (written off) for Plan 2 loans. Plan 2 loans can vary so make sure you check the terms of the loan you are on.

Always check the recent information on:
studentloanrepayment.co.uk

Take back control, look your debt(s) in the eye

Is your debt becoming a problem? Unsure whether you can keep up with your payments for your mortgage, rent, energy bills? Are you paying only the minimum balance on your credit cards? Do you feel you are losing control or feeling trapped by your money worries?

Managing debt is difficult and it can become a massive psychological burden, especially as it feels as though you are completely on your own. Receiving endless payment reminders and watching the totals mount up would test the optimism in any of us, because we process the situation as a sign of personal failure rather than as a problem we can solve. Many will start to push the problem out of sight and avoid opening those angry-looking envelopes. There is still a lot of shame associated with battling debt and it remains a bit of a taboo topic to bring up. As a society we are very limited in the way we talk about money and the emotional toll that worries and debt can take on professional self-esteem and mental health. But it needn't be this way. You really need to make a plan and focus on it, according to the Citizen's Advice Bureau.[38] The best way to tackle this is by taking small, incremental steps: dealing with one bill at a time.

Get some help: In a moment we will look at the different ways to approach the problem, but know that you definitely *don't* need to do this on your own. Don't hesitate to ask for help – there are some great places where you can get FREE debt advice as well as phone support and online tools, such as Citizens Advice, StepChange Debt Charity, National Debtline, PayPlan, and Mental Health & Money Advice.

By approaching repayments methodically, clear-sightedly (that is, not being in denial) and with a do-able repayment plan, you should gradually get out of debt. It might take a while, but you will feel so much better, and more in control, knowing that every day you are getting closer to your goal. You will gradually stop making the common mistakes that can actually increase the amount you have to repay too. Making progress will help you to feel lighter and more empowered. As you reduce your debt, you will have less interest to pay too. Plus, it will have the added bonus of giving you give a real boost to your credit profile.

Which debts should I pay first?

The first rule of getting out of debt is to make sure you are dealing with the most important debt first. Some repayments are more important than others because of the consequences of missing them. *Priority* debts are mortgage payments, rent, council tax, taxes, store cards, charge cards, hire-purchase fees, water bills, etc. The result of not paying your mortgage payment for example, could mean losing your home (in a worst-case scenario). *Non-priority* debts are credit cards debts, payday loans, overdrafts, and money owed to family and friends. Not paying these debts back straightaway is less serious, though the delays can cost you a lot of money and goodwill.

Priority debts: Priority debts such as your rent or mortgage should be paid in full every month. If you fear that you may miss a payment, contact your provider in advance to let them know and make an arrangement with them. Now, if you can't pay them because you have too much debt, you need to get debt advice as soon as possible.

Non-priority debts: If you can't pay your non-priority debts, your creditor could eventually take you to court or ask you for more money. It is important to keep the lender informed and to make an arrangement to pay at least the minimum amount on all debts to avoid falling behind.

Let's run through this in more detail:

1. **Stop blaming yourself – but do start taking responsibility:** This has nothing to do with your self-worth. Be practical and take action. Repeat: 'This happens to many people and I can get myself out of debt.'

2. **Commit to not taking on any additional debt:** Before you do anything else, cut your spending. This sounds obvious but it can be hard to do. Many people react to maxing out on one credit card by applying for another, which leads to disaster. It really is quite simple: stop using that credit card! Freeze it or cut it up. You have nothing to lose but stress.
3. **Face it and write it down:** Take a pen and paper, copy out the below chart and write down everything you owe. Make a list of all your debt on one sheet. Collate your latest statements, take a deep breath and open bills.

   Find out the following:
   - What non-priority debts do you have?
   - What annual percentage rate (APR) are you paying on the interest?
   - How much do you owe in total?
   - What is your monthly payment?
   - Order your debts, listing the debt with the higher interest rate first.

You will now clearly know what you owe, in which area of your life your debts are located, the terms of the loan and interest payment due on each.

EXERCISE

Get started and complete the debt/liabilities table with your numbers on page 62.

PRIORITY DEBTS			
Debt Name / Type	**Interest Rate (APR)**	**Balance**	**Monthly Repayment / Minimum Balance**
NON-PRIORITY DEBTS			
Debt Name / Type	**Interest Rate (APR)**	**Balance**	**Monthly Repayment / Minimum Balance**
Total =			

4. **Use a debt repayment method:** There are a few debt repayments methods, the most user-friendly are called the debt avalanche and the debt snowball.
   - *The avalanche method* is when you allocate money to cover the minimum payment on each debt, and use any funds left over to repay the debt bearing the highest interest rate/APR; that is, the card that is most expensive is the one you pay off first.
   - *The snowball method* is when you allocate all of your extra money towards covering the minimum payment on each debt, and the extra money available then goes toward paying off the debt with the lowest balance first. If you feel overwhelmed at the thought of tackling all your debts at the same time, this method allows you to focus on just one.

The avalanche method often makes the most economic sense but the snowball method can be the more motivating because it allows you to eliminate debts one by one. Since you begin with the lowest debt balance, it will help you to feel as though you are making progress.

5. **Order your debts:** Based on your debt table, order the debts according to the debt repayment method you've chosen. Include the minimum due every month in the table.
6. **Get started:** Make a budget, identifying what you want to achieve versus what you need and check all your spending (See Chapter 4). What can you cut back on? It's going to be hard but needs to become your top priority. It will allow you to release some cash to start repaying some of your balances – and just picture the financial freedom...

Instead of paying off the minimum each month you can also transfer the debt to a zero-interest card, look at the balance and see exactly how much you should repay to get the amount down to ZERO. However, be careful, as if you are feeling vulnerable to the £££ pressure you could be tempted to access fast cash without examining the ever-more painful consequences (hello payday loans).

7. **Celebrate:** Share your new debt-free status with your friends, family and community 🤩.

Stop Paying Fees!

You have probably been paying hefty bank fees without even noticing. Find out whether you are incurring overdraft fees, annual fees on your current account, monthly fees, bank transfer fees, fees on late payments, cash withdrawal fees (the worst), credit cards fees, even ATM fees. Most of these are avoidable. You already give the bank your money and you don't want to be paying extra on top of that for giving them the privilege of holding on to it!

Check your account because it is likely you have been paying extras. Most of these fees could be avoided.

Use a fee-tracking app (see page 364) to show you what you have been paying to your bank as well as unused subscriptions.

A bank account should be free: A bank account or a credit card that is in a healthy financial state should not be charging you for their services: meaning where your account is in credit, you are not in overdraft, or you repay your credit card balance in full each month.

Always avoid unnecessary fees and shop around to find the account that suits you best. If you think you have been charged bank charges unfairly (on an overdraft, for example) or if you have paid a monthly fee for your bank account, you can speak to your bank and ask them for a refund. This is called reclaiming. (If you are in financial hardship you could try to reclaim unfair overdraft charges too.)

ATM fees: We've all been there: it is 3am, you are out on the town and need cash for a taxi home. You dash around trying every cash machine in the vicinity and find that all of the ATMs charge a fee to withdraw money. But you take the hit because you are in dire straits. Well you really need to stop doing that. Here's why: there are almost 70,000 ATMs across the country, and almost 97% of them do not charge you to use them. The 3% remaining are owned by independent operators who usually charge £1.50 to £2 per transaction.[39]

You will also incur charges if you use your credit card to withdraw money. This is called a cash advance, and most credit cards companies will charge a fee of about 3% on top of the cost of the cash. Remember: you will be charged a high rate of interest on this withdrawal too, starting immediately, not from the date of your monthly statement.

EXERCISE

Kill the bank fees:

Account	Bank	Fees for?	Could be avoided?	Change bank?	Fees £

Who Can Help You?

Are you sceptical about financial advice? Do you wonder why you would want to pay someone to manage the very little money you just about have? Do you think you are nowhere near wealthy enough to consult one? Are you worried about giving all your personal finance credentials to a stranger?

There are different kinds of financial advisers, from specialist consultants for specific products such as pensions and mortgages, to much more generalized service providers. Financial advisers can do a myriad of things for you and your money: they can help you understand your financial goals, build a holistic plan for you, look into your investments and give you investment advice based on your goals and tolerance of risk, and they can also work on very specific areas of finance such as buying a home, planning for retirement, wealth planning and so on. Of course, none of this comes for free – these people are regulated professionals who expect to be properly rewarded for their services.

The term 'financial adviser' has become a bit of a catch-all term to describe any finance professional who can help you to manage your money and achieve your goals. Although the finance industry had a bad reputation in the past due to mis-selling scandals and the way that advisers used to be compensated for their services, things have changed. Since 2013, financial advisers no longer receive a commission from the finance companies when they give you investment advice (hence they now charge you a fee instead). Note that some advisers can still accept commissions for life insurance policies and mortgage broking; you will pay for these products and the advisers will pay themselves a cut. You may remember from the introduction that I had a bad experience with an adviser but that shouldn't scare you off; I met other amazing ones along the way.

Financial advice is not just for the über-rich, and sometimes it is best to reach out to a professional and ask for help. You should never feel embarrassed or ashamed about doing so. Financial professionals are there to help you. The main barriers for most people are finding an adviser that is a good fit for your needs, understanding their explanations, and finding one who does not charge fees that are more than you can afford. So – you need to understand what you are getting yourself into.

What is a financial adviser?

Financial advisers provide you with advice on how to manage money. They research the market and are able to offer financial products that will suit your personal financial situation, investment, retirement, insurance, etc.

The sector is carefully regulated and all financial advisers are listed and monitored by the Financial Conduct Authority (FCA). This will ensure you are protected in case of mis-selling or if anything goes wrong as they will be protected by the Financial Ombudsman Service (FOS) or Financial Services Compensation Scheme (FSCS).

You can choose between two types of advisers depending on what area of personal finance you would like to focus on and get help with.

- *Independent Financial Adviser (IFA):* If you require general financial advice, you may want to see an IFA.[40] IFAs provide impartial and unrestricted advice and are able to consider and recommend all types of retail investment products (i.e. pensions, investments) which could meet your needs and objectives. They work in your best interests and don't get paid commissions to push products.
- *Restricted advisers:* These advisers can only offer limited advice. They focus on particular types of products and/or product providers (i.e. mortgage adviser, pension adviser, investment adviser, etc.) so it may be more difficult for you to understand what they can help you with. (It's interesting to note that most of the big, well-known financial advice firms don't provide independent financial advice but restricted advice.)

Advisers will typically provide advice on a product (*Do I need a pension or an ISA? Do I need insurance?*) but they should also provide you with broader comprehensive financial life planning (*Am I saving enough money? Will I have enough money to retire on? How can I achieve my goals?*). You will be able to discuss your financial goals, lifestyle and priorities and, based on this, they will work on a cash flow model and build a financial plan for you.

There is still a fear of being mis-sold financial products that are not right for you. However, a good financial adviser should genuinely be interested in growing your wealth, because it's good for the health of their business reputation too.

Do you need a financial adviser?

If you are young and have a financial life that is relatively simple (that is, you are not struggling with debt, you are single, don't have kids, you don't have a large sum of capital to invest or you are just looking at saving money) you may not feel you need an adviser. For now, it may be enough just to manage to save some money and learn the basics about investing because the cost of financial advice can be prohibitive if you don't have a lot of money. According to the *Financial Times*, most banks have now stopped offering financial advice to their clients, except to wealthy customers, but they can give you an overview of the financial products they offer. However, this will be informative only – they can't tell you which products are suitable for you.[41] As and when you embark upon more complex financial decisions and situations (planning for retirement, inheriting money) or major life transitions (buying a home, having a baby, getting married or perhaps divorced), you may want to get some more expert help. Although financial advice will cost you some money, which is counter-intuitive, it will also in all likelihood save you time and provide you with knowledge that can add value to your future. If money is a source of stress, working with a professional could also boost your confidence. I can't tell you what's best for you but working with a finance professional is definitely a great option to consider.

FINANCIAL ADVICE GAP HAS BEEN IDENTIFIED IN THE UK

In 2016, the FCA and the Financial Advice Market Review (FAMR) published a joint report[42] that identified an 'advice gap', showing that consumers are unable to get the advice and guidance they need, at a price they are willing to pay. They have introduced market recommendations aimed at closing the gap with the aim of achieving, 'a real improvement in the affordability and accessibility of advice and guidance to people at all stages of their lives'.

What will happen during a first meeting?

The first meeting with an adviser should always be free as it is a consultation. Do make sure that this is the case beforehand, and that you are not committed to take any financial advice by attending this first meeting. The first session is usually called a 'fact-finding' meeting where the adviser can get to understand your goals, where you are today and how he or she can help you. You will also get a sense of whether the adviser is the right one for your needs.

You will be asked about all the money taboos that you usually keep to yourself: how much you earn, save, have in your accounts, what are your assets, liabilities, etc. They will write all these numbers in black and white in front of you, and this can seem a little overwhelming but if you have already practised the exercise earlier in this chapter, you will be well-prepared.

The initial consultation is the best way to get to know an adviser. You may also find yourself having the first frank money conversation of your life. Do focus on whether you think you could work with your adviser on a personal level and whether he or she has helped you to form a better understanding of your goals and finances. If they have also helped you to understand what options are available then they have done their job well and it may be worth a second date.

How much should you be prepared to pay for on-going advice?

Depending on the type of advice you require and the amount of money you would like to invest, advisers will charge you in a different way and at different rates. According to a report by the FCA[43], there are two different charges made by advisers: the initial charge, which is for when you need specific advice as a one-off or first step of an on-going process; and the on-going charge, which is what you pay for the on-going relationship with the adviser.

Remember that the more advice you need, the more money it will cost you. According to MAS[44], there are different charges by advisers:

- **Percentage of investment value:** This is the most typical way to charge fees. For initial advice, it is on average 1–3% of the money that is managed for you and for on-going charges the average is between 0.5%–1%.
- **Hourly rate:** If you require specific advice, you can ask your adviser to work on an hourly basis, for a fixed rate. In the UK, this will vary from £75 to £350 per hour (£150 per hour on average). It is better to agree a total number of hours before starting the process.
- **Fixed fee:** The adviser will fix a fee for a specific service (mortgage, pension, ISA, and so on) ranging from a few hundred to a few thousand pounds.
- **A monthly fee:** this could be a flat fee or a percentage of the money you want to invest.

According to Unbiased[45], it is recommended that you seek financial advice when you have more than £30,000 to invest. According to the organisation, which publishes industry averages, you should expect to pay £450–500 for an initial financial review, for setting up a £11,000 stocks and shares ISA, or for advice on investing £80 a month into a pension.

How can you find an adviser?

Discussing money matters is very personal and it can feel incredibly exposing, so choosing the right adviser for you is vital...

There are a few ways you can look for an adviser. The ideal way is via a personal recommendation from a friend, member of your family or a colleague who has already worked with the adviser and is happy with their services.

If you can't find personal recommendation, there are online directories such as VouchedFor and Unbiased. These sites list the advisers available near you and you can search for your specific needs.

Always make sure that the advisers are qualified and listed by the regulator on the FCA website.[46]

Once you have listed the subjects you would like to cover and the goals you would like to achieve, you can start to contact a handful of advisers by email or by phone. It is very important to make sure you meet them in person before making any kind of decision. It is also a good idea to ask them to send you a sample financial plan in advance. Take time to read the small print and make sure you understand the services you will receive for the fees you will be paying. Then you can start to prepare the right kind of questions in advance of your first meeting.

Here is a list of questions that I find super useful and that has helped me get to know lot of advisers:

- *Are you an independent (IFA) or restricted financial adviser?*
- *What certifications do you hold?*
- *What are the types of products you offer?*
- *Do you sell your own firm's financial products?*
- *How much will you charge for your services?*
- *How and when would I pay for them?*
- *What style of service will you provide: face-to-face meeting, calls, emails?*

- *What materials will I receive or what apps/software do you use?*
- *Can I see an example of a financial plan that you have prepared?*
- *Will I work with you exclusively or with someone else on your team?*
- *What is your experience as an adviser and what type of clients do you typically advise?*
- *How will you manage my investments? How often will we review these?*
- *What is your investment track record?*

Financial coaching

Financial coaching is essentially life coaching for money. Nowadays, there are also financial therapists who will help steer you through your personal finance journey and help you get to grips with the emotional issues that underwrite your spending and saving style.

Financial (or money) coaches are not regulated by the FCA and they are not allowed to sell any products or tell you which ones to buy. Their USP is in providing guidance on saving, budgeting, money and relationships, debt, education and so on.

Make sure you are happy with a financial coach's fees (which are usually fixed per hour, starting at a few hundred pounds) and credentials. Some can be ex-IFAs (independent financial advisers); others may come from a non-financial background. You may be happy with either but try to determine what kind of person will help you most with your money in order to understand what type of coaching you need.

Financial coaching can have great benefits as it allows you to have an honest conversation that you would struggle to have with anyone else. A good financial coach can help you rewrite your money narrative and methodology and teach you how to deal with the self-limiting beliefs and self-talk associated with money and earning potential, such as: 'I don't earn enough', 'I'm not worth it', 'I'll never have enough to live off', 'I will never clear my debts.'

One of the aims of a financial coach is to educate you about the financial services on offer; from saving and investing to your pension or insurance.

They will also try to destigmatize money jargon and help you to combat any financial taboos you feel oppressed by. The relationship with your coach is an ongoing one that should help you to form healthier financial habits without the fear of a hard sell, being mis-sold to, or in fact any selling at all. Think of it as an emotional helping hand through your personal financial needs.

It is important to note that financial guidance (or money coaching) is very different from financial advice (which comes from financial advisers). Financial advisers are regulated by the FCA and they will be able to recommend products for you. Financial coaches can't do that, they can only offer more generic information and help as a guide to navigating the personal finance landscape.

EXERCISE

Start building a short list of financial professionals who could help you.

Adviser Name	Certification	Specialty	Contact Details	Recommended by?	Fees

How should you choose financial products and spot scams?

We all suffer from information overload and with so many of us making our own financial decisions and the ease of subscribing to anything online, it is no wonder that the number of financial scams is on the rise. Most of these are quite easy to identify and there are some basic rules that should help you spot what is good, what is bad and where you can put your money safely: more about these below.

First, the good news. It is important to know that your savings and any money deposited in an account have a level of protection, provided by the Financial Services Compensation Scheme (FSCS). The FSCS is funded by firms (banks and financial institutions) that are authorized by the UK regulators (Financial Conduct Authority/FCA and Prudential Regulation Authority/PRA) who pay an annual levy and will automatically protect the first £85,000 of your money (or £170,000 for joint accounts) if your UK bank or building society goes out of business, provided your lender is authorized by the FCA and PRA. The FSCS is impartial and independent of the government and the financial industry.

So, ensure the firm you are dealing with has a FCA or PRA number. If you're unsure, visit the FSCS website for the full list of banks, building societies and credit unions protected and compensation limits. If you have more than £85,000 in a single account, move some of it to another account in another bank to spread your risk.

How does it work? If you wish to make a claim, you can visit the FSCS website. You can either complete a claim service form online or request a paper application form. If anything happens to your bank, FSCS will automatically refund your savings. In the vast majority of cases to date, savings have been refunded in less than 7 days.

WHAT IS THE FCA?

The Financial Conduct Authority is a financial regulatory body in the United Kingdom, but operates independently of the UK Government, and is financed by charging fees to members of the financial services industry. fca.org.uk

WHAT IS THE PRA?

The Prudential Regulation Authority (PRA) is a part of the Bank of England and responsible for the prudential regulation and supervision of banks, building societies, credit unions, insurers and major investment firms. It sets standards and supervises financial institutions at the level of the individual firm.

bankofengland.co.uk/prudential-regulation

Beware of scams!

Don't be fooled! People running scams are very good at making you part with your money. Always remain vigilant because scammers are using newer and ever-smarter techniques to get at your identity and your money. You can never be too smart for them... They will usually approach you directly at home, by post/phone or email and will ask you for personal details, or login details. They will often offer you a deal too good to be true.

- Always keep your personal information confidential and protect your accounts with strong passwords that you change regularly.
- Check that the company contacting you is legitimate; you can do that on the FCA register website.
- Don't call a company back on the phone number they give you – get the number from the official website instead.
- Check your bank statement for small withdrawals that seem unfamiliar. (Scammers will sometimes do a test transaction first.)
- Check your credit score online and look for unfamiliar applications.

- Always avoid using public WiFi if you need to do an online bank transfer, because these free WiFi spots have become prime targets for scammers and hackers. Make sure you switch to your mobile provider's data network (4G) and disconnect from the free WiFi.

If you've been scammed: Try to stop the payment and report the scam to Action Fraud on 0300 123 2040 (UK only) or use their online reporting tool.[47]

Well Done! You have earnt £ coins!

If there is any chapter in this book worth re-reading or annotating, it is probably this one, because in order to move forward, you really need to understand your current financial status and recognise the money pitfalls that have tripped you up. This chapter will have given you an overview of where you stand today with your money. This new and revitalized understanding will serve as a core foundation-stone for the next stage of your pre-rich journey towards financial health and wealth. Like any strong structure, your financial life plan needs a strong base on which to build, so ensure that you have properly digested and got to grips with this chapter.

Working through this chapter may have been painful, but now you have done the hard graft, you can look forward to a bright and sparkly future, because the next chapter is all about your money goals...

Wealth is more than money.

Money Talk
with Romilly Morgan

Job: Senior Commissioning Editor at Octopus Publishing Group, Hachette UK.

Fun fact: Passionate and curious, Romilly is hunting for the best non-fiction ideas. She finds exciting new authors and operates her magic to transform their expertise into beautiful and brilliant books 🤩.

Money motto: 'A woman must have money and a room of her own' – *Virginia Woolf*

What makes you happy?
Long conversations that change the way I think for days after. Achieving more than others think I can. Pushing myself harder than I think I can go. Being surrounded by people who challenge me.

What is your most treasured possession?
My library of books. Whenever I go into someone's home I look for their books; it is the closest you can come, I think, to stepping inside someone's mind.

What is the best money advice you have ever received?
Ask for more.

What is your biggest money failure/mistake?
Thinking it/I was a failure. Failing and making mistakes is the only way to learn anything.

What is your greatest money achievement?
Getting out of the red and knowing I could. Essentially realizing what stands in your way becomes the way.

What is your greatest money regret or fear?
I have an irrational fear of bailiffs.

What is your top money hack?
Negotiate. Negotiate. Negotiate. Everything.

Who is your go-to person to talk about money?
My older brother, he is my finance guru.

Who is someone you admire most in life?
Aemilia Lanyer, who lived in the 17th century, rumoured to be the 'Dark Lady' of Shakespeare's sonnets and all round non-conformist. She wrote *Salve Deus Rex Judaeorum*, a poem that seeks to debunk the myth that original sin was created by the first woman, Eve. It's a dazzling feminist tract that still blows my mind with its potency.

What is your favourite book?
Primo Levi's *If This Is Man* has a sentence that I have turned over many times in my mind since reading it: 'Sooner or later in life everyone discovers that perfect happiness is unrealizable, but there are few who pause to consider the antithesis: that perfect unhappiness is equally unattainable.'

What is your next money step?
To one day be able to buy a room of my own.

Who are going to give this book to?
Myself. Knowledge is power. It starts with the individual. And then you need to pass it on.

CHAPTER 3: PLANNING FOR THE FUTURE

£££

* *

What you will learn in this chapter:

How can you put together a life plan?
How can you live life on your own terms?
How can you protect yourself and your family?

* *

WHAT IS A DREAM WITHOUT A PLAN? A WISH!

Now that you know where you stand financially, don't judge yourself too harshly if you are not happy with the result. You have honestly done the hardest part: digging deep to get real with your numbers. From here on you will start to figure out the answers to life's bigger questions.

Do you have any idea of where you want to be in 1, 5, 10 or 20 years' time? What are your dreams? What is your purpose? Have you ever thought about how can you achieve your dreams? Do you actually need money for all of these?

A study by Brewin Dolphin shows that there is a disconnect between the way we live today and the way we think we will live in the future. More than 50% of respondents questioned say they have a plan but only for a 'few days or weeks in advance'. Just 14% have a plan for the coming years and a mere 4% for the next decades. Unsurprisingly, without a plan in place, it's very hard to achieve our goals.

In this chapter, we will think about what our goals are, what we want to achieve in life, and explore some bigger ambitions which you may or may not have on your own 'bucket list' to inspire you. These are based on the dreams, issues and challenges faced by those within the Vestpod community. Thinking about these will offer you new ideas and guidance on how to fine-tune your own life goals to prioritize and achieve what you want. This is a very open conversation and we may well have differing views or personal circumstances, but the main thing is to stay inspired and on track with your goal-setting.

We'll finish off this section by talking about protection. In this ultra-connected world, we sometimes need to take a step back and understand where we are on a personal level, to allow ourselves to take life as it comes and aim to achieve our goals no matter what life throws at us.

Where Do You Want To Be?

The future will look different for each of us. We all need time and dedication to build a plan for how we envisage it to be. Life will not necessarily turn out as we expect it to, but we need to aim for something; once we reach our initial goal, we can then aim higher and bigger. Having a plan will allow you to achieve more, more quickly – especially when it comes to your finances. You can either wish to win the lottery (even if you have never bought a lottery ticket), or you can throw aside your dreams of getting rich quick (unless you actually do win the lottery 🤩) and start the long journey of wealth building instead. This section helps us too understand how to create a plan and get started on working towards our goals.

Why do you need a plan?

You are the only one responsible for your financial future. Your employer, family, friends unfortunately are not. Financial plans are not only for the rich, they are for everyone – and here is why:

A plan will help you get to your destination

Knowing where you want to go might seem obvious, but sometimes the detail of how to reach your destination is not the first thing that springs to mind when you talk about your hopes and dreams. What do you really, really want? Is it to retire at 50 or is it to re-train for a career that will keep you motivated and inspired into your old age? Do you want to be able to buy a property for your children one day, or buy them the best education possible so they can earn enough to buy their own homes before they're 30? Does your love of baking, yoga, pottery really need to become your main job, or would it be better left as a hobby or side-hustle?

A plan will help you to become wealthier by saving more

I can't emphasize enough that not buying stuff now will make your life happier in the long term than if you did buy those things. We are talking luxuries here, not necessities. If you can switch your goals from immediate gratification to security later in life, you will sleep much more soundly at night. Saving small amounts of money will help you to grow your financial pot steadily.

A plan will give you peace of mind and more confidence

Having a plan may not be essential for success in all areas of your life, but when it comes to money, it definitely is. By planning ahead for how much you will need if you want to achieve your dreams, and by understanding what financial position you need to be in to buy a property or retire early, you will develop a clear plan of action and peace of mind. Think about how much you earn, how much you spend, and how much you keep every month and every year. Start to make money management part of your well-being!

A plan will make you happy

According to a survey by Morningstar Financial Research, when people believe they can plan for their financial future and be in control of their money they feel better about money than those who have little control over their lives.[48]

A plan helps you to sail through surprises

We all know that surprises can be both good and bad. One of the major benefits of having a plan is that you can avoid unexpected situations and be in control, even when a bit of bad luck strikes.

A plan doesn't get distracted

Procrastinating is never a good idea when it comes to your personal finances. It can be tempting to put off making decisions, or even doing research into ways to save, to a time when you are feeling less stressed. But your stress will compound (in a bad way) like the interest on a loan, if you don't act now to put a financial plan in place. You are never too young or too poor to start the ball rolling. Even by saving a small amount you will be better off in one year's time than if you procrastinated because it didn't seem worth saving right now. Your future self will be proud!

A plan will force you to use numbers

Some of us can be reluctant to use the real numbers for planning purposes – but when you have a plan with actual figures you gain both clarity and confidence. Planning can be complicated, but it does not have to be – and whilst financial advisers can produce in-depth plans for you with the help of software and algorithms, there are also many things you can start doing on your own, from making an incomings and outgoings list, to adding up how much you're *really* spending every month, on luxuries like Uber and eating out! If that figure is horribly high, translate that into the fantastically high saving you'll make next month by stopping unnecessary spending!

A plan will help you avoid ending up in debt

Building your own plan is the first step towards a debt-free life. You could also take this plan to an adviser later on to discuss how to fine-tune it. In these ways you can start looking ahead to a future where paying off debt comes naturally and doesn't ever lead to taking on more.

Write down your financial goals

Let's start by writing down our goals. Sometimes, this can sound easier than it is. Most of us have never done this exercise before and at first, it can seem overwhelming, but try not to panic! We'll run through examples to help you. Start off with your short-term goals in mind, and when it comes to long-term, think of more complex goals. In order to do this, try to imagine your life in 1, 5, 10 and 20 year time-frames. This will help you decide what you need and when.

Ask yourself: Do I have an emergency fund? Do I have costly debts? Will I be making big purchases (house, cars, big birthday parties)? Do I want to change job or set up a business? Do I want to have children? Am I saving for retirement? Do I have to pay for my childrens education, childcare and more? Do I plan to leave a legacy? Do I have insurances to protect myself? Will I have to support ageing parents? Do I have dreams?

EXERCISE

All the things I want to achieve in the future are:

....

....

....

....

....

....

....

Once you have a list of all the things you would like to achieve, break the time-frame into four parts. It's always good to start today. As we've discussed in the previous chapter, repaying our expensive debts, building up our emergency fund and making a budget are really key here!

Today (the next 1 to 2 years): Day-to-day spending, building emergency savings, repaying expensive debts?

Short-term (the next 2 to 5 years): Holidays, shopping, new laptop, car?

Medium-term (the next 5–10 years): Set up a business, deposit for a house, getting married?

Long-term (10 years+): Retirement, children's education?

EXERCISE

Can you try writing at least one goal per time horizon?

★ My four main goals at the moment are:

Today. . . . .

Short-term. . . . .

Medium-term . . . .

Long-term. . . . .

How does it feel? Businessman and founder of Virgin Group Richard Branson always recommends that you should write down your ideas as you have them, rather than trust that you will remember them – and he should know! There is power in writing down your ideas, whether through bringing them to life, or by working towards attaining self-realization.

To help me write down my goals, I use the SMART approach[49], to help me to clarify and break down my goals, and make them achievable on time. The five SMART steps will guide you too:

- **S**pecific: What exactly will you do with the money? What do you want to buy or what do you want to accomplish?
- **M**easurable: How much is the goal valued at in £? What is the exact amount (more or less)?
- **A**chievable: How can your goal be achieved? Is it realistic? Would a budget or spending plan help you to achieve it? Can you break your goal into smaller goals to make it easier to achieve? What are the constraints?
- **R**elevant: Is your goal relevant? Does it motivate you? Is it meaningful enough? Can it challenge you?
- **T**imely: When do you want to achieve this goal by? If the horizon is too long and difficult to think about, can you create staged deadlines inbetween, to help you to achieve things more quickly?

Without numbers and timelines, your goals are not realistic: it is hard to reach a goal if you don't know whether you're close to it or how to achieve it. Your goals have to be as closely connected as possible to your today and your current reality; creating a sense of urgency will help to achieve this! When a goal is vague and undetailed, it does not seem real. The less real it is, the less achievable it will be.

This exercise of goal setting is also a learning process. Here are some generic examples with three goals: one today, one short-term, one medium-term and one long-term!

Specific GOAL	**M**easurable COST ££	**A**chievable HOW	**R**elevant WHY	**T**imely WHEN
'Build my emergency savings'	£4,000 (this corresponds to 4 months of outgoings)	Save £333 per month into a specific saving account	Last month, I had to pay for repairs on my car but as I did not have the cash to hand, I had to pay with my credit card, and now I am struggling to repay. Never again!	Today 1 year
'Trip to see my friends in Australia (for one month!)'	£3,000	Save £80 per month into a specific saving account	Can't wait to go but I know it will be an expensive trip so let's start saving now.	Short-term 3 years
'Saving money to buy a house'	£30,000	Save £500 per month into a specific saving account	I have been renting for years but I really want to get my own place. According to my calculations, that should also cost me less per month, so I will be able to save money.	Medium-term 5 years
'Saving for retirement'	£4,800 per year	Save £400 per month into a retirement account invested in the stock market	I want to retire at 60 no matter what, and make sure I have enough money to live the way I am living today.	Long-term 30 years

EXERCISE

After thinking about your financial goals at the beginning of the section, you can start filling in this table with your today, short-term, medium-term and long-term goals. You can then rank them (some of them will be more urgent and important than others), to decide where you want to start first. We are always tempted to work on short-term goals first and, while repaying expensive debts and building an emergency fund should be your top priorities, don't ignore retirement when you look at your savings goals 🤓.

Today's goals

Specific GOAL	**M**easurable COST £	**A**chievable HOW	**R**elevant WHY	**T**imely WHEN	*Priority (1, 2, 3...)*

Short-term goals

Specific GOAL	**M**easurable COST £	**A**chievable HOW	**R**elevant WHY	**T**imely WHEN	*Priority (1, 2, 3...)*

EXERCISE

Medium-term goals

Specific GOAL	**M**easurable COST £	**A**chievable HOW	**R**elevant WHY	**T**imely WHEN	*Priority (1, 2...)*

Long-term goals

Specific GOAL	**M**easurable COST £	**A**chievable HOW	**R**elevant WHY	**T**imely WHEN	*Priority (1, 2...)*

Once you have decided on your goals (with costs and timelines), create a game plan. How are you going to achieve this? What will it cost each month?

Take the **M**easurable amount, and divide by the number of years, then divide by 12, and you'll be left with the amount you need to save every month for each goal. Don't panic if the sum is greater than you expected. Think, is this realistic? Is it affordable? Maybe you could try to see if you could get there! Two thousand years ago, Aristotle wrote: *'First, have a definite, clear, practical ideal; a goal, an objective. Second, have the necessary means to achieve your ends: wisdom, money, materials, and methods. Third, adjust all your means to that end.'*

If you see these goals are not yet reachable, revisit your goals and negotiate an achievable target. Now, you can now start working towards your goals. You can decide to start working on them simultaneously or start according to the rank you gave them.

We've had a go at our first planning exercise by understanding where you like to be. Your adviser would be proud. So, what's next? Well, you should review your goals and update them regularly – the likelihood is that as you achieve some of your goals, others will start to seem outdated. Remember – you can always change your mind, and your work and your life! Look back periodically at the goals you've written down to see if they are still valid. Maybe you'll have already achieved some of the short-term goals or made good progress towards them. Upon a second glance, was it hard to achieve these or effortless?

Finally, accountability is key. Of course, we all want to achieve optimum financial health, but in reality, it's very, very hard. Willpower has its limits. We're only human, and however carefully we budget, there will always be those days when you just *have* to splurge on a treat, blowing half your monthly spending money in the process. This is where personal accountability comes in.

What is personal accountability? To sum it up, it means that you and you alone are responsible for your actions and their consequences. That goes for successes and failures.

Why is it important? Because it's often the missing piece of the puzzle when you're not achieving your financial goals. You might have stopped that £5 a day coffee habit, but why are your debts not diminishing as you'd hoped? It's probably because you're not being totally present and honest with yourself when it comes to money. Being accountable means not sweeping *anything* under the carpet and looking honestly at your *every* financial action, including Amazon books orders, drunken internet shopping and giving money to charity. You have to own your transactions, to make your money work for you.

Six ways you can stay accountable with your money

1. Get a motto to live by: Know who you are and why you are doing what you are doing. Yes, this might sound like a level of self-knowledge that even 2,000 years of philosophy can't quite figure out, but by picking a phrase which is meaningful to you, you can prepare for the day ahead with it in the back of your mind. It might be something as big as 'achieve total independence' or as low-key as 'stay humble'.

2. Find your tribe: Do you have a personal trainer when you go to the gym? Do you have a nutritionist checking up on your diet? Do you have strict deadlines from your boss? If these things help you achieve your goals, extend that to your personal finances.

Whether it's a financial adviser, a friend, or even an online community like Vestpod, having the right person by your side can really help you to get things done.

3. Use an app: Online goal trackers like Stikk or to-do-list app Wunderlist are brilliant for helping you commit to your goal. You will be sent reminders when you need them, which will help you stay organised and focussed.

4. Visualize your goals: Try to see or imagine a visual mental image of your goals. Figure out your intentions first and then focus, not necessarily on getting exactly what you want, but on connecting with the feeling of achieving your goal. Start by creating a mood board, whether on Pinterest or a physical version, with pictures associated with your goals: Saving for kids? Add a photo. Seeking inspiration? Pin a photo of someone who you find empowering or inspiring, whether an entrepreneur such as Sara Blakely (founder of Spanx), or an influential figure like Michelle Obama. Saving for a round trip? Print a photo of a plane or the perfect surf beach shack in Bali. Saving for retirement? Put up pictures of a dog, a house, a plane, another job... You get it!

5. Break it down: Make your saving to-do list manageable. If an item is still on your list after a month, it might not be something you're ever going to manage, and staring at it every month might make you feel bad. If this is the case, scrap it! Set achievable targets and keep reviewing them to see how you're doing. Remember, you learn more from your mistakes than your successes. Spent far too much on lunches this week? Take time to sit with your thoughts and really burrow down into why. Don't blame work, or the weather, or other people. The reason you do what you do lies within you.

6. Reward yourself: All this might sound a little more tough-talkin' than the usual Vestpod hand-holdery... but while looking hard at your motivations and taking full responsibility for yourself is one of the hardest elements of personal development, the process of applying this to your finances does not need to be painful. Remember that there's a reward just around the corner (and not one that will ruin next month's budget either, because the new accountable you doesn't hide their 'guilty' spending in the back of your wardrobe, like a never-worn pair of expensive shoes).

When you're being personally accountable, everything is out in the open, so you can really enjoy your spending. Once you've saved enough money, you can reward yourself. And why not make it an educational experience like a fun cookery course or a session with a life coach or nutritionist? Spending your hard-earned cash on an experience, rather than a commodity, will make a difference to the way you feel (and it won't ever gather dust!).

EXERCISE

Coming back to your list of goals. Can you attach one or two images to each of your goals, to help you to visualize them, make them real? Do you have someone you would like to share your goals with?

....

....

Live Your Life On Your Own Terms

How can you get the most of your time on this planet? Whether you see money as an enabler or a constraint in your life, the truth is that for most big decisions in life, you will need money, but let's first look at its subtleties:

☻ You and your life: are you dreaming big enough?

Every child has a dream, whether to be a ballet dancer, an astronaut, a vet or a footballer. But somewhere along the way reality takes over and that child who once fell asleep at night dreaming of a standing ovation at the Royal Opera House becomes an adult who just has a photo of ballet shoes as her screensaver.

The fact is, most adults don't have dreams. They surface, sometimes in middle age, when the realization that death is non-negotiable suddenly leads people to buy a Porsche or start skydiving. But those responses are just expressions of fear, really.

If you look deep within yourself, you will find that there is something amazing you want to do, no matter how old you are. If you're dreaming of becoming a pro-footballer at the age of 45, this might not be so achievable, but the great thing about the dreams we have as adults is that many of them are only just out of reach – so if you really want it, you can make it work. Our dreams often related to having a certain lifestyle: living in the sun, teaching yoga, keeping animals, never getting stuck in the rush hour again – not such crazy ambitions!

It's time to take charge and to decide on the life you want, and then to do everything you can to achieve it, because that mid-life crisis victim is right: death is non-negotiable. Cut the small talk and start thinking big – it's a fun and joyous thing to do. Think positive and believe in your power to change and move forward!

After figuring out your goal, the first step is often nothing to do with money. It's about opening your mind to all the new skills that are going to help you on your way. Read more, try new podcasts (don't be afraid of the 'self-help' label). Take a course, consider going back to studying, learn new skills. Take care of yourself, exercise, meditate. There may be some fees to pay initially but consider this as an investment in yourself that will deliver clear, long-term returns.

Try to stay positive throughout the process. See the challenges that arise as learning opportunities. Can you overcome your limiting beliefs (see Chapter 1) by developing a growth mindset? It may sound like a lot to do, but positivity and forward momentum really are a choice – think of the times you have seen people pick themselves up after unimaginably bad times. You too can change the script and achieve levels of wealth that you have only just started dreaming of (the kind that tastes like freedom – not £1,000 handbag 'wealth').

EXERCISE

What are your biggest dreams?

....

....

....

☻ Prepare for a family and protect them

If you decide to start a family, your life will become more complicated and your financial decisions will not be as personal to you; instead they will become couple and family finances.

Preparing for coupledom

Imagine you've just got married or you've been dating your partner for some time. How do you manage your rent payments and day-to-day expenses? When is the right time for you to combine your finances? How do you both protect yourselves? Many of us have used long Excel files and iPhone apps to reconcile monthly expenses, summing up the total into a who-paid-what sort of bill. Somewhat painful and not quite romantic, but think carefully before you consider the alternative. Combining your finances is a big decision so think about the pros and cons. Here are the options:

Combine part of your finances:

- Open a new bank account under both your names and transfer a predetermined amount of money each month. The amount of money you transfer could be equal for both of you, or according to salaries. The rest is kept in personal accounts.
- Combining your finances is a good way to help you track of your expenses and keep on budget. You will need a new, shared and separate bank account to do this and it is a useful way to stash away the money needed for rent and bills at the beginning of the month. You'll have a better idea of where your money is going and how to keep a budget (as the expenses won't get mixed with your personal expenses).
- Bear in mind that you will both have full access to the account and that the money can be withdrawn by either of you at any time!

Combine everything:

- Combine all of your money: this involves sharing savings, current and brokerage accounts.
- Combining your finances is a big step. You should make sure that you have discuss this in detail in advance and know exactly what you are doing and why you are doing it. Whether it's for commitment,

convenience or support, you need to agree with each other and set up some rules for what you can or cannot do. Before you take the plunge, ask each other honestly, do you have any debt? If yes, are you ready to share this debt? Are you really 100% sure?

- Make sure you protect your income and net worth. Sadly, many couples have to separate at some point or even divorce and this can become a tricky situation to manage. See the end of this chapter for more on this.

Keep it separate:

- Each has his/her own accounts (savings, current, brokerage).
- If you are not sure about combining your money or that it sounds a bit too much for you at this stage of your relationship, this may be your best option. Money is personal, and you need to feel in control and trust your partner with your money.
- You can pay for household expenses by splitting them (use an app for that such as Splittable).

No one solution is better than another, these are very personal choices and often evolve with time.

MONEY + LOVE: A MATCH MADE IN HEAVEN?

Some recent research from the US[50] sheds light on how earning parity might affect the success of a relationship. Patrick Ishizuka, an academic at Cornell University's Cornell Population Center, has been studying the role that money plays in how long people stay together, and whether they get married. His findings, published on the Cornell blog in the journal *Demography*[51], make for enlightening reading.

First, he found that people will often *delay getting married* until they have accumulated enough joint income to pay for a wedding (in the UK in 2018 people spent an average £18k on their weddings, not including the honeymoon)[52] as well as a house, car and a stable personal finance situation. This is actually the first time it has been empirically proven that most of us will wait until we attain the same financial status as our peers before heading down the aisle.

The other thing Ishizuka discovered is that *couples with a healthier financial life and higher level of education are less likely to separate*. We've talked before about the pressure that poverty and lack of financial education can put on a relationship, and it seems that's not just anecdotal. It really is harder to make love work when your working life isn't working for you.

Ultimately, the study concludes that 'equality appears to promote stability'. When partners can contribute the same amount, marriage appears to be more equal and stable over time.

Prepare your finances for a baby

The glow of fresh parenthood is quickly tainted by sleepless nights and endless feeding sessions, so it's no surprise that getting down to the nitty-gritty details of your family finances may feel like the last thing you want to do. But whether you plan for your child's financial future pre- or post-partum, it's something that simply has to be done. Here are four essential considerations:

1. **Life and health insurance:** If you haven't already got the former, it's time to strongly consider it. Your child is your financial dependent and preparing for the worst-case scenario – grim as that thought might be – is your parental responsibility. And while health insurance isn't mandatory in the UK, if you or your partner are covered through a work scheme, you might want to add your child to your insurance plan, too.
2. **Start saving for their future with a Junior ISA:** Help your child or children to get a leg-up in life by starting to save early for their future. There are cash or stocks and share options for the Junior ISA just as there are for the regular version. But remember, you're not investing for yourself and won't be able to withdraw any of the money you put into a Junior ISA. Only your child will be able to access their money, when they turn 18.
3. **Budget your maternity (and paternity) pay:** Baby-related expenses can escalate quickly, especially if you catch yourself off guard and fail to plan ahead. This is the time to say 'yes' to offers of help from friends and family to buy things for your new arrival, especially things like clothes which babies grow out of in no time. (Baby shower, anyone?) Also, keep in mind that there are many items and products on the market that you really can do without, despite aggressive marketing to try to convince you otherwise! Make sure you also look into Child Care Tax Credits to help you pay for childcare or at least keep up with your National Insurance contributions.
4. **Make sure your will is up to date:** It may feel scary to think about, but writing/updating your will is likely to give you greater peace of mind. Besides the financial elements of your will, another vital thing to consider is who your child's guardian would be until they turn 18.

EXERCISE

Are you planning to get married and have kids? How do you see your life with more members? Can you plan for it? What are the things you will need to adjust? Would you need more money for this?

....

....

....

To buy or to rent?

For generations, buying a home has been viewed as the ultimate measure of success. Property ownership has become a sort of Holy Grail; as a result, you may feel increasingly stigmatized if you are a tenant. But is it really that big a deal? Have we simply been oversold the idea of home-ownership?

Getting onto the property ladder is more difficult today than it has ever been. According to the Institute For Fiscal Studies,[53] only a quarter of young adults manage to buy a property compared to a third two decades ago. The biggest decline in homeownership has been observed for young adults with incomes between £22k and £31k a year.

There are many reasons why so many people – predominantly millennials (aka Generation Rent) – are finding it nearly impossible to get a foot (or even just half a toe) on the property ladder. Low savings? Self-employed? Riddled with debt? Or, perhaps, simply facing high living costs?

We know that buying a house is an expensive, long-term commitment – which begs the question: is it worth it? As with everything in life (except ice cream and shoes) both buying and renting have their pros and cons. Here they are:

Some buying considerations	Some renting considerations
• When you pay off your home, it's all yours – you own an asset (and usually a large mortgage) but you are also financially responsible for repairs and maintenance. • If your house does increase in value, you can earn a return or break even. The opposite is also true – when house prices go down, you may lose money. • It could be cheaper to pay a mortgage than to rent but, if interest rates rise, you may end up paying more. • You could rent it out to generate some income (check the taxes). • Emotional security: owning a home is a tangible asset, so it has an emotional benefit, by making you feel secure and safe.	• Renting isn't 'throwing away money' as some would say – because you actually get a place to live. • What you can afford as a tenant could be nicer and more spacious than what you can afford as a homeowner (especially true in urban areas). • You run the risk of being made to move out by your landlord. • No need to worry about stamp duty, conveyancing fees, valuation fees, mortgage fees, repairs and maintenance...The list goes on. • You don't have the same commitment as you would to your mortgage, allowing for more flexibility.

What's right for you? At the end of the day, only you can decide. Maybe the idea of committing to a mortgage is simply too stressful, or perhaps you'd rather own a modest home in the suburbs than rent in the middle of a city. There's no 'one-size-fits-all' answer, so listen to your reasoning, assess various resources and only do what works for you.

→ For more about getting onto the property ladder, head to Chapter 9

EXERCISE

What is right for me? What are your reasons for buying? For renting?

....

....

....

....

Prepare for a 100-year life

Did you know that life expectancy has been increasing at the rate of two to three years every decade? There are all kinds of implications for living a longer life: we get to spend more time with our families and explore unforeseen hobbies in retirement. But there's also the more complex issue of planning financially for our more enduring future: living for 100 years hasn't exactly been the norm in previous generations, so we don't have a clear blueprint to follow. Andrew Scott and Lynda Gratton's '100-year life' website provides exactly such a blueprint: helping us tackle the exciting but ever so slightly terrifying prospect of living longer than ever.[54] Their key takeaways are that in order to support a longer life and your financial assets, you will need to work longer and save more. However, while working into your late 70s may give you more security, it also creates an imbalance in your other, less tangible assets, such as relationships, health, productivity and the ability to spend your time on something else.

In essence, this means that by extending the number of years spent in work you will tick the box of 'financial security' but will probably not be very happy (or relevant).

A multi-stage approach to life is one way to solve this conundrum. Take the multiple-career perspective as an example: each career stage will differ in terms of sector and role as well as motivation. You may spend the early years of your career motivated by financial rewards and, towards a later stage, you might want to switch to more socially rewarding work instead. In short, we each need to make sure we take care of our skills and our knowledge (perhaps in the form of re-training, short courses or vocational degrees), our mental and physical health and that we adapt to rapidly evolving technological advances. It's time to bid farewell to a linear approach to life and welcome the era of fluidity!

EXERCISE

What is your plan for an extended life? What are the things you want to focus on today/tomorrow? Do you think that the possibility of living longer will change the way you plan today? In what way?

....

....

....

....

(Based on this section, do you want to look again at your goals and see if you would like to add a few, or review them?)

Be Protected From the Unexpected

I don't particularly enjoy writing about this subject for two reasons, the first being that I realize I am clearly under-protected, and the second being that we all hate to think about the worst-case scenario 😢. You can do all the planning in the world and have the most kick-ass dreams and achievements, but if something happens that is out of your control, it's a disaster. This is often referred to as 'a financial storm'. Here we will talk about emergency savings and insurances. In life, surprises are to be expected; not all of these are good, and some can turn everything upside down – which sucks.

So, how do you stay protected? Insurance! It protects you from accidents, medical emergencies and other unexpected situations. But we will also talk about protecting yourself and your family from problems linked to relationships: inheritance or divorce for example.

Do you have an emergency fund?

📣 I know I keep saying it, but building up a rainy day fund is the *most important thing* you can do when it comes to planning your personal finances. When the unexpected happens we are likely to throw money at the problem without thinking about the implications. But after paying out for that expensive roof repair, those last-minute tickets to visit your best friend in Bali, or the medical bills incurred abroad, you can be left with a bill that's ruinous. The [simple] solution? Build your emergency fund.

Experts say you should aim to keep three to six months living expenses to one side and that it should be possible to withdraw this money instantly; so make sure you hold the cash in a savings account you can access. Have no idea what three to six months' living expenses looks like? Don't worry, we'll calculate this in Chapter 4 as part of budgeting, but living expenses are basically the cost of living: your rent or mortgage, food, groceries, utilities, debt, basic needs. Financial experts will say that the three to six months' fund may not be enough but that it's a good rule of thumb to *start* with.

If you're thinking *'What?! That sounds crazy. How am I supposed to save that much money?'* then visualize making it happen and create a plan. As for any goal, you need to start somewhere. Stash small amounts every month and increase how much you save gradually. Over time, you'll reach your goal. If you start saving £20 a week, in two years, you'll have saved £2,080. If you decide to save £50 a week instead, you'll have savings of £5,200. And if you save £75, that's a whopping £7,800 you'll have saved. Remember the £4,000 I had in the goal table earlier on? I didn't smash my goal of saving that in a year, it took me two – and that's OK!

Insurance

No one likes to think about life insurance, much less talk about it or buy it. But it's important to be pragmatic when it comes to taking care of your loved ones, and life insurance could make all the difference to their future. To determine whether you need it, ask yourself two key questions: *do you have dependants, and would they suffer financially if you weren't around to provide for them?*

If you have a mortgage or any outstanding debt and a family to care for, or you simply want to ensure your dependants will be provided for when you're no longer around, life insurance could be the single most important financial product you buy. If you die, life insurance will either pay a lump sum or regular payments to your dependants. It will also help alleviate financial stress in an already emotional and distressing time.

But, what if you were to become very ill or physically impaired? Remember that life insurance may cover death only, so you may need to take an additional insurance product for long-term illness, critical illness cover, or for total or permanent disability.

You might already have some insurance in place through work or credit cards (some cards offer travel insurance, for example). The first step is to enquire about everything you already have, then evaluate whether you have any specific needs that may require extra cover.

When you take out insurance, it will protect you for one or a few things. The insurer will decide the price of the insurance based on the risk that these things will happen. This price is called the *premium*.

How it works in practice:

- Decide what type of insurance you need (health, travel, life and so on) and choose an insurance provider.
- You will sign a contract with them called a *policy*. Make sure you read the small print. It can be extremely frustrating to find out you aren't covered for something when you thought you were. Don't be shy about asking questions; ask as many as possible until you feel you fully understand. To start the cover, you will have to pay a monthly or yearly premium. The premium frequency can affect the total cost of the cover; some providers give discounts, for example if you pay on an annual basis.
- Check the pre-existing conditions: many health problems can be considered as pre-existing medical conditions and could impact your rates or cause you to not qualify for coverage.
- Hopefully nothing will happen. But if something does and you need to use your insurance, you can make a *claim* (it's best to check how to do this at the start of your contract, before you need anything and don't feel stressed by a situation). When making a claim, you will need to explain the situation in the hope that your insurance company will be able to cover this. They will then pay you compensation or whatever you have agreed.

You may or may not need insurance and the decision is ultimately up to you, but we will look at the most common types of protection that you need to know about. You can then dig further and do your own research. If you're not sure about life insurance or the level of cover or type of insurance policy you might need, you can use an insurance broker. An adviser can also help you to make these decisions HELP? .

How to buy insurance

- The first place to investigate is your *workplace*: you may already have something in your perks and benefits, or be able to subscribe to insurances at a better premium.
- If what you are looking for is not covered, you can work with an *insurance broker*. They are experts and may be able to advise and find the best deals for you (you can find one via the BIBA/British Insurance Broker's Association Find a Broker service[55]).
- Your third option is to do it yourself and if you really know what you are looking for, use an *online comparator* such as **confused.com**, **comparethemarket.com** or **gocompare.com**.

Be vigilant: we have looked at scams earlier. You may be approached regularly to buy insurance for your phone or home or something else. Make sure you check out the companies and make sure they are registered. In recent years, for example, there has been wide-spread mis-selling of PPI (Payment Protection Insurance) in the UK, so it's important to be vigilant!

PPI?!

It's likely that you will have received dozens of emails in your junk mailbox, a few text messages or even nuisance calls about PPI (Payment Protection Insurance). The PPI topic has also stirred a media storm. But why? There has been a wide-spread mis-selling of PPI whereby millions of consumers were sold – based on bad advice – a product designed to cover repayments on mortgages (for example) if something were to go wrong and the homeowner was unable to pay for it. These products were sold as part of the mortgage or alone.

PPI was largely pushed by insurers in the 90s as a way to make more money.

However, regulators began working on the case and are now forcing banks to repay the PPI charges to consumers. According to the FCA, as of August 2018 the amount paid to customers who have complained about the way they were sold PPI is £32.6bn since January 2011. A massive shockwave for the banks...

29 August 2019 was the date set as the deadline for complaints about the mis-selling of PPI. Visit the FCA website for more info: fca.org.uk/ppi/

Types of insurance

Life insurance (also known as life cover and death cover)

Yes, we know, life insurance is one of those coffin-shaped subjects we like to ignore. According to Compare the Market[56], less than one third of UK adults have life insurance. The number of households actually covered (8.1 million) is way below the number of outstanding mortgages

(11.1 million). No one likes to think, as those morbid adverts put it, 'Who would provide for your loved ones if something happened to you?' but we all have that niggling feeling that it's something we should look in to.

On the other hand, you might not need it. Check out our quick guide to find out whether life insurance is something you can forget about, or whether it's one of those priorities that you need to tackle in your next admin session.

What is it? Life insurance is a way of paying an income or lump sum to your family if you die.

Who is it for? People who are major breadwinners in a family group. If your income is important for paying the mortgage, school fees or general expenses, insurance could give you some peace of mind.

Who is it not for? If you don't have any dependants, are already seriously ill or have a much richer spouse, maybe you don't have to bother.

Is it pricey? Not often. Depending on your age and state of health, it could cost just a couple of pounds a week – and the earlier you contract it the cheaper it will be.

How does it work? There are three main types of life insurance:

1. **Level-term insurance:** These policies run for a fixed period of time and you decide exactly how much would be paid out. They only pay out if you die before the end of the term. If you don't, the policy lapses and you get nothing back.
2. **Decreasing life insurance:** This type of policy is usually purchased to cover a specific debt such as a mortgage, which is itself reducing over time (to make sure your mortgage will be repaid after you die).
3. **Increasing life insurance:** This is the opposite of the above. It is still a term policy and the same rules apply as above when the policy holder dies (within the term). These policies are designed to protect against inflation by financially protecting the life-assured and their family, with the sum insured increasing in value over time.

How to get one? Many employers offer life insurance to their employees as part of a benefits package, and it usually comes in the form of a lump sum paid out to your dependents. It's calculated as a certain number of times your salary, so if you earn £30,000 and have a 'four times' salary policy, your dependants would get £120,000. However, always make sure to check what kind of cover your employer offers, and whether you think it is sufficient to sustain your family. It's important to note that if you leave your employer, your insurance will end. If your employer doesn't offer life insurance, you should take a look at other options. Always bear in mind that the cost of the insurance will depend on your age and your current health.

You have two options available to subscribe to these:

Consult with a financial adviser to get some help to find the best cover for you. Insurance brokers could also help you out.

Visit comparison websites such as Compare the Market, MoneySupermarket or Confused to learn more about different types of cover and find something that works best for you and your family.

Is insurance only for Grim Reaper situations? Nope. Some can help you and your family if you lose your job or are incapacitated but still kicking:

- **Income protection insurance:** Provides you with some cover if you can't earn an income because you are unable to work due to a serious illness or injury, usually until you return to paid work or you retire. If something happened to you would you be able to survive on savings, or on sick pay from work? If not, you'll need some other way to keep paying the bills. Be aware that these policies tend to pay out a percentage of your salary and usually have deferred periods of 1+ months, which will be reflected in the cost. The cheaper the cover, the less beneficial it will be.
- **Critical illness insurance:** Is a long-term insurance policy that protects you and pays you a tax-free lump sum on diagnosis of a specific illness or injury listed in the policy. The cash benefit can help you to pay off your mortgage, debts, or pay for additional medical help, but it's up to you how you spend it.

So next time you feel like doing something grown-up, go online and research what's available. There's almost certainly an option you can afford, and it might make you sleep better at night.

House insurance

This one is mandatory if you own a property. If you have a mortgage in place, the mortgage provider would have required you to subscribe to a building insurance, so that in the case of something happening (fire, massive cracks, etc), you are covered. It's not covering the fact that the house is getting older however; you will still have to pay for your own repairs and a new boiler. There is also another type of insurance you can add to the package called contents insurance, which will cover anything you lose in case of one of the above events, or if you are burgled.

- Determine which cover you need.
- Check the small print! Insurance companies always have 'reasons' not to cover you for something that happens. For example, for burglary cover you may need a certain type of lock or alarm system which may add additional costs or nullify a claim if not met!
- All your goods may not be covered – check the maximum value of certain items (jewellery?!) and look for separate insurance for these.
- Home insurance can also protect people working in your property.

Health insurance (also called Private Medical Insurance/PMI)

We are very lucky to have free access to the NHS in the UK and I have personally had very positive experiences with it. Unfortunately, sometimes you can't rely on it and the wait for an appointment can be too long, especially in urgent instances or if you have children. While it may not be a necessity if you are short of cash, private medical insurance is sometimes an important thing to have. Some form of medical cover may also be included in your work benefits, so make sure you check what you have. There are different types of cover available, from basic (access to a GP and referrals to specialists) to Gold plans (including dental care and private clinic birth delivery). You may also want to check what is covered and what is not (such as dental, optical, osteopathic or acupuncture sessions and access to nearby hospitals). Even cancers can sometimes be covered. Bear in mind that some cheaper plans don't cover in-patient treatment so if you ever require a stay in hospital following surgery or accident then you won't be covered privately.

Private health insurance can be quite costly. You have a monthly or annual premium that you pay upfront and there is also an *excess* (a certain amount you pay towards your medical bills before any repayment kicks in). The larger the excess paid for… the lower the premium.

- The price of your insurance can go up every year, but you can switch by searching for a better deal.
- Non-smokers get cheaper premiums, as do people who exercise! With some providers, by showing you have a healthy lifestyle, you can get a discount on your premium.
- Don't be fooled by discounts and rewards (such as free coffee, vouchers and gym memberships) these are just ways to encourage you to sign you up. Get clued up and look at the total cost and cover.

Car insurance

If you have a car, you need car insurance. When taking out insurance you're protecting the vehicle and the damage it/you can cause to others and their properties. There are three levels of protection you can choose from that will also have different price points (called premiums) from low to high: from the basic 'Third party' (protecting you against damage that's caused by you to others), to 'Third party, fire and theft' (same as previous but with extra protection: they will replace your car if stolen or damaged/destroyed by fire) and 'Comprehensive car insurance' (most things covered). The price you pay is determined by a lot of things including driving/accidents history, personal circumstances, car, parking etc.

- Determine which cover you need.
- Don't accept the automatic renewal (and the outrageous price increase) of your policy every year. You can change your provider by browsing around to see if you can find a better deal. You could also use a cool black box (or Telematics car insurance) that will base your premium on the way you use the car.

 Head over to GoCompare or another comparison website.

Travel insurance

Anyone who likes to travel knows that travel insurance is an essential rather than a luxury. When you travel abroad, the wisest thing you can do is always make sure you know the rules and regulations of the country you're visiting when it comes to health and safety. If you have a credit card it's possible it includes travel insurance. Travel insurance protects you from painful and expensive risks such as cancelled flights, ski injuries, lost luggage and much more. Make sure you read the small print in the terms and conditions.

- Check whether you already have travel insurance via your bank or credit card or work benefits.
- Check the terms and conditions for winter sports, for example. Insurance is offered when you buy ski passes but you may already be insured through your credit card or travel insurance. Just make sure you don't pay twice; the money saved can go towards more *genepi* (the infamous traditional herbal liquor made in the Alps) on the slopes!

Head over to gocompare.com or another comparison website.

These are the most common types of insurances, but you may also want to think about other things you would like to insure. What about your pets, your phone, your luxury items? Once you have determined what you want:

- Check whether you already have cover, as mentioned above.
- Check the cost? Does it bring value: what happens if you use the insurance?
- Do you insure or not? If not, what might be the cost of an accident?

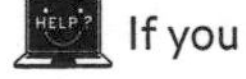

If you need help, why not check with your bank or insurance broker?

 Get clued up by visiting the Money Advice Service website.

What's my legacy?

Personal finances are of course about us, but what about the next generation? How do you protect others at the same time? How do you protect your loved ones and leave a legacy? Your situation will change over time, you might get married, you might have kids, you might get divorced; it's a complex area. While I can't tell you what is exactly right for you, there are a few things we can review that should help you understand the bigger picture.

You should definitely consult an adviser for this exercise too!

We will talk about these: the will and the power of attorney, inheritance, pension nominations and protecting yourself in your marriage. This is clearly just an overview, but we think it's important!

Do you have a will?

Financial advisers unanimously agree that writing a will is vitally important. Many even insist a will should be one of the first things you tackle when you begin planning your financial future. It can be a shock to the system and take some time to digest. If you're in denial, you're not alone: research shows that more than 60% of the adult population in the UK has yet to write a will and, of those who have no will, about 20% think it's not important because they have too small an estate and too few assets. Like it or not, though, writing a will is crucial – it gives you the power to decide what happens to your money, property and possessions after you die, and helps protect the lives of loved ones that you leave behind. When there is no will in place, some rules automatically apply to divide the assets. These are called the rules of intestacy and it's worth checking them out.[57] So it is imperative to get it done and dusted – regardless of your age, health or the state of your finances.

Where do you start? For a few hundred pounds, you can get a solicitor to write your will for you – this is often the best option. Alternatively, you can use an online DIY will platform (yep, that's a thing), which is usually free or will cost less than £50 but make sure you read it carefully and make amendments as necessary.

Pensions nominations

When you die, your pension will be left to your beneficiary (the person who inherits it) and pensions are normally (but not always) exempt from inheritance tax. But do you know who that is? Make sure you review this area and inform your pension provider of who your beneficiary should be – it can be anyone HELP?. This is a complex area and you may want to speak to an adviser to understand tax implications.

What if I can't decide for myself?

If you are well and in full command of your affairs but fear that might change due to illness or accident, you can nominate a friend or family member to take over your affairs if or when you are no longer able to carry on. They will be allowed to make healthcare and financial decisions and transactions on your behalf. An LPA (Lasting Power of Attorney) should give you and your loved ones peace of mind, because without it people can't take decisions for you. Power of attorney appoints a person, whereas a will is a written statement that does not appoint anyone to make the decisions. People can then reflect on your choices from health and welfare to property and financial affairs: where you want to live, what type of care you would like and so on. This helps to avoid stress and money issues HELP?. To make an LPA, you can choose an attorney (or a few), fill in the form from the Government website[58] and register it with the Office of the Public Guardian (this can take up to ten weeks). At the time of writing, it costs £82 to register an LPA.[59]

Inheritance rules – make the most of them

The government will tax the estate (assets) that you leave behind when you die (cash, property, investments, insurance pay-outs and so on) minus your debts. Inheritance tax (IHT) is payable on possessions that are passed on when you die above a certain tax threshold. For 2019/20, the threshold or 'nil-rate band' is £325,000 (you can pass on up to £325,000 when you die without paying inheritance tax). If you're a married couple or in a civil partnership, you can pass on double that amount – £650,000. Above this amount, you pay 40% tax.

On top of this, there is a relatively new allowance called the 'main residence' allowance, valid on a main residence and where the recipient of a home is a direct descendant of the owner (classed as children, step-children and grandchildren). This allows you to increase the allowance by £150,000 for the 2019/20 tax year, rising to £25,000 each year until it reaches £175,000 in 2020/21. Make sure you check the rules because these can change.

To find out more about this, visit **gov.uk/inheritance-tax**. (Gifts can be made to any individual, trust or charity.)

Getting married: protecting each other

I have met many women who have committed to their partner, mixed up their finances and debt with them and ended up in a very difficult financial situation – having to bear the debts of the other party after they have split up. The burden of paying back a debt which wasn't yours can become a toxic situation. The only way to avoid this is to plan ahead to make sure you are 100% certain of everything you sign up to and the consequences it may cause. Get advice, talk about it. Once you've decided that you want to get married, you will be free to enjoy the tax, inheritance and pension perks of married life.

Now, the sad part: 40% of marriages end in divorce and you want to be protected in case it happens. In the UK people think their assets (cash, house, pensions) will be split 50/50 between partners. This is not always the case. The court can deviate from this for three reasons:

1. Who will be in charge of the children? If it's you, you would need more capital.
2. Are you earning enough to live off?
3. How much do you both earn and what will you earn in the future?

In the case of a divorce, you need to get advice, rather than trying to sort things out yourself – it's a complicated area and having extra moral support will help you through the difficult process. What if you can't talk to each other? What if you discover too late that your partner has bad debts? What if you end up with a lot of money that you have absolutely no clue to manage? What if you don't work and your partner was the breadwinner? There is a multitude of questions that could arise, so prepare and protect yourself the best you can.

If you need more info on money and divorce go to: **gov.uk/money-property-when-relationship-ends**

PRENUP (PRENUPTIAL AGREEMENT)

Even if you're a die-hard romantic, you can't deny the importance of a prenuptial agreement. A prenup is a written document agreed by both partners before their wedding. It sets out the possessions of each as well as how things should be split in case of divorce. It can be quite flexible, and it can also be revisited after the wedding. If worse comes to worst, and you decide to go your separate ways, a prenup will help ease what will already be a painful and complicated time.

In the UK, courts recognize prenuptial agreements, but they can also have their view and waive any prenuptial agreement if unfair or if you have children. So, while it is useful, judges may overrule it to look at financial needs of both parties.

You don't have to be rich to do a prenup. You may want to have one in place if there's disparity of wealth between partners, but you should also consider one if you both want to ringfence the money you would be making over time, or if you've previously been married and have kids already.

A prenup can be a complicated document so it's a great idea to get professional help from a family law solicitor.

Protect your identity!

Many of us will know someone who has been the victim of banking or credit fraud – it's one of the downsides of living in a globally connected digital world. If you were to find that money had disappeared from your bank account unexpectedly, you would naturally contact your bank at once and ask what procedure they have in place for refunding you and preventing the issue from happening again.

But the best thing you can do for your identity security (apart from not having your date of birth as your pin number or chucking unshredded bank statements in the bin) is to sign up to CIFAS. This is a government-sponsored fraud prevention system that will check with you every time someone tries to take out credit or a loan in your name. It's free and easy and it's what your bank will probably advise you to do in the case of fraud, so get ahead of the game and sign up now.

EXERCISE

What protection do you have in place today? For each of the following, do you know what's covered, how much you pay?

- [ ] Life
- [ ] Home
- [ ] Health
- [ ] Travel
- [ ] Others

Do I have a will? ....

What other agreements do I need? ....

Well Done! You have earnt coins!

With so much thinking and learning now under your belt, it is hopefully safe to say that you now have a plan in place. You've figured out what your real goals are and *the type of life you would like to live*. Better still, by now you should understand the basics of how to protect your assets from the vicissitudes that life might throw at you, from illness to divorce.

Understanding all these things – about yourself and the world of finance – will give you a strong foundation on which to build a safe, strong and rewarding financial future. Of course, learning is an open-ended process, so it's incumbent on you to keep checking in over the years, not only with the boring stuff like changing tax rules and inheritance laws and all that, but with yourself.

Dreams and goals do shift as life ebbs and flows around us... so your current plan might be to move to a hot country and work freelance from the beach, but who knows what tomorrow may bring. Or you might think you want to retire at 50 but as that benchmark approaches, you find you're on a roll career-wise and are enjoying it too much to stop. You may even find that your fundamental values and beliefs about money change.

So be open to things changing and factor frequent check-ins into your plan. Remember – change and self-awareness are good, and they are what this process is all about.

In the next chapter, we're going to get into the practicalities of budgeting and spending to help you to achieve the changes you want to make.

Money Talk
with Bonnie Lister Parsons

Job: Founder of Seen On Screen (SOS).

Fun fact: Bonnie's mission is to empower people through dance. She launched an all-female funding round through SOS's Instagram channel and hit her fundraising target within two weeks. Safe to say, women *do* invest.

Money motto: *'Invest like a woman.'*

What makes you happy?
My husband, my family, my girlfriends, my SOS community, drawing, writing, playing the piano, horse riding, spending time with dogs (and animals in general) and, of course, knowing I've just closed the world's first all-female equity funding round!

What is your most treasured possession?
My diary from 2007. I moved to New York, and later Los Angeles, on my own that year and my 19-year-old self documented the experience in detail. That time really laid the foundation for the rest of my life.

What is the best money advice you have ever received?
'Prove them wrong.' I announced I was going to do an all-female [funding] round while pitching at a women's networking club in London. The co-founder of the club told me after the pitch that women are risk-averse, they don't invest, and doing an all-female round would hold my business back.

What is your biggest money failure/mistake?
I failed to raise money from the traditional investment world. An old accountant of mine made a painful mistake three years ago which gave me an incredible drive to own the finances of my business. Use 'failures' as opportunities for growth and flip them to your advantage.

What is your greatest achievement?
My relationship with my husband, I think. We've been together for ten years and I met him when I was just twenty. I couldn't be prouder of my business achievements, but my husband is my rock and I've built a partnership with him which has provided the emotional support I've needed to weather the ups and downs of my 'dancentrepreneurial' journey. I come home to my biggest fan every day, and we're building a life together. After all, behind every great woman is a great man 🤩.

What is money for you?
Freedom.

What is your top money hack?
It's okay to talk about money. Hearing other women's money stories took a lot of the fear and shame out of money – thank you, Vestpod, for pioneering this!

For entrepreneurs – it sounds so obvious – but sell something people want to buy.

Who is your go-to person to talk about money?
I have a money posse! My husband, my 'women on the hustle' network, my accountant and the women on SOS's advisory board.

Who are your inspiring heroes?
Living: Queen Bey.
Of all time: Queen Elizabeth I.

What is your favourite book?
There are so many, I can't choose one but generally books about strong women. I have read many books on Elizabeth I, for example! I'm currently reading *What Would the Spice Girls Do?* by Lauren Bravo. It's genius and a must for all millennial women.

What do you invest in?

I believe your power is in the women your surround yourself with, so I invest time in my relationships with women I respect, and who inspire me to be my best. I've just started a supper club where I bring my network together every three months, and it's a great space where we can let our hair down, have fun, listen, advise and be there for one another, judgement free. It's basically hustler group therapy!

What is your personal mission?

There's a well-known saying – '*She believed she could, so she did*.' What if that said, '*She believed she couldn't, so she didn't*?' Confidence is so important because it will make the difference between picking yourself back up, and giving up. I know how powerful the SOS experience and community can be, and it's become my personal mission to ensure every woman who walks through Seen on Screen's doors, believes she *can*.

CHAPTER 4: OWN IT: GET A GRIP ON YOUR MONEY

* *

What you will learn in this chapter:

How can you make a spending plan (aka set a budget)?
How do you get a better understanding of the way you spend money?
What are the painless ways to cut costs and release some money each month?

* *

WHERE DID ALL MY £££ GO? 'I AM EITHER WEARING IT... OR I ATE IT.'

Life is a numbers game...

A relatively unknown Australian real estate mogul, called Tim Gurner, shot to infamy in 2017 when he openly blamed millennials' love of avocado on toast for being the reason they were struggling to get on the property ladder. His prejudice aside, we'd like to make it clear we would have to eat an inordinate number of avocados every day for this concept to be even remotely true. It has probably never been tougher or more of a struggle to purchase even the smallest of properties on the slippery, ever-ascending property ladder. Those who can afford a millionaire's mansion need to leave us and our avocados alone.

But still we find ourselves wondering where our money has gone at the end of the month. For when was the last time you checked your bank account and discovered that you had *more* money than you expected? Never?

The truth is this: the money that will make or break our dreams *is already in our hands*, because what we do *today* with our cash will affect how we live our life *tomorrow*.

Many of us prefer to live in the moment, are accustomed to instant gratification and, as a result, put off saving for the long term. We tend to see the present and the future as separate entities, rather than part of a continuum where we save money today to enjoy more tomorrow. There may not be a 'one simple trick' or a 'get rich quick' option but it is at least a simple paradigm to get your head around: save some money today to be able to enjoy it tomorrow. This does not need to be painful – we won't be making any grand plans to begin with, just small, smart hacks and with a sprinkling of what it means to transition into being a saver.

And part of the solution lies in spending to a B U D G E T.

The problem is that most people freak out when they see numbers on a page, let alone on a spreadsheet. The reality is overwhelming and makes them want to run away. As for hearing that you should be adding up the cost of every single thing you spend your hard-earned money on... Does that feel like another commitment that you don't have time for?

In reality, the secret to having personal wealth is knowing where your money is going – every week and every month – because understanding your outgoings allows you to form new money habits and start to save. So, this chapter is going to help you take a non-judgemental look at your spending decisions so you can develop ways to get 'better' at spending. There is no one budgeting methodology recommended, but hopefully within these pages you will be able to find one what works for you.

We will also brainstorm ideas of how you can start to save on the small things: the hacks, habits and little things that can help you along your way. Because if you don't take time for the small things, how can you create time to do the big things in your life!

Welcome to the £££ jungle!

Where Is All My Money Going?

Have you ever tried to find out how your friends afford their lifestyle? Do you know how much money you have in your account right now? Are you always surprised by how little money there is left in your account at the end of the month? Why is that we never buy expensive things but always end up 'in the red'? Do you think to yourself, 'I can't afford to budget and save, I barely make ends meet'? Think again…

Most people's answers to these questions are unsurprising. According to the ONS (2017), UK households are spending beyond their means for the first time in nearly 30 years (on average, each household spends in excess of £900 more than their annual income). Yes, this leaves people with a reduced ability to save money, and often leads them to turn to short-term debt, in order to make ends meet.

The first step toward getting real is to take action today. Face up to your finances and recognize what is going on. Confront your spending, start to examine where your money is going, and focus on breaking your negative thought patterns. Developing clarity and a firm understanding of where you stand financially will help you achieve these goals. To help with this we need to look at two things: financial planning (with the help of a budget) and understanding your spending decisions.

According to a study by a US Bank in 2016,[60] only 41% of Americans follow a basic budget. A Gallup poll from 2013 showed that only 32% actually keep a detailed budget, and most have an annual salary of $75,000 or more.[61]

A lot of us are stuck in the spiral of earning, spending, amassing things and not providing for the future. It can be difficult to start spending less and saving more if we can't see the future benefits of our actions – but starting to live slightly differently from today and becoming more conscious of where our money is going will make a big difference next year as well as in 5, 10, 20 and 30 years' time. The choice is yours, each £1 you earn either can be spent buying things which lose their value, or can be saved and invested for the future, steadily building your personal wealth.

Building wealth is a simple process in theory but it takes time and consistency to achieve in practice. The basic principle is to spend less than you earn each month, in order to save. To achieve this, you need to wise up to differences between wasteful spending and smart spending.

Do you want it or do you need it?

It can be very rewarding and interesting (emotionally, psychologically, socially and even politically) to start to scrutinize how you are spending your money. Analysing your behaviour can help you achieve self-knowledge, and with that comes the ability to be kinder to yourself when you slip up (though the slip-ups will happen less, as self-awareness grows). It is a virtuous circle. Looking closely at what we spend will also gradually change our money mindset. You have done this exercise once before in Chapter 1. Now can you repeat it, and dig deeper this time?

EXERCISE

Can you try to think about your latest big financial decision? And start asking yourself these few questions:

What triggered your wish to buy this?
Why did you decide to buy it?
Did it make you happy and why?
For how long did it make you happy?
What did you have to give up, to be able to afford to buy it?
Was it the cheapest option available? Why?

We all know the feeling of wanting or deserving something at the end of a challenging day or week. Perhaps we had to 'tough out' a tricky situation at work, or overcome a relationship problem. Perhaps we just felt awful about something. It can be very hard to resist buying a treat while on a budget, because spending is emotional and budgeting is rational; our psyche becomes torn between both camps. Inevitably our spending habits are influenced by impulse, instinct and irrational desire, but they are also tempered with the logical voice of self-doubt: 'Should I?', 'Although I want it, can I justify it?', 'I won't be able to eat if I buy this.' and so on.

This process of cross-examining yourself during every purchase (yes, even down to your favourite brand of takeaway coffee) will help you to access which things you want and which you need. Sorting your wants from your needs is a major thought exercise, and one that can reveal a lot about you.

WANT	NEED
A new item of clothing for a party	To get to work and buy a travelcard
To go on holiday	To pay council tax (yes, not sexy)
To get a cab not travel on public transport	To pay my rent
To go out	To buy groceries
Cash now (so ignore the surcharge)	To pay this fine

There is scope for both wants and needs in your budget, but obviously needs have to be prioritized.

What are our needs?

Essentially, they are requirements such as food and shelter. If you are Bear Grylls or an SAS operative crawling behind enemy lines, this means knowing how to trap game and make a smokeless fire, then build yourself a bivouac out of palm fronds. But let's face it, the other 99.99% of us, whether we live in the town or the country, are likely to have a job, daily commitments and stuff to juggle, and therefore more complex needs. These probably include: housing costs (including bills and maintenance), communication – the internet and a phone (with almost unlimited 4G), clothes (for different occasions and weather needs), tasty snacks (to give you energy and keep you happy), travel money (including holidays – time in the sun is allowed) and entertainment. (No books, no movies, no sport, no concerts? No life!)

Now, some of these essential needs will also be things that you genuinely want. Others, such as bills, you will not attach desire to at all. (I mean, who gets a thrill from paying their water bill?) When something is just a need on its own, it feels like a drag, right? But hey, it's a need, so it needs to be paid for. The applied logic is kind of simple. On the other hand: when a need is also something that you really, really want, you become more motivated to pursue it, even if that means doing without something else in order to save up for it.

What are our wants?

Our wants are rather complicated than our needs. If you take a look at all the things you bought (or *wanted* to buy) last month, you will probably find that you convinced yourself you 'needed' most of them. How many of these scenarios feel familiar?

I need a coffee right now or I will never get through this meeting.
I need a new work shirt so I'm going to give in to this 'impulse purchase'.
I need to get a gift (or two) for my friend's baby (and she deserves the best).
I need a holiday. Where am I going to find the money I need for that? (Looks at credit card which is already maxed to the limit.)

All of these purchases feel absolutely essential at the time, but could you have achieved them more cheaply or even – gasp! – not at all? Yes, quality coffee and nice clothes make you feel good. But have you ever been to an early meeting on no caffeine or wearing an 'emergency' outfit? We bet you have. And you know what, it was ok! You got through it. Life moved on. Because you are still the same person inside. No matter how much material worth you surround yourself with: You Are Still You.

As for the friend who has a new baby – maybe she would really like a home-cooked meal and some cute hand-written 'vouchers' to cash in for babysitting, when she's ready to go out again? Wouldn't those things be more personal than yet another bodysuit for the baby to grow out of? If your friend knew that you were on a tight budget there is no way on earth she would want you to blow half a day's wages on a gift, when she already holds in her arms the only gift she really wants.

You may think that you need to own a car, but is it really a necessity? What are your other options? If you live in a rural area, with no access to public transport you will answer this differently than if you live in a city. The running costs and the cost of insurance can take its toll on your monthly budget. Other options might be occasional car rental, or looking into membership with a car sharing website – such as Zipcar – which means that you only pay for the hours you use the car.

These examples may or may not apply to your life right now, but the point is this: if you take the time to think carefully about each item you spend money on, you may come to a deeper understanding of what you really, really want and need.

The role of gratitude

Conscious gratitude also has an important role to play in budgeting. We are lucky to be able to spend money and we should be grateful for this. Becoming mindful of how and what we spend our money on can increase feelings of gratitude and connectedness to others, and help to combat our desire for instant gratification. The results of 2014 study published in the journal *Psychological Science*[62] explored the connection between economic impatience, emotional state and long-term well-being. Participants were invited to choose between having $54 dollars now or $80 dollars in 30 days' time. They were also asked to look back at a past personal event that made them feel (a) grateful, (b) happy or (c) neutral. Those who wrote about who or what they had to be grateful for, showed greater patience and chose to wait for three months to receive $80, whereas those who focussed on neutral or happy events opted for the $54 and decided to forgo the future gain. The link between gratitude and a sense of personal fulfilment was quite marked. The findings seemed to show that when people feel grateful, they are more likely to behave in ways that benefit others. That usually involves an element of patience. Those who are patient are more likely to be able to delay immediate gratification.

Another mind-hack that works well is to look around you and take note of all the stuff you already own. Don't they already meet your needs pretty well? Hopefully you have a bed, some clothes, a fridge with food in it and the wherewithal to make something delicious – as well as enough technology to power a small spaceship. Then there are the intangible and precious things that cost nothing at all to maintain: your friendships, your family, your connection to the natural world. Now those are the things that you really, really need.

EXERCISE

List three things that you spent money on recently, costing any amount. Were these wants or needs?

	Is your life dependent on this? Yes = need. No = want.	**Does someone else's life depend on this? Yes = need. No = want**
1.		
2.		
3.		

Now that you have looked carefully at what you want versus what you need, we can look at setting your first budget.

Don't panic...Keep reading!

Budgeting guidelines

Budgeting is the process of creating a plan to manage and spend your money. There are many different ways to set a budget because there isn't a single approach that will fit everyone's needs. I can't tell you the one and only approach that will make you fall in love with budgeting. However, there is one formula that underlines all of the basics of budgeting:

Understanding what comes in (+) and goes out (–) of your pocket each week, each month and each year equals (=) *more* £££.

Living to a budget may not feel sexy but it is essential. If we don't know how much we are making or how much we are spending how can we ever start to think about saving money or investing money? Being in control of your finances is truly liberating. We can all think of a million things to spend money on and as much as we would love to consider a pair of Gucci loafers to be a wise purchasing decision, it's important to keep personal spending in perspective. Setting a budget makes saying 'no' to yourself a great deal easier.

The 50/20/30 budgeting goal

I find one budgeting goal in particular extremely handy: the 50/20/30 budgeting guideline was first introduced by the Harvard bankruptcy expert Elizabeth Warren and her daughter, Amelia Warren Tyagi, with whom she coined the popular term in the book *All Your Worth: The Ultimate Lifetime Money Plan*[63]. (It was known initially as the 50/30/20 rule.)

50/20/30 is also called percentage or proportional budgeting. 50/20/30 means that 50% of your income is allocated to essential expenses, 20% to financial goals and the remaining 30% to lifestyle (aka flexible spending). The order is important here and that's why we address the 50% first then the 20% and finish with the 30%. By working first on your needs and directly after that on your savings goals you substantially increase your ability to save – instead of waiting to see what's left at the end of the month...

This budgeting goal is empowering and effective because it is not as stringent as the typical method of counting every pound that goes in and out of your pocket. It is a simple and very adaptable guide to how you should allocate your money. Sure, there are always going to be exceptions (hello Gucci loafers), and the percentage breakdown should be adjusted to your needs and lifestyle.

However, the overriding guiding principles of the 50/20/30 budget are very helpful. This is just an indication and definitely not accurate science, so make sure you do whatever works for you!

For this exercise we will use your monthly income after tax (your 'take-home' income). You can find this figure by taking a look at your payroll and finding the net amount you are paid every month after taxes once national insurance has been deducted. If you have a workplace pension, your contributions will also have been taken out of your pay – and these count as long-term savings. You can decide to apply this budgeting goal to your salary pre- or post-pension contribution figure. This budgeting goal is flexible and you have to use numbers that work for you as long as your saving goals are affordable. Just be consistent when you do your calculation over time. If you are a freelancer or a contractor you will need to calculate this yourself: work out how much you earn and then subtract the taxes you are expected to pay. You can also use a net salary calculator on the internet,[64] which is a pretty nifty way to get started.

50%: The 50% category comprises of all your 'essential expenses', which basically means the needs that you listed earlier. Sit down and take a look at your bank statements, compile all your essential expenses in one list, to include the following:

- *Rent or mortgage payments.*
- *Utilities: electricity, water and gas.*
- *Groceries.*
- *Transport.*
- *Mobile phone and internet.*
- *Minimum debt payments.*

These are your basic living costs, which would apply wherever you live or work, whether in the UK, Australia or somewhere else in the world. These are the things you need, to get by day-to-day. Remember to factor in the minimum payments you need to make on your debts (such as minimum credit card payment, mortgage, student loans).[65]

Although the headline figure is 50%, for some people the percentage will be higher as they will need to pay more for rent, transport and so on. The percentages can be adjusted to work for your life.

20%: The 20% category could also be called 'Pay yourself first'. This is money you will be putting towards your financial goals and savings. Whether or not you are already saving 20% of your income, there is no better time to start somewhere.

Bear in mind that financial goals and savings can come in different forms:

- *Paying back extra debt if you are trying to get debt free.*
- *Building an emergency or rainy-day fund (having the security of an emergency fund helps you to avoid taking on debt when you need some money urgently for unexpected events).*
- *Saving for your short- to medium-term goals (the ones you worked on in Chapter 3).*
- *Saving for your long-term goals (retirement funds and pensions).*

20% may seem a really high figure for some, especially to start with. The actual percentage will differ for each of us, but the most important goal is to get started, and to develop the habit of saving some money. Whether you start with 1%, 5% or 10% of your income doesn't matter: you can start with a lower number and have a percentage goal in mind for the future. Don't try to reach the 20% saving goal if you can't afford it. If saving too much will put you in the red at the end of the month, reduce your saving goal – there is no point borrowing on your credit card to increase your savings.

A quick note about workplace pensions and auto-enrolment: Pension payments fall within the 20% savings category. Obviously, the more you can contribute towards your pension the better, but if saving an additional 20% on top of your existing pension contributions is too much to start with you can simply factor in what you currently pay.

30%:The 30% spending category is basically the 'wants' we talked about earlier and includes your lifestyle choices. Now that you have sorted out your essentials and started saving, you can focus on treating yourself. Whoop! What is left from your income is free for you to spend. Once you have managed to set aside enough money for the other two categories, this becomes totally guilt-free spending. Whether you are a shopaholic or a sports enthusiast, your 30% lifestyle spending can cover a range of things:

- *Charity donations and gifts for your loved ones and friends.*
- *TV, Netflix and online entertainment.*
- *Shopping – clothes, household items and electronics.*
- *Sport and gym subscriptions.*
- *Concerts, theatres, cinema, gallery visits and other forms of entertainment.*
- *Eating out.*
- *Travel.*
- *Beauty treatments.*
- *The list is really endless!* 😎

This is how the rule looks like visually:

The 50/20/30 Bugeting goal

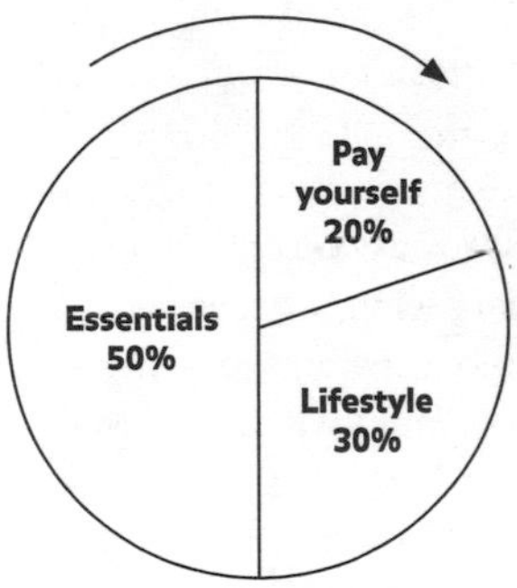

Let's look at a detailed example:

(Please note that the sample calculation below is provided for informative purposes only.)

Maria works as a sales manager. After pension contributions, income tax and national insurance, her net annual salary is £22,247. This is what she takes home, and equates to £1,854 net per month. She does not have student loan debt.

She pays £1,000 a month for her essential expenses, such as rent, utilities, transportation and groceries and these represent about 54% of her take home income. She is already contributing to her pension through her workplace pension (we assumed 8%) and she decides to save £150 a month towards building up her emergency fund. That corresponds to 8% of her take home salary.

Take-home (net) salary	**£1,854**
Essential expenses	£1,000 –
Extra savings	£ 150 –
Total	£ 704 / 30 = £23 per day

She is left with £704 to spend each month on living, which equals approximately £23 a day.

Maria's cost percentages are currently 54/8/38. Her plan when she gets a salary increase is to keep the amount she spends on essential expenses the same, but to increase the amount she saves, and perhaps have more money available at the end of the month. In this way she will gradually adjust the percentages to meet whatever her budgeting goal is.

The percentages used in this methodology are the goal but they are not set in stone. For example, the percentage spent on rent or a mortgage alone can be 40–50% (or more) of your salary, especially in London. The main purpose of these principles is for you to feel in control of your money rather than have it control you. If you have a partner and are both earning, you should take both sets of income into account – giving you more leeway. The proportions make sense and are a good guide, but your money is your money and not someone else's. Make sure you adjust the budgeting blueprint so that it works for you and you create a budgeting goal you can afford.

 Now, go get started on your 50/20/30!

Pros	Cons
• **Simple:** Easy to use and implement; you can screen your bank accounts and calculate initial budget within an hour. • **Flexible:** You can change the percentages to find the best fit for your money and spending habits but you should aim for the ultimate 50/20/30.	• **One size does not fit all:** Need to adjust the percentages when expensive debts need repayment, there are additional unexpected costs or periods that will cost you more, such as holidays.

 USE AN APP AND AUTOMATE YOUR SAVINGS

Personal finance apps are all the rage, and for good reason: most of us waste a large part of our income simply because we do not control our spending. We are living in a technological age, so why not use your phone as a personal piggy bank or financial coach?

Many of us find financial management stressful and time-consuming. The ability to automate routine (some might say mundane) financial tasks helps ease unnecessary stress. Who doesn't want a hassle-free financial life?

Check the Little Black Book section (see page 364) to see a round-up of the most in-demand apps that will help ease your life.

EXERCISE

Build your own budgeting goal inspired by 50/20/30.

In the first column, note down the actual numbers you found on your bank statement: how much do you earn, save, and spend. You can also add the resulting percentage of your post-tax income.

In the second column, note your post-tax income and apply the percentages – look at how this total compares to column 1.

In the last column, define the percentages that work for you and adjust the numbers to make up your own budget!

	Actual	**50/20/30 Budget goal (indication)**	**My budget goal based on %: ____/____/____**
Income			
Post-tax Income			
Essentials (goal: 50%) Rent or mortgage payments Utilities: electricity, water and gas Groceries Mobile phone, internet Transportation Minimum debt repayments	My % is	*(Post-tax income x 50%=)*	My % is . . . . .
Pay yourself first (goal: 20%) Extra debt repayment Emergency fund Saving goals Retirement funds	My % is	*(Post-tax income x 20%=)*	My % is . . . . .

Lifestyle (goal: 30%) Charity donations TV Shopping Sport and gym Entertainment Eating out Travel	My % is	*(Post-tax income x 30%=)*	My % is . . . . .

For some of us, it is easier to visualize these budgets on the 50/20/30 pie chart we looked at previously. For the first and third column, divide the pie chart into the 3 categories – 'essentials', 'pay yourself' and 'lifestyle' – and colour in your personal percentages. This way, you will be able to see the difference between your current spending and your new budget.

My actual spending

Essentials

. . . . %

Pay yourself

. . . . %

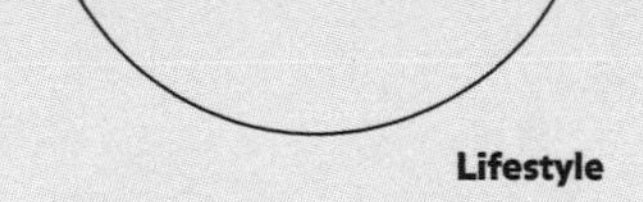

Lifestyle

. . . . %

My new budget

Essentials

. . . . %

Pay yourself

. . . . %

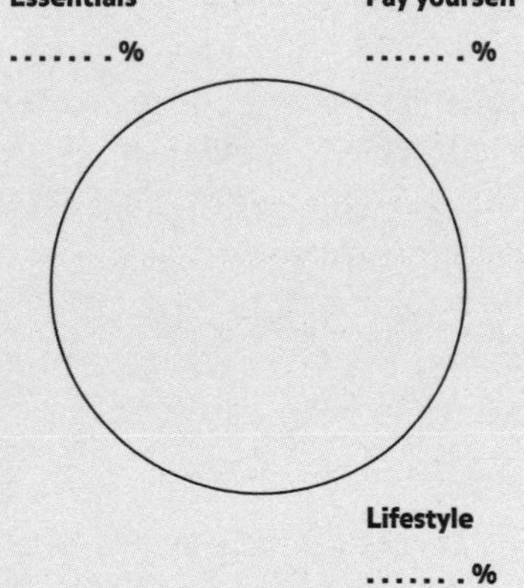

Lifestyle

. . . . %

The envelope system

This budgeting method uses only cash – that is physical cash in physical envelopes! It is recommended by the money saving expert Dave Ramsey[66], and has lots of fans. It is an old-fashioned practice sure. What is useful here is the concept, rather more than the (non) practicality of the technique.

With the envelope system you withdraw the money you need each week and put it into the corresponding envelopes. For example, envelopes labelled rent, gym, savings, healthcare, kids, clothing, transport and so on.

The good news is that this back-to-basics accounting system has been made digital, so you can apply the envelope system to your cash without using physical cash. Instead, you can use an app such as Mvelopes (see page 364) to compartmentalize your spending in exactly the same way as 'the paper envelope system' with the added convenience of being able to make online payments. Your bank may also offer this type of service as it allows you to set up spending categories via their online user's service.

The reason this simple system is so useful is because it stops you over-spending or feeling guilty about spending. For example, if there is money available in your 'clothing' envelope, you won't feel bad about spending it because it's part of your budgeted allowance. As another example, you could use the envelope system for going on a night out: if you put £50 in the envelope then you can only spend the premediated amount. This will stop you from overspending and ensure you stick to a budget.

Pros	Cons
• A super-detailed spending plan. • The method allows you to understand exactly where you spend your money as there is no transfer from one envelope to the other! • It is for those who like strict budgeting. • Can allow you to spot fees and things you should not be paying for such as overdraft fees.	• No buffer. • Sometimes a problem stems from the fact that the money allocated in an envelope might not be enough for what you have to pay for and you have to get a buffer. • Can be stressful and time consuming to plan.

Zero-sum based budget

This budgeting method is about giving every £ that you earn an active job to do. In other words, use every bit of money you make each month to pay for every bit of your outgoings for the next month, including savings. With a zero-based budget, all your income is used to cover all of your outgoings, so you end up with zero at the end of the month. This method is useful if you overspend each month and, for example, always end up with additional expenses on your credit card.

Remember with the zero-sum method you will be using last month's income to pay for the coming month's expenses. You will therefore need to have saved a whole month's income to achieve this. For some people, this can be a lot of money to put aside: especially if you are living pay-cheque to pay-cheque. Don't worry, start small. It may take you a few months to get ahead and build up one month of savings. You may also want to put a small buffer in case you think you will over-run or you know that this month you will earn less.

Importantly: the money should not be drawn down from a saving account, because the whole purpose of your budget is to gradually grow your savings, not deplete them. If you have taken some money out of an emergency saving account (which is a life's essential), do make sure that it becomes your top priority to refund what you have taken out.

This method is a great one for those who are self-employed or freelance because it allows for monthly adjustments, when you know you will receive less or more money during the coming month. Zero-sum budgeting helps you to identify problem areas in your finances. The main challenge is to look at the numbers with your eyes wide open.

The way that you spend your money impacts on the way that you feel, so building a zero-sum budget is amazing way to complete a reflection exercise, to think about your life and habits. People who have employed this method have found that they become better at saving and more mindful of their spending.

 You can use an app such as YNAB (You Need A Budget) to apply the zero-sum based method.

Pros	Cons
• Easy to use: Once up and running, this is a simple, easy-to-use plan. • Adaptable: It quickly reveals where you need to make changes, and allows you to identify where you are failing to make ends meet.	• Saving up: You have to get one month ahead to start doing it properly, because you are literally using all of last month's income to pay for the next month.

In the end, your best option is to learn and research the different budgeting methods available and to figure out which one would be best for you. Decide what feels right, what suits your money (and spending) style, and what you think you will be able to stick to. You could also create your own approach by taking some inspiration from these basic methods.

Arm yourself with an Excel spreadsheet or whatever works for you: you can use paper and pen, or an app.

The 'Pre-Rich' mobile apps

There are now many excellent budgeting apps available. To help you to get started, you could try using one of the following: Money Dashboard, You Need a Budget (YNAB), Moneyhub, Emma, Plum, MoneyBox, Chip or Mint; and there are others too (see page 364). They are designed to help you stay in control of your daily, weekly and monthly funds by reminding you of where you are overspending and suggesting ways to economize. An app can also be used to encourage you to establish your financial goals: these are the bedrock of your journey to greater money wisdom.

Stop Impulse Spending and Start Becoming More Frugal

Learning to resist impulse spending may be one of your biggest challenges, because impulse purchases have a funny way of bypassing the budgeting radar. They don't feature in your budget, so you try to forget about them as soon as you have made a purchase, and they are therefore wiped from your financial mindset. Yet in that moment, when that special something is calling out to you – whether it is a Black Friday iPhone deal or a chocolate bar by the supermarket check-out – it feels like the most important, all-consuming need in the world.

Why does impulse shopping feel so good and how can we stop giving in to it? A big part of the appeal is because it is forbidden. Tell any human that they can't have something and the forbidden thing suddenly becomes incredibly desirable. Another reason we fall for the lure of an impulse buy is because they are marketed boldly. They may flash up on a web page with a big red banner saying *last chance to buy!* or be strategically positioned by a check-out queue in a high street store. We don't want to miss out. We want to be part of the clever, smart crowd who came away from the shop with something 'extra'.

How can we arm ourselves against merchandiser's tricks? Try telling yourself more convincingly that you are not scoring a cool, cut-price treat, but falling into a trap laid by a ruthless advertiser. You will gradually learn to see impulse buying as a fail rather than a win.

Another angle is to stop making treats 'forbidden' in the first place, by tweaking your budget. Factor in a monthly amount for impulse spending, even if you have to take it from the proverbial avocado toast fund. Who knows, once you know that you are allowed to spend money on a so-called bargain, you might even decide that you don't want to.

You could also try following the 10/10 rule: if an item costs more than £10, spend 10 minutes thinking about it. If after that time you're still not sure whether to buy it, put it back on the shelf. That should save you some time and money![67]

The most effective hack works at a deeper psychological level. Start becoming aware of 'opportunity cost': this means pausing before you spend, to ask yourself what future benefit you might lose out on if you spend unbudgeted money on an unplanned purchase right now. You have created your saving goals based on what will make life better for you in the future. If you give in to buying that brand-new-pair of trainers (which incidentally look like another pair of trainers you already own) the purchase is going to impact or delay your future happiness. When you say no to the shoes, don't see your decision as a sacrifice, instead see it as a great opportunity to make your true goals happen more quickly! It is easier than you think to flick the switch in your brain from negative to positive if you know you are making the right decision.

So, the next time you're out shopping, or browsing online, stay alert to what is really going on in your mind, and remember what you really want in life.

Frugality vs. austerity

Austerity has become a buzz-word of late, as anyone who keeps half an eye on the news will know. Governments seem to debate endlessly over whether it is better to cut spending and save money, or whether a further injection of cash is needed, to give the global economy a capitalist boost and to get everyone spending again.

But what does austerity vs. frugality mean on an individual level? For most of us, austerity has a depressing ring to it: who wants to give up spending their hard-earned cash on stuff that makes them happy? Saving every spare penny sounds miserable, yet we are all aware of the trend towards curbing our consumption. Could frugality become the mid-ground that we are looking for? Whether rich or poor, people are wising up to the fact that spending money they do not have on shiny stuff they do not need may not be making us happy in the long run. We are reaching peak 'stuffocation' with nothing to show for it that is worth anything to us in the long run.

Of course, the idea that 'less is more' is not exactly new.

Let's look back to the philosophy of ancient Greece for a moment. Stoicism was a school of thought founded by Zeno of Citium (334–262 BCE) that still has value in today. Stoics taught how to stay rational in a world that is unpredictable. They knew there are things we can't control and should accept, but that we can master our own minds and behaviour. They prioritized virtues like courage and wisdom as a way to achieve a good life oblivious to wealth, pleasure or pain. In other words, we can choose to control our own minds: our thoughts and actions.

The four major Roman Stoics were Seneca the Younger (c.4 BCE–65 CE), Marcus Aurelius (121–180 CE), Gaius Musonius Rufus (20–30 CE) and Epictetus (c.55–135 CE): respectively adviser to the emperor, emperor and teachers. They continue to give us insights into how to live a happier life. Although they were wealthy and did not experience poverty personally, they advised simpler and more frugal living: *living below our means*. In the words of Seneca, 'Frugality makes a poor man rich.'

According to Stoicism, we need to understand what makes us happy because clarity will help us to enjoy our lives. Having a meaningful and good life is therefore aligned not with chasing luxury or our insatiable desires but with learning to want the things we already have. (Less of: 'I will be happy when I… upgrade to a bigger house, a bigger car, more possessions.' More of: 'I am satisfied with where I currently live. My car fulfils my needs.') Try this out when you next start planning a holiday. Are you seeking luxury that you can't have at home? When you come home, do you take a moment to appreciate what you have?

The modern concept of minimalism echoes the way of the Stoics. It is all about living life more simply and becoming more aware of what you already have: choosing to live with less and not always buying more to please others. Living minimally should lead to maximum pleasure long term.

One of the most famous personal finance bloggers, known as Mr Money Mustache (check out his website if you're wondering about his name)[68] has gained a huge following for bringing the 'less is more' philosophy to the masses. He employs this in his own life and his family does too: they prefer bikes to cars, camping trips to expensive resort holidays, and value time more than money. But what makes him such an interesting example is that he is by no means poor. He has the means to be living differently – and confesses that in the past he was on track to be that guy who owns multiple holiday homes and cars. But then he discovered that living frugally was actually way more fun, healthy and enriching.

He believes that it is possible to take advantage of amazing technology and the advantages of living in a first world country, but with the greater buzz of living simply. No one is suggesting you should build your own brick oven instead of buying a stove, or brew your own medicines instead of visiting the doctor when you're sick. But there is an important lesson to be learnt from looking at the lifestyle of people like Mr Money Mustache, because they embody the truth that capitalism can be made to work for you, not against you. He shares plenty of ways to relish the great gift of being a human without going completely off-grid.

Your time has a value too

It is important to start seeing your time as an important resource too. You are used to asking yourself 'where has all my cash gone?', or 'how do I spend my money?', but it is time to start asking yourself the same questions about what you do with your time too. This can apply to business owners and managers as much as individuals, because we all need to question what we are spending most of our time on. Is it valuable and useful and contributing to our goals, or is it wasteful and pointless in the long run? The crux of it is that our goals are usually more to do with personal freedom, rather than the amounts of money involved.

We have to appreciate today for what it is, instead of always telling ourselves that *tomorrow* is the time to do things. In other words, we need to stop procrastinating. Marcus Aurelius expressed this perfectly: 'There is a limit to the time assigned to you and if you don't use it to free yourself, it will be gone and will never return.' Equally, in the words of Seneca the Younger, 'It's not that we have a short time to live, but that we waste a lot of it.'

EXERCISE

What makes you happy? How much does it cost? Can you do more of it?

What makes you happy?	How much does it cost?	Can you do more of it?
[seeing my friends]	[lunch £10 or coffee £3 or £0]	yes

'Millions' of Ways to Cut Costs

Apps... New spending habits... Considered purchases... These are the changes that will work.

You know that feeling when you receive a bunch of mail in the post, hoping that one of the envelopes has enclosed within it a gift voucher from Anthropologie, or a postcard from your bestie in New York – only to discover that your post is 90% bills? Yeah. Isn't that seriously the worst? Is paying your bills a bitter pill to swallow? Is your best memory of childhood of it being a time when you had no bills to pay?! Well, making bill payments is also a sign of adulthood.

According to research OnePoll research for Endsleigh Insurance Services,[69] Brits now turn into adults at the grand old age of 25, some seven years later than 'legal adulthood'. The findings note that paying utility bills, spending less money on nights out, or taking out their first contents insurance policy were some of the 50 key indicators that indicated to young people that they were on their way to becoming an 'official' grown-up, whether ready for the responsibility or not!

We live in an era where we are becoming more and more used to/and in need of instant gratification: think disposable coffee, Uber, takeaways, Amazon Prime and other forms of convenience. All this comes at a cost and is slowly becoming something we cannot afford any more. When we speak to Alexa (a virtual assistant developed by Amazon) to create our shopping list, we don't even need to touch our cards to make purchases. Yes, it may be fast and effective, but does it make us in charge of our spending? Not really.

More than 1,600 British Gas customers were charged exit fees incorrectly[70] – totalling £64,968 – when they switched energy company. Another 2.5 million customers were told wrongly (in their terms and conditions) that they would have to pay exit fees throughout the length of their tariff. British Gas has now compensated customers. So, does this mean you should resign yourself to a life of soaring direct debits? Not quite. While you can't banish your bills, you sure can help reduce them.

Intrigued? (Who wouldn't be...) Here is a painless spending-cutting strategy for you to try (and remember small steps make you richer). Think of it is as a receipt that actually adds money to your bank balance rather than subtracting from it:

Be smart with your bills

In the past, the high cost of household bills such as water, gas and electricity were pretty much non-negotiable. But these days there is often some financial wriggle room, as competition has increased and there are now many providers vying for your custom. Set a morning aside to phone each of your service providers and ask them how you could cut your bills. You will be surprised at how many deals and options are out there. If they won't budge, say you're going to go over to another supplier. If they *still* won't budge, then do go over to another supplier! The market is there for you as the golden and most valued consumer to play to your advantage.

First time you have switched suppliers? Here is food for thought: if you make the switch, you could save £200 a year or more. Use a comparator such as uswitch.com to find the best deal for you and your wallet.

Turn off the tap

The average water bill in the UK will be approximately £405 per year (£33.75 a month in 2018/19 according to Money Advice Service[71]), so it is no wonder that many households are looking for ways to cut the cost. The easiest way to do this is to reduce your water consumption. (For example, don't leave the tap running while you clean your teeth, use a mug to measure how much water you need when you fill up the kettle, have a quick shower rather than a full bath, resist the temptation to use your washing machine for small loads...). If you pay a fixed rate for your water bills, you should look into getting a water meter. Or, if you're feeling particularly adventurous, you could try collecting rainwater – after all, there is plenty of it in the UK. But the meter option seems a little more practical.

Upgrade your boiler

Efficiency is the key to saving money on gas and electricity, and guess what is not at all efficient? Old boilers. If your boiler hasn't seen an upgrade in 10 plus years, replacing your 'vintage' model could see you saving as much as £50 to £250 a year.[72] Replacing a boiler can cost you about £2,300 excluding radiators so make sure you do your calculations. If you decide to go for a new boiler, you should get at least three quotes from qualified heating engineers.[73]

Pay attention to your mobile and broadband

Do you know how much data you are paying for and whether you are actually using it? 1.5 million of us[74] may be spending more than necessary by continuing to pay a monthly fee that includes the cost of a mobile handset, after the initial minimum contractual period has ended. Double-check your broadband and mobile plans, as well as your bills – it is highly likely that you are paying too much for your plan, including extra costs.

Call your provider and ask for a better deal, but do your research beforehand. Try saying, 'I know that [name their competitor] offers [such-and-such a deal] – can you beat the offer?' It works a charm. Make sure you know what the competition is charging, shop around for the best offers, be wary of being tied into long-term deals and don't hesitate to switch provider or plan.

Switch off the TV

Do you honestly make the most of your Sky TV or Netflix subscription? If you watch fewer than five shows or sports matches a week, the answer is decidedly 'no'. Interestingly, according to Ofcom[75], more people pay subscriptions for Netflix, Amazon Prime and Sky's NOW TV than to 'traditional' paid TV services. You can catch up on most of your favourite series via BBC iPlayer or All 4 online (just don't forget to pay your TV licence fee). Perhaps, more revolutionarily, you could opt for reading a book! Perhaps even this one.

Shop like a pro

Use your common sense and don't get sucked in by chance-of-a-lifetime deals: they are nearly always designed to make more money for the vendor. Marketeers know that it pays (for them) to play on consumers' fear of missing out (FOMO), so you'll often see phrases like 'last chance!' 'limited supply only' or 'order now to avoid disappointment'. These tricks are exactly that and are absolutely not there to help you make good buying decisions. However, when you know you need to buy something, make sure you browse online for the best discounts.

> Another trick that marketeers use is called 'anchoring'. Anchoring works by getting the purchaser to compare prices, rather than reflecting on the true value of what they are buying. So, when a price is first thrown at you, you might react with, 'Wow that is super high!' You are then offered a lower price, so you compare the prices and think that you have scooped a great deal. But did you even want to buy the item in the first place? Create your own anchor price and know your budget for the things you want to buy. Good shopping decisions take time, so consider making a rule for when browsing – especially online. Wait for 24 hours before hitting 'Complete purchase' to filter out those late-night, emotional buys that you'll regret.

Transport and Uber

Transport will always make a big dent in your budget, unless you work from home. If you work in a city, public transport will usually be your only option.

A recent study by Motherboard showed that those who have the Uber app on their phone tend to spend about 1% of their income on Uber travel.[76] It's so easy to grab an Uber, isn't it? Maybe it's raining, or you've been out for the evening, or you're late for work, or you've found yourself coming out of a meeting in a street that must be all of 15 minutes' walk to the nearest tube station… But if you have committed yourself to saving a little for the future (a future where there might be bigger emergencies than a bit of rain or an inconvenient walk), wouldn't it make sense to try using an alternative, cheaper mode of transport? Most people only use Uber for short journeys anyway, so why not try walking, cycling or taking the good old-fashioned bus? (I am not suggesting taking a personal risk if you are travelling home on your own or have had a few drinks of course. There are times when an Uber makes good sense.)

Travel more cheaply

Travelling off-peak and booking your tickets in advance are the golden ways to save money, but going digital is also helpful. Compare flight, train prices and hotel deals online. Spend some time looking for the best rates - some of them can lurk in unexpected places.

Kayak and Skyscanner offer a fantastic variety of flights, Trainline and National Rail are good for train tickets while TripAdvisor acts as a very reputable source for finding the best hotel deals.

Be smart about money exchange. Exchange rates abroad are notoriously poor value, so why not save yourself some inconvenience (and some pretty pennies too) by trying out the Revolut app and card, which is all about getting you the very best rates in a totally hassle-free manner.

Missing flights is costly - and emotionally draining (as well as embarrassing). Don't let yourself be stranded and cash-strapped. Always plan ahead. TripIt is a fantastic resource for managing all of your travelling plans in one place; but there are plenty of other apps on the market that will help you stay ahead of your travelling game.

Consider buying second-hand

Buying new essentials is always tempting but their value decreases as soon as you have paid for them. Ask yourself: could you get what you want second-hand instead? Most of the time the answer is yes.

Start browsing your favourite brands on Gumtree, the neighbours' website NextDoor and eBay; you will be surprised to see what people are selling. Washing machines, beds, cars, furniture, clothes, baby gear... you name it. On top of the obvious savings, you are also helping to save the planet by recycling and preventing waste. You can use your creativity to give a new life to goods that would have been wasted and even re-sell them after you've used them too (upcycling), with a much lower depreciation. Owning vintage furniture is pretty cool and looks good – it also saves you driving to a furniture store or spending a day building a ready-to-assemble wardrobe.

Pack your lunch

Those £10 take-away lunches. Seriously? £10 x 20 working days is already £200! We won't even talk about the health side of it. Plan ahead to make your own lunch and fill a bottle with tap water. That way you can keep your money for when you want to share a meal with someone. Have an objective in mind – perhaps once a week enjoy a nice lunch. But what's the point of spending £s each day on pre-made sandwiches and over-priced salads. Try building the habit of preparing a quick thing at home the day before. You will love it.

Set limits on Deliveroo

How easy has it become to order food directly from your sofa without moving a muscle (aside from the tendons in your hands)? Yes, I'm talking about that £30 delivery on Monday nights. (How can two pizzas and a tiramisu cost so much?) According to the NPD group[77] over the past 10 years delivery is booming and we are seeing the market for takeaway grow from £2.4 billion to £4.2 billion as of February 2018, an increase of 73%.[78] That represents 6% of the total British eat-out-of-home market, and we order on average10 pizza takeaway deliveries each year! We need to get off our sofas and start living.

Say no to 'witching hour' shopping

According to a (serious) report by Barclaycard, 'One in three Brits now spends more money shopping online at night, compared to five years ago.'[79] Whether it's your weekly supermarket shop, a last-minute birthday gift from Amazon Prime or a browse on your fave online boutique for that perfect coat, the virtual marketplace has all our shopping needs covered. To incentivize this new bedtime bubble in the market, many online retailers are now putting out special offers and discounts late in the day, and even running tie-in events to coincide with popular TV shows that people might be watching while they shop (think buying cake tins during Bake Off). If you run a retail business, this is where to look for your next sales boost: nocturnal shoppers spend 42 minutes extra per week browsing in the small hours once the clocks go back, with 10:18pm cited as the peak time to purchase.

Avoid sneaky add-ons

Temptation is everywhere... When something is on offer as a cheap add-on purchase, don't buy it. You are ready to pay for your shampoo at Boots, but as you're queuing you realize these small Ricola sweets are just here for you so you pick up a pack – even if you already have three on your desk... At the airport, you buy a bottle of water and when scanning the item you are offered a newspaper for £1. Your response? 'Okay, why not? It's only £1.' This is a great strategy for retailers, but not for your wallet! Paying an additional £1 here and there slowly adds up; for example, when buying 'add-on' items online. These are low-priced items that can be purchased only if you are ordering at least £20 of eligible products! So – think twice if your response tends to be, 'It's only £5, why not buy it?' These offers have probably cost you at least £1,000 at this point in your life...

Same-day delivery is clocking up your costs

Same-day delivery is becoming the norm for many online retailers from Argos to Net-a-Porter (the sight of whose sleek black vans driven by liveried drivers, zooming round town to resolve fashion emergencies, is probably the best advertising a brand could buy). With the customer experience being constantly streamlined, the journey from 'add to basket' to 'your order is complete' has never been swifter or easier. Amazon Prime is Amazon's premium service with a monthly or annual subscription cost, which gives members access to exclusive features such as free fast delivery. US Amazon Prime[80] members spend almost twice as much as non-members do, clocking up nearly $1,300 in purchases every year (purchased 25 times a year on the site vs. 14 times a year for non-Prime customers).

Cancel your subscriptions

Welcome to the subscription economy! Recent research by enterprise software company Zuora[81] found that 58 million of us in the UK (89% of the adult population) are now subscribing to at least one product or service and pay a recurring fee for on-going access to services such as Netflix, Spotify or Graze, as opposed to buying products outright. This figure suggests that Brits are now spending 12% of their monthly disposable income on subscription services. And this represents £448 million a month on unused subscriptions...

Make sure you check and cancel your unwanted subscriptions with Bean or Emma.

Travel for less

We all need a holiday sometimes, and when you're budgeting, a week in the sun can seem out of the question. But there are so many awesome ways to see the world without it costing you the earth!

Self-catering accommodation is always a winner: compare Airbnb in an expensive city with a hotel in a similar area. It's a no-brainer. Airbnb can be truly like a home from home.

And have you considered a home swap? Love Home Swap, *The Guardian* Holiday Home Swap and other websites facilitate this safely and efficiently. If looking for flight bargains, Skyscanner or Kayak offer the best deals. And don't rule out holidaying in the UK... there are some gorgeous beaches, thrilling outdoor adventures and slick city experiences to be had, for the price of a tank of petrol.

The daily grind

It's hard to believe that there have not always been several coffee outlets on every high street, or that there was a time when the only question you were asked in a café was, 'Would you like that with or without milk?' These days, being offered a range of a dozen or more caffeinated options with everything from cinnamon to skinny almond milk is the norm; not to mention all those tempting cakes and pastries. For many, it feels impossible to get to work without giving in to the temptation of a warming breakfast brew en route. Currently 95 million cups of coffee are consumed a day in the UK,[82] up from 70 million in 2008. Millennials account for 50% of all the coffee consumed in coffee shops, bars or restaurants, compared to 25% of Generation X (38–53) and only 12% of those over the age of 72.

Not meaning to sound totally old-fashioned here – but – it is soooo expensive! You may be spending well over £1,000 a year, just on shop-bought coffee. We know mornings are hard and you need a treat, but try cutting your habit for at least half the week. Instead, make coffee at home or take advantage of the free stuff at work – or at least go to an independent retailer! Many give a discount if you bring a re-usable cup, and you get the buzz of saving the planet too 😎.

Hack your car

Few people know this, but it's actually possible to drive more cheaply! By cutting your speed, maintaining a steady pace, removing that heavy roof-rack and not going down through all the gears each time you brake, you will use less fuel. Add to this the fact that many supermarkets will give you up to 5 pence off per litre, if you fill up at one of their own-branded petrol stations, and you could be saving hundreds of pounds a year with very little effort at all.

Keep fit for free

Have you noticed all those outdoor gyms popping up in parks and recreation grounds? They're there for a reason: to help people get fit for free. Expensive gym memberships can be a real drain on your finances, so consider taking a few months off and mixing it up with some outdoor exercise and maybe a few exercise videos done at home. (Ever heard of YouTube?) It's so much better for the soul to work out in the great outdoors... if you can't bear to give up your gym pass, shop around for deals and consider a class pass that lets you turn up at any fitness centre, wherever you are, at your convenience: that way you'll be more likely to get full use out of your monthly health club bill.

Check your council tax

According to The Money Advice Service, up to 400,000 households have been assigned the wrong council tax band. What if that hefty bill you always dread getting is incorrect? You might be looking at an unexpected budget bonus. It only takes a few minutes to check your status and appeal an incorrect amount.

Check out your local council's website. You can also follow the step-by-step guide on the MoneySavingExpert website.[83]

MAKE YOUR WARDROBE PAY YOUR BILLS

Raise your hand if you own at least one article of clothing that you've only ever worn once. Yeah – that's literally everybody reading this. From the high-rise flares that make you look more Ron Burgundy than Jane Birkin, no one is immune to fashion faux pas. The good news is that one person's ill-fitting get-up is another person's treasure, so why not free up space in your wardrobe and monetize your blunders?

Trawl local Facebook groups: You'll be surprised by the number of sales-orientated, Facebook Marketplace groups there are in your area. Such groups tend to be a very cost-efficient way of getting rid of unwanted stuff, mostly because Facebook doesn't charge you a percentage of the transaction and you can ask for payment in cash (so you don't need to wait five days for a cheque to clear).

eBay is (still) pretty neat: This is where Sophia Amoruso (Must read: *#Girlboss*) started building her Nasty Gal fashion empire! Although eBay's fees can be a little off putting, sellers still tend to prefer it to other websites. A word of caution, though: make sure you send your sold items via a tracked and signed-for postal service.

For pre-owned designer goods, try Vestiaire: Vestiaire Collective is a fash-tech start-up gone unicorn; hugely popular amongst fashionistas. The popularity of VC is partly down to quality control – they've got a round-the-clock staff checking all items for authenticity.

Declutter with Vinted: If you are more of a high-street junkie when it comes to clothes shopping, don't fret. The prices may seem low, but remember – every little bit counts. Plus, that newfound space in your wardrobe has never looked better.

DePop: Is another online marketplace, where the world's creatives come to 'buy, sell and discover the most inspiring and unique things'.

EXERCISE

Based on the above hacks, fill in this table and see how you could cut costs!

Bills	Monthly cost and provider	Switch? Yes / No	NEW monthly cost and provider	£ saved per month
Electricity				
Water				
Gas				
Internet				
Landline				
Mobile Phone				
....				
....				
....				
....				
....				

EXERCISE

Pick 3 fave saving hacks to start today. How much money will you save?

.... £ .... £

.... £ .... £

Pick 3 saving hacks to start this month. How much money will you save?

.... £ .... £

.... £ .... £

Well Done! You have earnt coins!

Your bank account will thank you for learning these budgeting hacks and incorporating them into your life. You should feel empowered with your new budgeting guidelines, a more mindful approach to spending and some cost-cutting hacks.

These are small, easy things you can start today for your money that can make a big difference. Over time, they should help you spend less money and save more for your goals – whether or not you're ready to get started budgeting. This was one part of the equation: saving more. Next we will move on the second part: earning more £££!

Money Talk
with Sarah Malik

Job: Designer and Founder at Malik + Mack.

Fun fact: Sarah used to work in professional services, tech start-ups and scale-ups. Last year she took the leap, retrained as a designer and launched her own agency. Sarah is also the first ever Vestpod ambassador!

Money motto: *'Rein it in.'*

What makes you happy?
A delicious breakfast with my husband (to be). Long walks in the North York Moors followed by cups of tea. Beautifully designed things, whether it be clothing, a signpost or a kitchen utensil. Feeling like I have endless time.

What is your most treasured possession?
My £4.49 Amazon engagement ring 🤩.

What is the best money advice you have ever received?
Get some. Also invest frequently in stocks and shares so that your risk to fluctuations in the market is reduced, i.e. better to invest £100 every month rather than £1,200 once a year.

What is your biggest money failure/mistake?
I wish I had learned about investing earlier. Like many of my friends, I kept far too much of my money in cash. I did not truly understand depreciation – and the much better returns that could be earned elsewhere – until embarrassingly late.

What is your greatest achievement?
Starting my design company. I love it. It has also forced me to engage with money in a different way.

What is your personal mission?
I would like to one day be a person of consequence. Someone who can say, 'That wouldn't be that way, if it weren't for me.'

What is your top money hack?
Don't drink with every meal out; your bill will be halved (and you'll feel great the next day).

Who is your go-to person to talk about money?
My fiancé, although I will say we have very different attitudes. He is more of the 'spend money to make money' school of thought, whereas I am a saver at heart.

Who is someone you admire most in life?
Ruth Bader Ginsburg, I think, is a stellar example of how to succeed slowly. Her advice that 'you can't have it all at once' is precious wisdom for young girls today.

What is your favourite book?
I once heard a friend describe *Anna Karenina* as 'the best book'. He distinguished that from calling Tolstoy the best writer. I disagree: I think it is the best book, and he is the best writer.

What was the start of your financial journey?
I sought to get involved with Vestpod because I truly wanted to start a journey of financial empowerment. I had an 'Ah ha! Money!' moment when visiting some friends in Yorkshire. Over a (very) cheap pint I suddenly realized I had no idea what my male friends were talking about (stocks, shares and recent investments). I felt annoyed at being so out of my depth, especially as we had all been on a par at school. Vestpod to me is a movement, and a very important one in addressing gender imbalance.

What does financial independence mean to you?
Financial independence means being okay if the company you work for suddenly goes under. It means you are strong enough to leave a bad situation, bad job, bad partner, bad part of town...Growing up in the North I saw whole communities being affected by a sudden wave of redundancy after a company restructure or a buyout. Being totally reliant on a pay-cheque leaves you very vulnerable, probably the reason I've always been driven to start my own company.

CHAPTER 5: ASKING FOR MORE £££

* *

What you will learn in this chapter:

How much should I be earning?

How can I negotiate my salary or rates and earn more £££?

How do I make extra £££?

* *

BECOME SO FINANCIALLY SECURE THAT YOU FORGET WHEN IT IS PAYDAY

Learning how to save money by understanding our spending habits is a game changer, but there is another killer option that we have at our disposal to leverage wealth, and that's by increasing our value and earning power. If we want to earn more money, we're going to have to stop underestimating our potential, because negotiating a salary with yourself won't work out.

Most of us in employment don't bother asking for a higher salary. Why? Well, sometimes because we assume that what we are being paid is what we are worth. 'Surely,' the thinking goes, 'if I was doing a good enough job they would be paying me more.' We assume that each year we can expect to receive a salary increase in line with our role and responsibilities (especially if we are offered a job in a big corporation). But the underlying message that many of us are giving ourselves is that we are lucky to have that job – we need it more than it needs us – so we mustn't rock the boat by looking greedy or ungrateful. We feel that asking for more could negatively impact on our relationship with our boss. But, how can your boss identify you as a rising star if you sit quietly at the back instead of stepping up (calmly and rationally – no one's suggesting an angry shouting match here) to ask for what you truly believe you're worth? Most people, especially women, don't think to negotiate their salaries. This needs to change. If it helps, think of it this way: your time is the most precious thing you can give your employer, so should be seen as having continual value.

Almost 60% of US employees admit that they accept their employer's first salary offer, according to a survey by Glassdoor, the employer review site. In the survey, more than 50% of men did not negotiate and nearly 70% of women shied away from attempting to persuade a potential employer of their true worth.

It's time to look reality in the eye and start to take some of the emotional and social shame out of asking for a raise. Earning more is not the sole goal: earning more coupled with managing this money and keeping expenses under control will help you to save money – and saving money is the secret to building wealth. In other words, if you can't face talking to your bosses about getting better pay or negotiating higher rates, you are lessening your future wealth potential and reducing your chances of having the independent life you want. The good news is that even if the salary conversation seems an impossible one to have right now, you will get there. After all, what's the worst that can happen? They might say no and you will walk out of the room looking like – what? Someone confident? Someone who tried? That will do for us!

If you stay organized and realistic, you could also make extra income stream by combining an employed role with freelance work *and* a side-hustle. There are so many options out there!

🤩 Money is out there, let's go get it!

How Much Should I Be Earning?

Understanding how much we need to live on is really helpful to avoid living pay-cheque to pay-cheque. This might sound like the preserve of the low paid, but high-earning millennials are the worst hit by the cycle of having nothing left at the end of each month.

How much do we need to earn?

According to CareerBuilder,[84] 31% of British workers say they always or usually live pay-cheque to pay-cheque to make ends meet. Researchers from LendingTree[85] found that 44% of young American professionals earning $100k are maxing out their current account every month.

Why is this happening? A major factor comes down to making expensive lifestyle choices: the sense that if you've scored a big, shiny job with a good salary, you should be toasting your success in fancy restaurants five nights a week instead of staying home. This is understandable to a great extent, but there is a balance to be had between spending it all and saving some. If you want to keep up with your lifestyle and having nothing left over to save, earning more is the only way forward.

In reality, it's useful to start by writing down two numbers based on two questions: 'How much do I need to earn to live?' and 'How much do I need to earn to live comfortably or extravagantly?'

EXERCISE

- How much do I need to live based on my budget/achieve my goals?

  £..

- How much do I need to live comfortably/achieve my goals?

  £..

This exercise is pretty straight-forward if you are an employee but not if you are a freelancer or self-empoyed. So do keep reading!

The revenue you make as a freelancer can be unpredictable and cashflow can be precarious. Nor do you get the benefits associated with a job (think health insurance, workplace pension and perks).

A big adjustment needs to be made to your budget to cater for new expenses such as a laptop, software, office space (charges can be as high as £450 a month for a hot desk), invoicing, accounting, business cards, website and hosting, internet and much more. Then, there is the cost of medical cover and insurance that you may need to take in case you are not able to work for any reason. And last but not least, there is your pension contribution to factor in.

If you are not employed but self-employed, you can contribute to a pension plan and you get the tax relief from the Government, but you don't have an employer to financially support you.

If you are freelancing, remember that paid holiday leave isn't included. You usually get paid per day or hour of work so be sure to divide this number by the number of days you are planning to work per year.

The reality for freelancers is we don't spend 100% of our time 'billing' clients – there are times when we need to update our portfolios, market ourselves, meet prospective clients, learn new skills, go to conferences, prepare invoices, and much more, which can take up to 1 day a week (20% of your time) and so should also be discounted from the days worked.

EXERCISE

Freelancers, here is how to calculate your rates:

How much do I need to live comfortably	£
Add up expenses	£
Add up medical insurance	£
Add up pension contribution	£
Your number	£
Divide by the number of hours you will be working – 20%	£

How much are we worth?

Modesty is a virtue, or so the saying goes. This may well be true, but when it comes to advancing our careers, modesty can do more harm than good. Why? Because the workplace is a competitive arena, a battlefield (with fewer casualties we hope) and we have to fight for what we're worth. As with anything worth fighting for in life, it helps to have the skills and confidence to show bosses and clients why we deserve both advancement and better pay.

Why should we negotiate? Well, because it's an opportunity to have our worth recognized. This is not emotional, it's just a fact. When accepting a new job we don't want to start on day one by feeling undervalued. At any time, we don't want to lose out in comparison to others who are more willing to put their worth on the table.

Here are some tactics to help take stock of our true worth at work:

- Do a little *research* to understand how much someone in a similar position and with similar experience earns elsewhere.

- Because money is that much of a taboo, it can be hard to have a direct conversation with your peers, so start online. You can use LinkedIn or the online salary calculators from GlassDoor.com, PayScale.com and Salary.com. They collect millions of data and are helpful as a guide to allow you to search and fine-tune your salary expectations by location, skills and level of experience. You can also use the salary tool on LinkedIn to help discover your earning potential. Using these platforms will allow you to have hard numbers to hand, ready for any negotiation. (Though always take the findings with a pinch of salt if you work in a niche sector or in an industry that does not reveal salaries, such as banking.)

- If you are a freelancer, finding out the going rates may be harder, but still very much possible. I worked freelance for a few years helping start-ups to build their business plans and presentation decks and had absolutely no idea on how to price my services (which is basically pricing yourself). Speaking to other freelancers doing the same job proved useful in terms of finding out about rates, but also helping to understand how people priced these. I certainly underestimated my services and by asking for more you also increase the value of your work for others.

HOW MUCH ARE PEOPLE REALLY PAID?

If you're anything like us (as in, a little bit nosy) – you've probably wondered how like-minded people earning different incomes are spending and saving their money.

But first, a little bit of context. We're living in notoriously uneasy times; income inequality is continuing to rise in the UK at an even higher pace than most other developed countries. As a result, economic discontent is rife – the *Financial Times* reported on how this economic disparity served as a big contributing factor to Brexit. The statistics on income inequality speak for themselves: in the financial year ending 2017, the average income of the richest fifth of households before taxes and benefits was £88,800 per year, 12 times greater than that of the poorest fifth (£7,400 per year)[86].

The reality is that we fall into widely different income brackets, which is why we publish weekly anonymous interviews on Vestpod to look at women with different incomes and how they each spend and save.

- Another way to stay updated with the market and understand how much people like you could be earning is to keep in touch with *recruiters and head-hunters*. They are experts in getting both clients and candidates what they want and they get paid for making the match. They hold a lot of information on levels of salaries for a certain industry and expertise. I realized the power of head-hunters when they started contacting me. But you can build a long-term relationship with them: pick up your phone and get some information – they may have great opportunities for you.

- Can you get *another offer* somewhere else? Even if you are ready to leave your current position, another offer can give you the extra confidence and negotiating power you need. By keeping abreast of the job market you also stay aware of skills, your employability and companies that are hiring. In banking for example, the best way to get a raise is to move to another company (often the case with most industries). So, don't undervalue the power of negotiating a first offer because once you've got the job, that may be much harder. An idea could be to look at switching industries, gain more knowledge and skills, go back to school for additional training in a field that appeals to you, or accepting an entry-level job and learning as you go.

- *Keep calm.* During this process you might well discover that your colleague makes 20% more than you do. This is infuriating but it's also a good opportunity to ask for more, which in the end is a great thing.

Remember. When you are employed, you can contribute monthly to a company retirement plan – with your employer matching the contribution. On top of this, you get an extra contribution from the Government called a tax relief (the cherry on the cake). As the workplace pension is calculated as a percentage of earnings, the more you earn the more you should be saving towards retirement. (See Chapter 6 for more on workplace pensions.)

Beat the gender pay gap

We've all heard of the gender pay gap, but the subtleties of how it operates may be less familiar. It does not mean that women who do the same jobs as men are paid less (this is actually illegal) – it's more to do with the bigger picture: women overall are paid less than males in the same sector. Much of this is based on historic attitudes and comes down to women's role in family life being seen as detracting from their worth as professionals. Some call this the 'motherhood penalty' as there is less of a disparity between single, childless men and single, childless women. However once mothering comes in to play, women start to command lower salaries. It's a vicious cycle, because in each new job your salary can often be set with reference to your previous salary 😢. For many working mums, this figure is lower than it could have been because they've taken on a flexible or low-impact role to accommodate the needs of raising young children.

We still have an embarrassing amount of work left to do before we eradicate gender inequality. If you still need proof that we're miles behind men in our earnings, here are some stats: according to the Institute of Fiscal Studies,[87] women on average earn 18% less than men, with the gender pay gap growing to a whopping 33% for working mothers.

If you live in the UK, the pay gap prognosis is particularly bleak. According to a 2016 report by Glassdoor,[88] Britain has one of the worst records of gender equality compared with other countries. The UK ranks 11th out of 18 countries in their league table, lagging behind the US, France and Spain. Not quite what we'd hope for in a progressive society.

Why is our gender pay gap so bad? We've heard again and again the explanations that women are less likely than men to succeed in asking for a pay rise. It has been said that women shy away from negotiating salary increases because they fear being thought less of if they do – it's a phenomenon that has been mentioned in Sheryl Sandberg's *Lean In*.

In Linda Babcock's *Women Don't Ask,* it was found that male bosses do indeed sometimes penalize female workers for being demanding or 'difficult', though recent research has proved more positive and contradicts previous studies. It seems that say women do 'ask' just as often as men. They just don't 'get'.[89]

This inequality extends beyond salary increases too. The median pension wealth for married men and women is £53,000 and £10,000 respectively, and at the age of 65–69 the average man's pension wealth peaks at a staggering five times higher than that of the average woman (£35,700 for women vs. £179,091 for men).[90] The reason for this is the incompatibility of high-earning, leadership roles with family life, meaning that women take more career breaks, earn less and, as a result, save less.

But there is a way forward! You just need to arm yourself with indisputable facts and an even temperament. Sure, there are times when unleashing your sense of injustice gets you what you want but doing so when negotiating a salary increase or your pension package isn't one of them.

CHILDCARE AS AN INVESTMENT, NOT AN EXPENSE

There is no right or wrong when it comes to determining your work-life balance post-baby. We know all too well how difficult it is to weigh up the pros and cons of working vs. staying at home, but one thing is certain – it's important to do what feels right for you and your family.

There are a couple of things you should keep in mind when it comes to the financial side of working after having kids.

Childcare is notoriously expensive. Families have to sit down and make calculations to determine whether or not it is worth a mother going back to work after having a child. Is there any financial incentive in returning to work whilst paying for childcare? You need to make a rational decision based on both of your salaries. If you are in the privileged position to be able to consider childcare, you should view it as an investment, not an expense. This may seem counter-intuitive, but taking into consideration the longer-term benefits of returning to work, such as the steady increase in salary and pensions contributions, makes the process of paying for childcare a little less painful.

Did you know that women who leave the workforce are penalized for doing so? An illuminating study by Hewlett and Luce (2005)[91] distressingly reveals that women lose an average of 18% of their earning power if they take time out from the workplace for an average 2.2 years. The more time you spend away from work, the bigger the reduction in salary when you return to work. After three years or more of being out of the workforce, the 18% reduction in earnings becomes a shocking 37%... It's quite the bitter pill to swallow!

Getting Paid

Here we will talk about the practical ways of getting paid and the add-ons that come with your salary. When your employer pays you a salary you should receive a payslip (weekly, monthly, or whatever you agreed with them). Most of the time, most of us open our payslips, look at the bottom right number in bold, then close our payslips and put them away.

Employees: what's in my payslip?

When is the last time you really looked into all the figures and details of your payslip? So I've looked into the components of the payslip, how tax is calculated and deducted, and the other things you can find on yours and here is what I found (you'll need a copy of your payslip to join me on this exercise).

Your payslip must show the following information: gross pay (full pay before any deductions), net pay (pay after deductions) also called 'take home' pay – this is the number that we usually look at first; and all other deductions (variable costs such as National Insurance taxes and fixed costs: expenses you have incurred that your employer agrees to pay for). Your payslip also notes how your salary is paid to you – often via BACS. Bacs Payment Schemes Limited, previously known as Bankers' Automated Clearing Services is the organization with responsibility for the schemes behind the clearing and settlement of UK automated payment methods Direct Debit and Bacs Direct Credit, as well as the provision of managed services for third parties.

Your payslip also includes information that is not mandatory such as your *tax code* (this code provided by HMRC will tell your employer how much tax they should deduct from your salary) and your *national insurance number*. (Also called NI, this number is unique to you. You will keep it forever and it will help HMRC to understand how much you have been earning and paying in taxes.)

You should check with your employer that they have the right details. A wrong tax code means that you may not be paying the right amount of tax and you could be overpaying (or worse, under-paying).

On your payslip you can also look at your earnings, deductions and pension.

Let's start with the *earnings*: you will have agreed with your employer a basic rate of pay but, on top of this, you may also be getting extra payments from commissions, bonuses, overtime pay, sick pay, maternity pay, reimbursement of expenses and so on.

Now the *deductions*: based on what you earn you may have to pay income tax. This is also called PAYE (pay as you earn) and the amount of tax you have to pay will depend on how much you earn (and your tax code) as well as your National Insurance contributions. (Your NI contributions go towards paying for the support that the state provides you with in the form of a State Pension, Maternity Allowance, or unemployment and other benefits).

HOW IS INCOME TAX CALCULATED?

When you earn money, you are required to pay taxes. However, there is an annual income threshold, below which you do not have to pay any tax. This is called the personal allowance and was set at £12,500 for the year 2019–20. (This may be modified if you earn more than £100,000 or if you owe tax from a previous tax year.)

You pay taxes on any amount earned that is more than the personal allowance, as a percentage of your income, based on incremental bands. Different percentages are payable, according to certain thresholds:

- **0% on income up to £12,500**
- **20% on earnings between £12,501–£50,001**
- **40% on earnings between £50,001–£150,000**
- **45% if you earn £150,001 and over.**

 Make sure you check HMRC's website for all of the current rules.

If you are paying money towards a *workplace pension*, you will see this on your payslip. This is not a deduction but a contribution. If your employer is contributing too, you may also be able to see their balance on your payslip. Otherwise you can check your pension statements for more detail.

→ For more on workplace pensions, head to Chapter 6

If you're *repaying a student loan*, it will also appear on your payslip. Your employer is responsible for collecting the money due, directly from your salary, and will send it to the Student Loans Company to repay part of your loan.

Other deductions that you might be able to see on your payslip are for workplace benefits such as health insurance, court orders and child maintenance, or trade union subscriptions.

Making a living out of a freelancing career

How do I find and keep clients and know how much should I charge? How do I do manage my taxes and what is the self-assessment tax return all about? What are my long-term freelancing goals?

Freelancing is hard work and rewarding but also lonely at times. While you don't have a boss anymore, you have something that can be more challenging: clients. Freelancers have an entrepreneurial mindset, they set their own rules and drive their businesses, they bear their own risk whereas employees have stability.

Getting paid

When I left private equity to build my first start-up, I worked freelance for a few years, often for start-up clients. I was and I still am shocked to witness how hard it is for freelancers and SMEs to get paid on time by clients. This is especially true when you are starting out and don't have years of experience in charging for your work or chasing invoices. Clients can also be fickle or short-term: there for one month and then disappearing the next.

How can you make sure you will be able to pay your bills at the end of each month? If your clients were to 'forget to pay you' for a few weeks or months, ask yourself, 'Can I survive?' The first rule-of-thumb is to make sure you have a cash surplus available in case of need. This is the all-important emergency fund and short-term savings I mentioned earlier.

If you have decided to go freelance or set up your own business, the way that you charge for your services and pay for your taxes will change from when you were traditionally salaried. You will need to think about your business structure (Sole trader, Partnership or Private limited company) and pay your own taxes (income tax, VAT, corporation tax).

When you are self-employed you pay taxes on your profits: income minus (–) your business expenses.

As soon as you start working for yourself or receive income from your company you need to register as self-employed. This means registering for Self Assessment with HMRC to pay tax and National Insurance on your self-employed earnings. Working as self-employed requires you to be extra careful with your financial planning because you will earn money first and pay tax later. It is vitally important that you put money aside for this! If you earn money from self-employed activity in the 2019–20 tax year you will be expected to pay the tax due no later than 31 January 2021. So, don't be surprised by this expensive bill and plan ahead for it!

What about my pension?

If you are self-employed you won't receive a workplace pension, so it is your own responsibility to set up a pension fund. You won't have the luxury of this being cared for by someone else. Ideally you manage to save money every month instead of waiting until the end of the year, because when it's time to pay your tax bill, unless you have budgeted for it, there may not be enough to make your pension contribution. If you earn more than the basic rate, you will have to ask for your additional tax relief through your Self Assessment tax return.

If you have your own business you could get tax advantages through your pension too.

Sort out your accounting

Keeping your finances in order is extremely important and not something you can afford to compromise! Not only will you need to charge clients and send invoices, you may also have to pay invoices. Keeping track of all this is super-important when the taxman comes to your door to check you've paid the right amount of tax.

Whatever your business status: whether you are working freelance or a business owner, you need to keep records of what's coming in and out of your business, the sales you are making and the costs. As your business grows you will also need to consider payroll and office space costs.

There are online accounting packages and solutions you can use, such as **xero.com** or **sage.com** that could save you time and keep you organized but it's also a good idea to find an accountant who can help you to plan ahead and budget accurately for your taxes.

Visit the Government website for 'business and self-employed' advice. You will find here all the resources to set up a business, pay your taxes, pay yourself and register for VAT. Don't hesitate to also give them a call as they are pretty responsive: **gov.uk/browse/business**

How to Negotiate

I first met V at a workshop when she came along to learn about investing; she then came to a few book club sessions, so we got to know each other quite well. She is a massive supporter of Vestpod and the last time I saw her, she mentioned she had got a salary increase. I was really excited for her. But that was not all, she told me her secret: she had secured three promotions and three pay increases in just six years. Last time around, she sends a calendar invite to her boss; he replies (jokingly): 'Are you going to ask me for more money again?' She just replies, 'Yes' (non-jokingly). *#girlboss* 😎

We talked about having a growth mindset in Chapter 1: negotiating is one of the key skills we need to grow. I always see the good in negotiation. It requires a positive mindset and a willingness to improve things. I aim to be clear about what I want to get out of a negotiation and work hard to achieve it without losing out or becoming aggressive. It's important to remember that some things are worth fighting for, but others less so. ('Choose your battles wisely', as the saying goes.) I aim to bring some nuance to my work negotiations and in life more generally, to make sure the process is empowering and useful. The best kinds of negotiation are always 'win-win' (so that all parties feel happy with the outcome) rather than 'win-lose'. There is almost always middle ground to be found.

Earn it! This may be the most important 'detail' needed before starting any salary negotiation or rate increase. To earn more you have to first have earned it! In reality, this means not only putting the hours in, but also ensuring that you are offering a genuinely desirable set of skills.

Next comes the nitty-gritty of setting your own pay-grade. We'll start with advice for salaried workers then move on to the specifics of negotiating as a freelancer.

Negotiating your salary

You've decided that you are not paid at the right level, based on what you need to live on and what you think you're worth. You decide to book a meeting with your boss to discuss your salary. The hardest part of any salary negotiation is often getting to sit down for a meeting with whoever is in charge of the purse strings – so well done if you've already overcome that hurdle! Once you've arranged your meeting, remember that the offer you receive is never set in stone and that there is always room for negotiation.

Salary negotiating is not a one-off thing you prepare for: it's actually super-useful to see it as a continuous process. Try viewing it as shopping for the best deal every year. Here are some tips to make that big money-meeting go well:

Build your case

Based on how much you think you're worth, can you prepare a simple case to support your negotiation? How much do you earn today? How much do you want to earn tomorrow, and what are you basing this on? What are your targets? How will you achieve them? What will that bring to the table? What are your strengths? Based on this, it is useful to start any negotiation with three numbers in mind (i.e. on paper) – these will be your negotiation range. These numbers are for you and should not be seen by your employer, or prospective employer/client. You should ask yourself:

- *What is your current salary? Is it at the market rate? Does it cover your budget and financial goals?*
- *What is the lowest salary you can accept (the base rate – i.e. the amount of money you would accept for the job that will help you cover your needs and wants. Make sure this level helps you to work towards your goals, is fair and is in line with the market)? Keep a number in mind or you can end up KO.*
- *What is the ideal salary you're aiming for? This amount should allow you to live comfortably and achieve your financial goals a bit quicker than with the base salary if you manage to stash away more money over time, but you should also make sure you are paid what you're worth, i.e. the market value.*

EXERCISE

Based on this can you write your 3 numbers:

Add: My current salary is: £ . . . .

My base salary is: £ . . . . (I will never go below this)

My ideal salary is: £ . . . .

Write down your achievements and successes

Take notes on a weekly basis of all the things you do in your role. Just open a Google doc, or an Evernote and drop in any event, success or appraisal from your boss or colleagues. We tend to forget about the wins and focus on our failures, but these won't get you your raise. Go over these notes and find recurring themes or strengths: perhaps you bring new business to the firm, consistently reach targets, are great at networking, presentations, deals, new hires, management... Numbers don't lie, so to make your arguments persuasive, arm yourself with the best numbers you can find. Take note of any positive feedback you have received from management and peers that links to your role and responsibilities. V tells me she prepares a business case with spreadsheets, and a presentation that details successful KPI data (these are Key Performance Indicators: the number of new clients on board, number of deals signed, number of hours billed and so on; you should know the ones that are used to measure your performance) as well as changes in her role and responsibilities. Keeping track of your productivity will be instrumental in promoting your value and help others to recognize your worth both internally and externally.

Make yourself irreplaceable

While your self-confidence and how you carry yourself matter greatly, the one thing that underpins your value in the workplace is your ability to deliver the work better than anyone else. If you know you are not genuinely giving 100%, you may feel less inclined to push for a promotion or salary increase. When you know that you can demonstrate your true value, you will, in turn, feel more confident about asking for a raise. So, make sure you're truly giving it your all before you go in all guns blazin'...

Find your supporters

We are not always comfortable negotiating for ourselves. A study by the American Psychological Association (via *Harvard Business Review*)[92] shows that women usually negotiate better for others than for themselves; they are great advocates.

So, try to find colleagues who can champion you. Can you be more sociable at work and make more time for coffee catch-ups? Take some actions that will benefit you and others, as well as the organization. So, go. Find your advocates!

Don't accept the first offer

Congrats on getting a job offer or a salary increase but remember, you don't have to accept it on the spot. I suggest asking for one or two days to think about it; then come back with a new proposal or counter-offer if you think it is necessary. Remember, too, that if someone asks you what amount you are looking for, you also don't have to state a precise figure for the salary you want. Some people find it easier to state a salary bracket; you could also let your employer make the first offer, which could give you a good basis for negotiation. It is important that your employer feels comfortable with the level of salary they are willing to offer. Being greedy can potentially make yourself more vulnerable when it comes to cut-backs.

Stay true to yourself

Authenticity is key to successful negotiations. You don't need to be anyone other than who you really are. The whole painful interaction with your boss is going to be a lot weirder and more stressful if you start to play a part. Just be your strong, open, true self. Value your skills and have faith in knowing the great things you have to bring to the company.

We don't have to become a tribe of alpha-women to get ahead. Research shows that there are differences between the way men and women negotiate. While men tend to be more competitive, women prefer more ethical negotiation. It's sometimes difficult to bring together these two approaches but more positive and collaborative results have been observed (a win-win situation) when there is more empathy and less confrontation.[93]

Put yourself in your boss or clients' shoes

Spend some time thinking about your request from the other person's perspective. If you feel as if you are being undervalued, why do you think that is? Perhaps they haven't noticed the extra time you have put in at work, or your commitment to your role and the company. There can be a myriad of reasons why your dedication and ethic seem to go unnoticed. Frankly, it's your job to put this right! Demonstrate your value the next time you're in a meeting with management (this goes back to my earlier points above) and you may be surprised by the result. If you focus on the added value you provide, your employer will start to think about you in terms of increasing the bottom line of the business and be more likely to agree to your request. Remember: you are not asking them a favour. You have earned this. Another simple hack is to use the word 'we' instead of 'I' throughout that tricky salary meeting. 🤩

Confidence and awareness!

What's your favourite outfit? What makes you feel powerful? It's important to feel good and to feel like yourself when you are in a challenging meeting. The value of power poses is often mooted by self-improvement experts (think of striking up that Superman pose in the bathroom) and there is no doubt that positive non-verbal communication can make a big difference to the impression you make on others.[94] Smile! Be a great communicator.

Adopt an open posture and be aware of what's happening around you. These actions will show your authority without you appearing bossy, and should also boost your confidence.

NINA ON 'WHAT IS THE BEST FINANCIAL DECISION YOU HAVE EVER MADE?'

'Honestly, the best financial decision I ever made was negotiating my salary. It sounds so trite, but it's something that I think we as women have a great fear of doing. I read a book once that said, 'Walk into that room and say the highest number you can say without laughing. And why shouldn't you? Most mediocre men would!' It really gave me the confidence to go in there and demand more. A starting salary is such a fickle thing, because you obviously need it to live [on] but it also sets the tone for your pay moving forward. Many people who say the gender wage gap doesn't exist claim that if it does, it only exists because women take lower paying jobs or do not negotiate. Now, I know for a fact that the gender wage gap does very much exist, but there is something to be said of this point. If you compare it to a race, if a woman is standing at the start line but a man is already 20 metres in, any advances the man make will obviously compound to be greater than the woman makes!'

Think about the long-run

Ask yourself why you want this advancement. Have clear goals for every year of your career and a plan for how you will get there. Invest in yourself and your skills – nobody is perfect but trying to better your 'problem areas' will put you miles ahead of the competition. And, if things don't go as planned – don't get discouraged! Failing is part of life. If you don't fail, you don't learn.

Silence is golden

It's so hard to manage the silences when you're nervous, especially in an interview, but state what you want, then listen and wait for the other person to come back to you. If you fill that awkward space with self-deprecating lines such as, 'of course I totally understand if you can't', you make it easy for them to say no.

😀 Remember, negotiation doesn't have to all be about cash

Sometimes you may have hit the upper pay limit and your employer won't be able to increase your salary band. Of course, getting paid at the level you want is key, but are there other things you could ask for too:

- *Pensions:* You will see in the next chapter the importance of workplace pension as well as the associated tax relief. Your employer has the obligation to put some money in your pension, but you can try to negotiate a higher contribution. This is not cash you can use today but it will prove vital for your retirement!
- *Benefits:* Could you have health insurance? What does it cover?
- *Perks:* These could be flexible working hours, shares, holidays or other perks such as training and personal development, financial wellness programs, yoga classes, physio sessions, pets at work, unlimited holidays etc.
- *Vacations:* How many holiday days do you get?
- *Stock options:* As part of your compensation package, you may be offered some sort of participation in the company you are working for in place of other benefits (such as a higher salary). This is quite common if you work for a listed company, but some start-ups and private companies will also offer you the right to acquire shares in the business. Having

company shares or options (the right for you to buy shares in the future and at a certain price) means that you have an incentive to work hard, help the company grow and entices you to stay with them for the long term. Remember that if you own shares in a business that is not listed you will have to wait (sometimes a long time) to sell your shares and will only make money if the sale is successful. I invite you to check the terms of these offerings as well as the tax treatments.[95]

These things can be worth more to you than hard cash, and you can see whether your employer is committed to increase your value in other ways.

If you get shot down, don't give up

Even if the absolute worst happens, and your tough negotiation stance costs you a job offer, don't let that turn you into a scared little mouse when you go for the next one. Stating your worth will not injure you – it is what you deserve. No more, no less.

Keep talking about money

We all need to get used to talking about money as if it's just a normal part of adult life – which it is! It really doesn't need to be laden with emotion. You wouldn't get tongue-tied and embarrassed talking about that cosy winter coat you just bought. You wouldn't feel shy talking about the great holiday you just had. The more often you practise money-talk on a daily basis, the more confident your conversational repertoire will become and the better every verbal financial transaction will be.

FAKE IT UNTIL YOU MAKE IT

Do you secretly feel like a fraud? Do you fear that your boss and colleagues might discover the 'real' you and send you packing? Do you think you are where you are today only because of luck?

Imposter syndrome may be holding us back, but we can definitely beat it.

Impostor syndrome is a phrase that is often bandied about when we feel a bit insecure, but it is a potentially serious psychological condition. There is no doubt that this debilitating syndrome is a bitter reality for many people. Some 70% of women and men report experiencing impostor syndrome at some point in their lives.[96] The bad news is that it can actually send your career in to a decline, either by causing you to sub-consciously sabotage yourself at work, or by over-achieving to the point of burnout.

WHAT CAN BE DONE TO OVERCOME IT?

The good news is, this doesn't have to be a permanent feature of your internal landscape. Experts have come up with all sorts of tips to undo the negative thinking that goes with impostor syndrome, and here are some of the best ones to try:

- **Recognize you have it and know that having it means you're not seeing things as they really are. This is the first step on the road to separating your paranoid imaginary version of yourself from the awesome you that others see.**
- **Celebrate your achievements! List the great stuff you've done at work recently. Expressing specific, positive thoughts about yourself will boost your confidence.**
- **Acknowledge that luck, chance and even nepotism do play a part in most people's success, but it's what you do with these benefits that counts.**
- **Accept that no one feels confident and fabulous 100% of the time. Everyone has days when they look in the mirror after a bad night's sleep and can't summon up their game face. Everyone has months or years where they take knock after knock and don't know whether they have the resilience to bounce back. That's life and that's OK. Confidence ebbs and flows.**
- **Don't forget, there will be a reason why you are prone to feeling like an impostor and it's probably not your fault. Maybe you were raised or educated in a super-competitive environment. Perhaps you work in an industry that tends to be judgmental and bitchy. If things get really toxic, you might want to consider really taking charge of your life by exploring a new career avenue or a working arrangement where there's less of a cut-throat culture.**

Negotiating as a freelancer

If you think freelancing or being self-employed is a euphemism for 'I'm just sleeping in and chilling', think again.

Many people dream about freelancing: think less commuting, more time with your family and greater control over what your day looks like... Freelancing is getting more popular and this is especially true among women. The number of self-employed increased from 3.3 million people in 2001 (12% of the labour force) to 4.8 million in 2017 (15.1% of the labour force).[97] But what does freelance life really look like?

It should go without saying, but before taking the plunge to go freelance, take an honest look at what you have to offer. If you have the skill-set and the determination to make freelancing work, then you're starting from the right place. The world of freelancing can be mired in uncertainty, which is why we will look into the different aspects you should keep in mind if you're considering, or already are, freelancing.

The tactics discussed above on the salary negotiation also apply to freelancing because you need to negotiate your rates. As a freelancer, one of the first but trickiest things you have to do is decide how much to charge.

You can do this in various ways:

- Start with the number you have identified above – this should be the rate that will allow you to live comfortably and save towards your financial goals.
- Go online and seek out chat boards for your industry, where other freelancers are discussing what they get paid.
- Consult a specific networking site like The Dots to see what kind of figures are normal for your line of work.
- Ask your prospective client what their budget is, and what they usually pay (then check, if you can, with another freelancer or client whether this is true!)

Different pay structures

You can choose to charge by the day (or hour) or for the whole project. Most businesses use the pay-by-time model because it's more straightforward for everyone involved. Knowing how much you're being paid per day will make your budgeting a whole lot easier too.

Show them what you're made of

When you go in for a client meeting, be prepared to show your true value. It's not going to be all about money. Freelancers are usually asked to provide a portfolio of their work, so get that looking sharp in advance. Your portfolio, just like a CV, should include client names, testimonials and case studies. Be specific about showing the value you have brought to past clients, even if it feels as if you are spelling out the obvious. Pitching for work is a sales job so it's important for you to start showing off those skills.

Learn new skills

Enriching your portfolio with an ever-expanding skill-set can give you the edge over competing freelancers. Keep learning new computer programs, languages, accounting practices, communications techniques. And tell people about those skills!

Network

Your network is everything as a freelancer, so take every opportunity to socialize and work with a broad range of your industry fellows. Don't limit your contacts to your current corner of the industry: things could change suddenly in your field and put you out of work, so make contacts in other areas that you might one day wish to move into too.

Be creative

Don't stick to one way of finding work or just one set of clients. There could be a great project out there for you, in the most unexpected place, so keep your eyes and mind open and don't automatically discount any potential offer that comes your way. Research foreign markets too and plunder family contacts and neighbours for hidden income streams. You're a hustler!

Earn More £££ With a Side-hustle

Do what you love! Believe in yourself! Follow your passion and the money will come! These are aphorisms that chase twenty-somethings around the job market for the first ten years of their working lives, making them anxious about finding what their passion is and wondering whether they're passionate enough about it anyway. Passion... love... happiness... Unfortunately, they are not much help to a generation beset by rising living costs, astronomical student debt and record levels of job insecurity.

So, what should you do? Give up on your dreams and opt for financial security by training as an accountant? (No offence to the accountants out there – we love you and need you!) Or is there a third way? A happy medium between doing what you love and doing what's right for those who depend on you, as well as society at large?

Research by Harvard Business Review[98] shows that when people spend just 15 minutes a day pursuing something they love and believe in, they report higher levels of well-being than those who don't. So, even if you've decided to be practical and opt for a job that's a bit boring but well paid for now, you don't have to give up doing what you love. Choose to devote as much of your spare time to it as possible, and it might even develop in to a lucrative side-hustle. Plus, there's real satisfaction to be gained from doing the 'right' thing and saving money for the future well-being of yourself and your loved ones. This feeling starts to feel like joy as you get older and start to see others benefit from your choices.

Having said all that, we shouldn't disregard the amazingly motivating power of passion and enthusiasm. If you can find a job based around something you enjoy, *do it*, as long as it doesn't pay literally nothing. It is surely worth earning less than your friends – or less than you could be earning elsewhere – if you love the field you're working in. After all, when the chips are down, only those who feel passionate enough about their work will feel motivated to carry on working on that tough project, will stay up all night or do something for free to help a colleague. Those are the star qualities that get noticed, rewarded and ultimately bring success. So, if you're at a crossroads in your working life and you're wondering how to choose between what you love and what's practical, we have news for you. You don't have to choose. Do both.

Making a side-hustle work

Whether you're saving up for something expensive or simply hoping to learn new skills and grow your professional network, side-hustling can become your thing. Yes, the 'side hustle' might sound like a funky new dance move, but it is in fact the current buzzword for taking on an additional, part-time job. You could also call it earning on the side, or a hobby that pays.

Second income streams are where it's at! Britons are earning £249 million[99] from what was once thought of as mere hobbies. Passion projects are paying out, and more and more people are jumping on the after-work bandwagon. Many start-ups began life as a side-hustle.

A side-hustle can also be a great source of income for saving up for a specific project or event. Many people with a wedding or round-the-world trip coming up will put in a few extra hours each week at a second job. Anyone who has a special skill, from baking to baby care, may as well capitalize on it.

If you want to put in a few hours working for others but aren't ready to fully launch your own business, consider signing up to taskrabbit.co.uk or peopleperhour.com – these work like the old 'small ads' in the local paper: you will find people advertising for help with everything from their weekly shopping to writing and designing a website. Many skilled professionals use these sites. Our weekends might now include yoga, bread-making, learning a language… and all these things need a teacher! Personal finance fast-trackers who have drawn up their DIY financial plan and want to rack up six months' additional earnings for their emergency fund could reach their goal faster by taking on some weekend or evening work.

Even if you're in stable employment, it can help your promotion prospects if you show that you're an ingenious, independent person who thinks outside the 9–5 box. Some workers fear that their managers will disapprove of their side-hustle, but in fact the opposite is often true: it makes you just the sort of motivated, ambitious self-starter they want leading their business (provided the day job does not suffer, of course.)

Some successful examples: You don't need to look far for examples of people doing it for themselves. Here are a few, collected over the past year at Vestpod:

- *Rent out a room.*
- *Occasional podcast making.*
- *Voice-over work.*
- *eBay antiques selling.*
- *Events: £100+ per month average.*
- *Writing: £50 per month approx.*
- *Some small consulting jobs.*
- *Selling old designer finds on eBay, selling items on Vinted (£100 per month).*
- *Owning a small shoe brand.*
- *The odd bit of freelance writing for magazines (£30+).*

You see, whatever your interests and however much or little time or commitment you have to give, there's a way of making a side-hustle work for you.

Taking the Leap: Entrepreneurs and the Self-employed

Building a business has become the trendiest thing. We see famous entrepreneurs on TV and in the news who make business seem so cool and easy: they had an awesome idea for a product or concept and they made it work. They pose for pictures in magazines and do keynote talks... they're spotted jet-setting around the world meeting and partying with the coolest people. They buy islands! They make spaceships! And best of all they are their own boss!

Maybe you too are passionate about something that you think people would love to spend money on. Perhaps the idea of running a start-up has always attracted you. Becoming an entrepreneur is certainly not for everyone – but it could be a great way to control your future and build an asset (i.e. your company) that generates income for you and your family for generations to come.

Is entrepreneurship for you? Can you deal with financial uncertainty or no salary for a while? Are you passionate about your mission and what you are building? Are you resilient? That is the only thing that will keep you going against all odds. If you answered yes to these questions, you might be ready to take the plunge and do the start-up thing.

Here are some preliminary tips:

- *Start with a side-hustle to gauge your market and abilities. To transform a side-hustle to a business, try your idea again and again until you're sure there are enough customers out there for you to make money. It is important to test and measure your market. (Ask yourself, too, could you keep running this as a side hustle rather than full time?)*
- *Try getting a job in a start-up to get a taste for the entrepreneurial life.*
- *Prepare yourself for some tough times. You may be lonely and poor for a long time and never have a paid holiday again.*

Now ask yourself these final questions:

- *Do you want to keep doing this freelance or build an actual business with employees and an accountant or book-keeper to manage your accounts?*
- *Are you financially ready? By which I mean, do you have an emergency fund? Have you cleared all your bad debts?*

OK, so maybe you're ready to take the plunge. You can try to launch the business on your own (bootstrapping it with your own money) or else, if you don't want to do this, you will need to raise some money for this new baby of yours. Don't start to seek funding too early: instead start saving some money yourself, prepare a tight budget and a business plan, get yourself educated about your legal, tax and accounting status. Then start looking for investors. Remember this may take some time...

Regulation

Before you set up a business or decide to run your own freelance practice, make sure that you get clued-up on all regulatory issues. This starts with data protection and the infamous GDPR guidelines to more specific regulations relating to health and safety practice. You can visit **gov.uk** to find the best tools to achieve this.

RESOURCES FOR SETTING UP A COMPANY

Visit the Companies House website for everything related to starting a business: gov.uk/government/organisations/companies-house

You can also ask a formation agent to help you by giving their expert advice and assistance to register your company and provide other services: such as naming your company, ongoing company secretarial support, registered office address services, help setting up a business bank account:
gov.uk/government/publications/formation-and-company-secretarial-agents/company-formation-agents-and-secretarial-agents

Well Done! You have earnt coins!

You've got through this big old chapter on earning. It's a bit more exciting than saving, isn't it – though maybe a bit less sexy than spending. Understanding our worth, working towards a fair salary or rate that will help us to live comfortably and achieve our financial goals, and negotiating for more are key to helping us save more £££. It is then in our hands to make sure we make the right spending and saving decisions and save for what we care about and for the future. But the valuable lesson is that money can come from many more places than just your regular pay packet. I hope this has got you thinking not only about your options in terms of side-hustles, freelancing and maybe start-ups, but also your attitude toward valuing yourself and your services in the market.

Hold tight for the next chapter in your financial journey about your understanding your bank balance!

Money Talk
with Louise Troen

Job: Vice-president of international marketing and communications at Bumble.

Fun fact: Louise joined Bumble while the start-up was still quite small (employee #8) but she has been an energetic and passionate busy bee, travelling the world to help people make meaningful connections. Her latest mantra: 'Glass ceilings make good dancefloors.'

Money motto: *'An investment in knowledge pays the best interest.'* – Benjamin Franklin.

What makes you happy?
New experiences – they challenge me.
Refreshing attitudes – they develop me.
Perspective – it keeps me grateful.
Family – they keep me grounded.
Creativity – it keeps me invigorated.

What is your most treasured possession?
I'm not sure 'possessions' are what I treasure. I think it's fun to buy nice things, and I most certainly love to shop – but I wouldn't say that they make me happy. I've bought a couple of items that have represented milestones and they make me feel good – but not because of the brand or function – because of what they stand for. My independence, my freedom, and the ability to have an autonomous choice in how to spend the money that I work so hard to earn.

In terms of what I hold that I treasure most, it's probably my mental health. We work so hard to be fitter, stronger, more resilient physically, and yet we forget that the sharpness and efficiency of our minds manifest our ability to reach higher levels of positivity, gratitude and recovery when life throws challenges our way.

What is the best money advice you have ever received?
Invest in projects or people who have inspiring visions and spend disposal income on unique life experiences. These experiences will shape you and give you the critical thinking and perspective to invest better. And get a financial adviser – if you don't know how to invest or spend your money, find someone who can help you do it.

What is your biggest money failure/mistake?
Assuming that your job is a guarantee – and living from month-to-month pay-cheque. It's important you always have six months of savings to live off just in case life throws you a curve ball. It's crucial to have a fallback to enable you to always have a choice in your work, should you run into a situation that morally compromises your principles or your ability to work happily.

What is your greatest money achievement?
I don't think I've reached it yet.

What is your greatest money regret or fear?
I don't really have any regrets but I've always been very sensible with my finances and never overspent or maxed-out credit cards. I think credit can be quite dangerous and a lot of our generation get carried away with 'free money' – and I'm extremely conscious to always spend within my means (or know that I can pay off a bill should it be a high upfront cost).

What is your top money hack?
I don't think I have hacks or tricks to spending money well. I think it's all rather simple. Push for being paid market rate, push your company to develop certain commission-based programmes to incentivize you financially if you're that way inclined, save each month (even if it's 10%) and spend on life experiences like travel that can develop your education and cultural understanding.

Who is your go-to person to talk about money?
My mother.

Who are your inspiring heroes?

My grandmother, who was Danish and a formidable woman. She was fierce and independent and braver than anyone I know. She lived on her own most of her later life and always greeted me with advice and honesty. She had the most self-respect I've ever seen in a person and it always inspired me to discover what my own sense of self-respect felt and looked like – it's different for everyone. She was irrevocably resilient (she suffered breast cancer and went on to live many years after they thought she wouldn't) and that resilience always guided me and gave me the strength that I hold as an individual.

What is your favourite book?

The Alchemist by Paulo Coelho, a profound fable about the way we should all live life.

What is your best career advice?

You don't need everyone to like you, but you do need everyone to respect you – my father.

What is your top negotiation tip?

Listen, listen, listen. Negotiation isn't about one offer versus the other or pushing your final offer onto someone – it's about understanding, compromise and context. Listen to their reasoning (which parts seem flexible and which don't) and build your counter-offer off this. Remember, some negotiations can be emotional, so understanding the emotional context around your counterpart's proposal is also important.

CHAPTER 6: NAVIGATING YOUR BANK BALANCE

* *

What you will learn in this chapter:

What is the difference between saving and investing money?
Where to save money: savings accounts vs. ISAs?
Where to invest money: pensions vs. ISAs vs. investment accounts?

* *

ABOUT TO CHECK MY BANK BALANCE: 'I'M GUESSING I SHOULD HAVE £500 IN MY ACCOUNT' BANK ACCOUNT: 'YOUR BALANCE IS £1.54'

How many of us have been holding our money in the same bank account for the past 10 or 20 years? Have you ever thought about changing bank for better terms? Do you know if your account costs you anything or if it has the best tax treatment? Do you receive zero interest on your money? Do you save or invest your money? How do you move money around?

Are we really taking care of our money? Can making a few changes and understanding the financial landscape improve the way we manage our finances? I really think so. We have been passively using our money and banks in a way that has not been empowering us.

Up until now, we have been looking at the big picture: what your goals are, what you are trying to achieve, how you can save and all the different ways you can eke out your salary.

We've realized that we needed to start saving yesterday – but what do we do with this money? Just keep it in our bank account? Transfer it into an ISA (Individual Saving Account) or contribute into a pension? But what if we need it earlier? Most of us are familiar with current accounts and savings accounts, but what about pensions, ISAs and other accounts?

We will begin this chapter by talking about the short term, how to save your money today. We will investigate the best ways to save money and what types of savings accounts/ISAs you can use. We will then move onto the long term and consider retirement planning and what pensions and stocks and shares ISAs can do for your money.

This chapter is UK specific and is an explanation of the main financial products available to you. If you don't understand a product, don't put money in it. I cannot tell you what's best for you, so do your research and talk to an adviser if necessary. Also check the latest rules on savings and tax allowances, this is not tax advice...

Check the Government website section 'Money and Tax'.

To Save or Invest?

In the previous chapters we worked on our goals and decided how much we wanted to set aside for each of them. These could involve saving and investing money. While we will deep-dive into investing in the next chapter, we need to know the *difference* between saving and investing in order to be able to choose the right place to hold our money (current accounts, savings accounts, ISAs, pensions, etc.). Deciding to save *or* invest is based on your *goals* and the *time* you give yourself to achieve them. I can't tell you what's right or wrong for you.

When you are *saving*, you have the foreknowledge that you will spend the money you are setting aside in the near future. You want this money to be safe and available anytime (it should be *liquid*). These savings are going towards something you may need in your future and you should ensure that you maximize their potential saving rate. This is why saving your spare cash in a savings account, although not very risky, is not letting your money work very hard for you. If you have some expensive debts such as those on credit cards, pay off these first before saving if you can and check if there is a repayment cost. Check how much interest you are paying on your debts; if the cost is higher than what you receive or could receive on your savings, it may be a good idea to tackle these first (for example, a credit card not repaid in full can cost you around 18% in interest rates – a rate that will be impossible to get on savings). Also focus on building up your emergency savings to prevent you from ending up in debt again...

Once you are comfortable you've built up your savings nest (including your emergency fund), don't touch it...you can start building another pot of savings that you could decide to use for investing. With *investing* you will be deploying your capital and putting your money to work. You want to make it grow by buying things that increase in value over time. When you start to do this, please don't invest in the first opportunity (e.g. your friend's start-up) but only begin when you have a clear idea of your investment strategy, i.e. what you are expecting from your money. Think of your money as an energy source 🤑. When you invest money, however, it can be locked away for a certain period of time (i.e. if it is in property you would need to sell that real estate to receive the money; if it is in the stock market you would need to sell your investments). These investments are not as liquid as cash – and they are also more risky! Investing always involves some risk: what if the stock market crashes or the price of your house drops by 10%? Consider the risk carefully – you don't want to be forced into a position where you have to sell these investments quickly at a difficult time.

With investing you are looking for something in return: growth of your money but also additional income (perhaps a property paying you rent, shares paying you dividends). It's more risky than saving but your money works harder and you can accrue more capital that you have earned. Usually the more savings you have the more you can invest, but it will depend on your personal situation. *However*, without savings in place or with expensive outstanding debts, you shouldn't start investing...

Short-term goals (1–5 years): You want your money to be available anytime, to keep your money in cash and save into cash deposits.

Medium-term goals (5–10 years): Again cash deposits might sometimes be the best answer. You could invest for certain goals.

Long-term goals (10 years+): You may want to consider investing. Why? If you are willing to take more of a risk, you could make your money work harder. Because of inflation, the measure of prices in the economy that is making life more expensive year after year.

→ In the Chapter 7 we will discuss in detail the concept of investing: inflation, compound interest and risk/reward!

Let's look at some examples to give you an indication of how to handle your goals:

Goal	Description	Save or invest?
Buy a car	Need a new car in the next 12 months	Save
Pay for your wedding	Getting married in a year	Save
Pay for my kids' university fees	In 15 years In 2 years	Probably Invest Save
Life of travel in retirement	I am 35 and I want to retire when I am 60, i.e. in 25 years	Invest

EXERCISE

Based on the goals you identified in Chapter 3, can you decide for each of them if you would need to save or invest money?

Goal	Description	Save or invest?

Which bank?

We all need a bank account 🤩. You may still have the one you chose 10 years ago or you may have recently switched to something new, but you still need to assess if this is the right account for your money. There are a few guidelines that can help you choose the best account.

First of all, remember you're in charge here. The bank is offering a service that you can choose to take or leave. Don't fall into the trap of thinking it is doing you a favour – this is your money, your rules, kind of. Now, what is it that you want this account to do for you? Here are some questions to ask:

1. **What comes as standard with the account?** Usually it's just a debit card but what are the arrangements for overdraft facilities? Do they have 24-hour telephone banking? Is there a handy app? And what about interest? How much will you be earning on your money and how much must you pay if you become overdrawn? Does it offer any extras like insurance?
2. **What's your communication style?** Do you like to physically go in to a high street bank sometimes, to talk things over or pay in a cheque, or do you prefer to do it all online? How easy will it be for you to set up standing orders and direct debits at a time and in a way that suits you?
3. **How easy will it be to switch to this account?** Some banks make it easy to switch and even incentivize the process because they want your custom so much. Others are less helpful. Go online and get a good idea of how painless the process will be.
4. **What do the reviews say?** These days everything is reviewed by customers online, so make the most of the commentariat and see what other users are saying about this bank. Are they reporting 30-minute on hold marathons to a call centre? How do they rate data security?

 NEW BANKS VS. TRADITIONAL BANKS

Have you tried one of the new app-only banks? The likes of Monzo, First Direct, Revolut, N26 and Starling Bank have tapped into a desire for seamless digital customer services and done away with bricks and mortar banking. Although still in their infancy they are already incredibly successful. This trend is largely led by more youthful customers, but we also know that customers of all ages are using internet banking because instead of hanging on the telephone, let alone actually going in to a high street branch, it is so much easier and meets our need for instant gratification. The new banks focus all their energy on ease of use, offering a simple, easy, multi-platform banking experience that makes the ins and outs of everyday personal banking just a click or a scroll away.

Understanding what you need from a bank is crucial to your selection process. You wouldn't often go to the supermarket without a list, or agree to date someone without their ticking a couple of boxes: apply this mindset to your bank, shop around, play the field and know what you want from them and then make sure you chose the one that suits you.

- How much would you like to save?
- Will you be making regular contributions or a lump sum?
- Do you need instant access to your money?

With your newly formed requirements at your fingertips, you can now start to research various banks across a few comparison websites. Make sure you do this exercise over a few sites because they may return different results and they may also list different products, i.e. savings accounts or ISAs. Play with the different options and make sure you use the filters according to your bespoke banking needs. (Just like flights and hotels comparison sites, the sponsored posts are usually in big boxes at the top – they are often not the best option, just the most visible. These platforms take a commission when you subscribe to a product on their site so it is in their interest to prompt you to pursue the ones they want to sell you most.)

Once you have a selection of products you think could be suitable for you, do your *own* research and visit the provider's website.

WHAT THE HELL IS OPEN BANKING?

Open banking is a new type of data-sharing technology (and attendant rules) that enables you to see all your financial information in one app. So, your current account, savings account, e-bank, investments, even utility providers, all appear side-by-side at the swipe of a finger. Previously this could only be done by a very basic form of screen-grabbing called 'screen scraping' but is being phased out due to questions about its security. Open banking is said to be much safer and more secure as you only grant permission to companies you trust with your data, and you don't have to give away your log-in details or password to any third party.

This new way of seeing and reviewing your money could help you in a number of ways. As it's easier to see all your accounts in one fell swoop, it should make budgeting simpler as you can easily detect which areas need less/more money flowing to/from them. Open banking is also designed to make it easier to compare services across different providers, to see if you're getting the best deal. There's the possibility of automating some areas of budgeting too, e.g. moving money to a savings account every month, or capping your spending if you've gone over an agreed limit.

This is the brave new world of personalized personal banking...

Where Could I Save My Money?

Do you find it hard to save? Do you also try to save money for different goals but then seem not to have enough for all of them? Do you have money saved but you don't know what it's for?

Saving money is hard work but it can be hugely rewarding when it's done properly. There are three main things to look for when trying to decide where to save your money:

1. **Make sure you can access the money when you need it to achieve your goal:** Is that in two months? One year? Five years? The objective when you save is to make sure your money is available for you at any time you may need it (not locked away in investments). That's why we hold some in cash but it can be deposited for a longer time which will pay you interest at the end of the agreed period.
2. **Maximize the interest rate you are receiving on your savings:** You should find the best place for your money, where it's taken care of and remunerated, i.e. getting some interest. In today's world interest rates on savings are low (around 1%), so it's challenging for you to try to find the best rate. (The rate used to compare savings accounts is called an Annual Equivalent Rate (AER), the higher the better.) You can save in fixed or variable rate accounts; usually the longer you keep your savings with a provider, the higher the rate you get. But make sure the length of the rates is in line with the fixed period you envisage when you will need your money back. You don't want to fall short.

Be aware that the headline saving rate can be misleading; check the small print to understand how the interest rate is calculated.

3. **Make sure you save in a tax-efficient manner – when you receive any interest you are taxed:** Do this unless the money is held in an ISA or the amount of interest you are getting falls below the Personal Savings Allowance (see page 233). This may not be relevant today in a low-rate environment but it could be in the future if interest rates increase and you will be able to start making more money from your savings.

4. **When trying to save money use multiple accounts:** Instead of keeping all your money in your one and only current account, consider opening separate saving accounts. If you only use your current account as a way to save, how do you know what your monthly cash flow money is vs. the money you've saved? You need to allocate your money in distinct places to make it clearer in your mental spreadsheets. It's essential to separate the monies you will need day-to-day (remember the 30% lifestyle spending category of your budget) vs. the monies you've saved (the 20% savings category).

→ Please refer to Chapter 4 for some budgeting guidance.

TAXES ON INTEREST AND PERSONAL SAVINGS ALLOWANCE

When you save money and receive interest on your savings, you have to pay tax on it! But these days most people can earn some interest from their savings without paying tax.

In 2016 the government introduced the Personal Savings Allowance (PSA). These are the rules in place for the 2019/20 tax year:

- **If you are a basic rate taxpayer, you have a PSA of £1,000. That means that if you receive more than £1,000 in interest on your savings, you will pay 20% tax on it.**
- **If you are a higher rate taxpayer, you have a PSA of £500. That means that if you receive more than £500 in interest on your savings, you will pay 40% tax on it.**
- **If you are an additional rate taxpayer, you don't have a PSA.**

If you are not earning a lot and your total income is less than the personal allowance, any income is covered by your personal allowance.

There is a starting rate for savings of up to £5,000 if you are on a low income.

For more information and the latest rules go to the Government website section 'Tax-free Interest on Savings'[100].

In this section we will look into a few products you can use to save money, namely the current accounts, savings accounts, premium bonds and the ISA family members. The main goal for you now is to save some money and make it grow in the form of interest. So, we will look at the best places for you to make your money work harder.

Current accounts

I have to mention here the possibility of saving money into a current account. Yes, you read that correctly! Your current account is where you do your day-to-day banking and transactions; it isn't usually a place in which to hold money for a long period of time. But recently some banks have started to offer higher interest rates on these accounts, so this is an option to consider. Make sure you check the interest rate and read the small print (What's the maximum amount? Do you need to deposit money monthly? And so on.). Also, using your current account for savings could prove to be a dangerous option – should you look for a separate savings account in order to avoid spending all your money?

Savings accounts and premium bonds

We will look at four different categories: instant or easy access savings accounts, fixed rate savings accounts, 'regular' savings accounts/'monthly savers' and premium bonds. Think of this as a tree. You planted the seed, now let it grow.

IS MY MONEY SAFE IN A BANK?

If you live in the UK, *always* look for this on your provider's website or paperwork: 'Protected under the Financial Services Compensation Scheme (FSCS)'. That means that up to £85,000 of your money (or £170,000 for joint accounts) is protected in this UK bank or building society, and you will get your money back if this bank fails. If you have more than the limit to save, spread it to another account in another bank for maximum protection.

1. **'Instant' or Easy Access Savings Accounts:** If you've saved money but you know you will need to use it very soon, then look out for the best saving rates across banks to get the most of your savings; you should find that the rates are quite low because of the flexibility you are asking for. This account could be used for your emergency savings for example. You pay taxes on interest after the PSA (see page 233).
2. **Fixed Rate Savings Accounts:** You could save into a fixed-rate deposit (also called a fixed rate bond), which means that if you leave your money in the account for long enough (usually one to five years) you will receive interest that is higher than with normal savings accounts. You put money in at a given time and can take it out after the fixed term. If you want to take the money out earlier (because you need it or found a better rate somewhere else), you will have to pay a penalty. These 'deposits' will help you get a bit more out of your money. Examples of how to use this type of account are short- to medium-term goals. You pay tax on interest after the PSA (see page 233).
3. **'Regular' Saving Accounts/'Monthly Savers':** If you know you are a great saver and can commit to saving the same amount of money every month (say £20 or £200) for a fixed period of time, you can look into the *regular* savings accounts. You will be rewarded by a slightly higher interest rate than the instant access account. This type of account is not as flexible though: check with the different providers whether you are allowed to withdraw money early and the penalty for doing so. You pay taxes on interest after the PSA (see page 233).
4. **Premium Bonds:** A premium bond is a savings product where the interest is decided by a lottery. Yup, you read that right! Bonds are issued by National Savings and Investments (NS&I), formerly the Post Office Savings Bank and National Savings, a state-owned savings bank in the UK. They offer savers protection against principal loss and liquidity. You need to purchase a minimum of £100 (or £50 for monthly standing orders) and the maximum amount you can hold is £50,000. In essence, you don't lose out – you either get a small return or, if you're lucky, a large, life-changing return! The annual prize fund interest rate is currently 1.40%. This type of saving is flexible, as you can withdraw it at any time; you just lose the chance to win in the given month. There is a chance every month to win a £1 million jackpot and other tax-free prizes.

Again it is best for short- to medium-term savings goals, e.g. a wedding or a holiday. You don't pay tax on interest.

Choosing a savings account provider

I find it useful to allocate my savings to different goals and the easiest way to do this is to open one separate account for each goal (i.e. different pots of money). If you are thinking about buying Christmas gifts at the same time as planning for a trip next year, but only have one savings account, there is a chance you would use most of this spare money for gifts and be left with nothing for the trip. Allocating your savings is also super-motivating because you can label the accounts and see what you are saving for. It's more inspiring to transfer money from your current account to a 'Two-week trip to Nepal' than to an 'HSBC savings account'...be creative!

To get the best rates on your savings you can start shopping around and use a comparator such as MoneySavingExpert, Money Supermarket or Which? They will offer a comparison of all the accounts by the banks and building societies but make sure you also do your own research. Depending on how hands-on you are likely to be (do you want to move your money around regularly to get the best rate or don't you have time to constantly regulate and keep on top of your accounts?) bear in mind some accounts offer a high bonus rate which is designed to seduce you – but bonuses drop off after a certain period. Make sure you understand the terms.

ISAs (Individual Savings Accounts)

You've probably heard of ISAs. ISA stands for 'Individual Savings Account', a savings account on which you never pay tax.[101] ISAs are wide-ranging instruments which have different characteristics. So, what exactly are they and how do they work?

ISAs are tax-efficient, meaning that all the money sheltered in your ISA is protected from taxes for the long term: you won't be paying taxes on the interest earned. Ever. For inheritance, you can pass on your ISA to your spouse/civil partner without losing the tax advantage. The surviving partner is given an Additional Permitted Subscription (APS) allowance.

If you are living in the UK and are 16, you get what is called an ISA allowance: in the 2019/20 tax year, the maximum you can save in ISAs is £20,000. You can put money into the five different types of ISA accounts available (no help-to-buy and lifetime ISA at the same time to make things simple!): cash ISA, stocks and shares ISA, help-to-buy ISA, lifetime ISA and innovative finance ISA. They have different specifications and we will look into these below. Some of them are used to save money and others to invest money.

You can also choose whether you want to split your £20,000 allowance between stocks and shares ISAs, cash ISAs, innovative finance ISAs, help-to-buy ISAs and the lifetime ISA or put everything in one (just a quick note: there is a limit on the lifetime ISA of £4,000!). Note that allowances need to be utilized by 6 April each year, falling in line with the tax year, and cannot be carried forward. You will get a new allowance each year, but you won't be able to use the old one if you haven't used it fully.

- *Some ISAs are used to save money, such as the cash and help-to-buy ISAs. The money is held in cash deposits.*
- *Some ISAs are used to save and/or invest money, such as the lifetime ISA (also used for long-term goals) and the junior ISA.*
- *Some ISAs are used to invest money, such as the stocks & shares ISA and innovative finance ISA.*

Each financial year you can open and contribute to only one cash ISA and one stocks & shares ISA. Always check the latest tax rules and allowance.

The investments you hold in an ISA are protected from capital gains tax and income tax.

TAXES YOU DON'T HAVE TO PAY WHEN YOU HOLD INVESTMENTS IN AN ISA OR PENSION

Tax on dividends: When you invest money in shares, you have to pay tax on the money you earn (dividends), unless you are investing in an ISA or a pension, in which case this profit will be tax-free.

For the tax year 2019/20 the Dividend Allowance is £2,000 a year, which means you don't pay taxes on the first £2,000 of dividends you earn. Above this limit you will have to pay 7.5% if you are a basic rate taxpayer, 32.5% for higher rate taxpayers and 38.1% for additional rate taxpayers.

Capital gains tax: When you invest money in shares, for example, and sell shares for a profit, you are making a gain, and this could also be taxed under Capital Gains Tax (CGT), unless you are investing in an ISA or a pension, in which case this profit will be tax-free.

Always check the latest tax rules based on your situation.

Each tax year nearly everyone who is liable to CGT gets an annual tax-free allowance of £12,000 (in 2019/20), known as the 'Annual Exempt Amount'. You only pay CGT if your overall gains for the tax year (after deducting any losses and applying any reliefs) are above this amount. This is a yearly allowance and if you go above it you may have to pay up to 10–20% tax depending on your income.

You don't know what the future holds...the PSA on your savings could change and potentially go down as interest rates and saving rates go up. You could also be earning more and lose your personal allowance when you become a higher tax payer. But that won't be the case with ISAs because anything that is saved or invested within an ISA will continue to earn interest tax-free as soon as it's under the ISA umbrella.

Look for the highest interest rates but *never* transfer an ISA yourself – always use the forms provided by the issuer. When switching from one provider to another, make sure you don't just withdraw the money and re-open an account somewhere else: the provider has to do this transfer for you so you don't lose the tax-free umbrella your ISA savings are under.

If you need to, you can withdraw your money from your ISA but once it's out, you won't be able to pay it back in if you have reached your annual allowance limit. You will also lose the tax benefits on the money you have withdrawn.

If you are married, you can maximize your ISA allowances by utilizing your partner's allowance too if she/he does not use it. An opportunity for a money conversation, perhaps?

Which ISA(s)?

For *saving* money, there are three ISAs you can choose from: cash, help-to-buy and lifetime. Remember that the stocks and shares and innovative ISAs are only used for *investing* money (see page 225).

Cash ISAs

When you use a cash ISA, you don't pay tax on the interest you receive. With the cash ISA, you have to look for the best interest rates: that's how you make money. As with saving accounts, you can compare and switch to the best provider. You can also choose from instant access, regular savers and fixed-rate ISAs.

Lifetime ISAs

The lifetime ISA was launched to push savers to beef up their savings towards a deposit for a first home *or* for retirement.[102] Think of it as a hybrid between a pension and an ISA. The government will basically pay you a 25% bonus (up to £1,000) for £4,000 saved per year and this will be available for potentially 32 years (rule for the year 2019/20).

How does the lifetime ISA work? To qualify you have to be between 18 and 40 (you can then contribute until you reach 50). There is no maximum monthly contribution, you save as little or as much as you want each month, up to £4,000 a year (the only minimum is the limit imposed by the ISA provider). Any savings you put into it before your 50th birthday will receive an added 25% bonus from the government.

What can I use it for? You have two options for using the money in your lifetime ISA:

1. **Save for a first home:** Your savings and the bonus can be used towards a deposit on a first home worth up to £450,000 across the country (note that accounts are limited to one per person rather than one per home). So, two first-time buyers can each receive a bonus when buying together. The lifetime ISA cannot be used within the first 12 months after you open the account.
2. **Save for retirement (after your 60th birthday):** You can take out all the savings tax-free at this stage. If you want to know if it's relevant for you to save for retirement into a Lifetime ISA versus a pension, you should consult an adviser because it depends on your personal circumstances.

If you wanted to take the money out earlier for another reason you would have to pay a 25% penalty on the value of the amount withdrawn. So make sure you understand the purpose of a Lifetime ISA and don't get a nasty surprise!

It is worth noting that, with the lifetime ISA, both cash and stocks and share products are available, so you could decide to invest it or not depending on your goals (i.e. when you need the money) and the risk you are willing to take.

Help-to-buy ISAs

A help-to-buy ISA is another ISA you could use if you goal is to buy a house, as this one is for first-time buyers, aged 16 or over only. You can open a help-to-buy ISA and save until December 2029. When you save money into a help-to-buy ISA, the government will top up your contributions by 25% (i.e. you save £1,000, you get £250 top up (bonus)) and the contribution limit is £12,000 (or a £3,000 bonus).

 You can't open a Help-to-buy ISA *and* a cash ISA in the same tax year.

You can open a help-to-buy account with £1,000 and qualify for the government bonus, but it will only be paid when you actually reach the £1,600 minimal contribution. You actually have to claim your bonus through a solicitor. Once received, it will be added into your help-to-buy account for your house deposit.

What can you use the money for? It's pretty straightforward: you can use it to buy any home worth under £250,000 (or under £450,000 in London). It is important to note that you can't use a help-to-buy ISA if you're going to rent out the property – you have to live in it! There is one help-to-buy ISA available per person, not per home, i.e. if you want to buy a house with someone you can do so and add up your deposits.

You can have both a lifetime ISA and a help-to-buy ISA. However, if your goal is to purchase property, you cannot receive the government bonus for both the lifetime ISA and the help-to-buy ISA. If you use the help-to-buy ISA to buy your first home, then you can use the lifetime ISA for retirement and then make the most of the bonuses. You can also transfer your existing help-to-buy ISA into a lifetime ISA.

→ Go to Chapter 9 to learn about investing in property and more about the lifetime help-to-buy ISAs.

Junior ISAs

Do you want to save for kids? You can give your children a leg-up in life by starting to save early for their future. Just like a regular ISA, a junior ISA is a way for you – and anyone else, including grandparents – to put a little money aside each month for your child's future and not pay tax on the interest. The allowance for 2019/20 is £4,368. The account will be in the name of your child and it does not count as part of your personal £20,000 annual allowance for the year.

The above is a non-exhaustive list – for more information on savings accounts and ISAs, go to: gov.co.uk or the Money Advice Service.

Choosing an ISA account provider

With ISAs, look for an account that suits your needs (i.e. how long will your money be locked away? what can you pay in monthly? what do you need the account for, looking at your goals?) and then find the account that pays you the highest interest.

You can then use an online comparator such as MoneySavingExpert, Money Supermarket or Which?, just as you would for a savings account.

Where to Invest Long-term and Retirement Savings

We all talk a lot about 'living in the moment' 😎, and although we should certainly all be more present and aware when it comes to our mental health, our financial health really does require us to look ahead. However much we try to pretend that old age, illness and death are negotiable, there comes an age when we realize age comes to us all.

Saving for our autumn years is a must, if we don't want to spend our pre-autumn years in a state of worry, fear or anxious denial. But there's a bright side because, as well as shoring up funds against care homes, there's a lot of fun stuff we can plan for too.

For your long-term goals you may wish to consider investing your money. This carries a higher risk, of course, but it could also make your money work harder than with cash savings and even beat inflation.

➔ Head over to Chapter 7 for a detailed explanation of investing.

There is a high chance you are already saving for the long term and investing some money, especially if you are employed. In which case, without even knowing it, you are already investing in your pension. If you're not, don't worry. In the following pages we will explain the different long-term savings products available, such as pensions or personal pensions (like self-invested personal pensions – SIPPs), stocks and shares ISAs, lifetime ISAs, and so on.

To start investing you will first need to understand which accounts and structures are right for you. We will look into the eternal comparison between pensions and ISAs and how you could potentially make them work alongside each other.

📣 Again, get clued up on these products and get to understand what is best for you. You can consult an independent financial adviser for more help and always check the latest rules.

Pensions

Pensions are too often thought of as being just for older people, but the reality is that if you don't contribute today towards your pension, your retirement pot may well be empty by the time you retire. Although you probably have 10, 20, 40 – hell – even 50 years of work ahead of you, the truth is that after your working life you will be spending money for about 20 or 30 years or longer. Who knows when you would want to retire. This long-term pocket isn't perhaps as exciting as your emergency fund or as crucial as paying off your expensive debts but it is just as critical to your quality of life. Luckily, pensions offer a *tax-efficient way* to invest in your retirement and workplace pensions offer some sort of free money!

Fundamentally a pension is super-simple: it's a tax-free long-term savings plan that you, your employer (if you have one) and the government pay into. The money contributed to your pension over time is invested and will have the opportunity to grow until you retire, but this is not guaranteed.

The money is locked until you reach retirement age and then when you want to start using the funds in your pension pot you can usually withdraw about 25% as a tax-free sum and then use the remaining amount to pay yourself an income and/or irregular lump sums – which are taxable.

Why are we saving into a pension at all?

Because of something called *tax relief*. When you earn money (above a certain level – the personal allowance), you start paying tax. When you put money into a pension, instead of paying tax to the government on salary or income you receive, some will go directly into your pension – this is the tax relief (see the examples below). This also works if you are saving into a pension and if you don't have any income. Essentially, the more tax you pay, the higher the tax relief.

Tax relief depends on your individual circumstances and could change in the future!

When you pay money into a pension, you automatically get a 20%+ top-up in the form of tax back (tax relief) from the government as an additional deposit into your pension pot:

 Always check the latest pension rules on the government's websites (**gov.uk** and **pensionsadvisoryservice.org.uk**).

For a basic rate taxpayer: You invest £80 into your pension, it corresponds to £100 on a pre-tax basis (since you pay taxes at 20%), so the government tops up your pension by tax relief of £20.

For a higher rate taxpayer: You invest £60 into your pension, it corresponds to £100 on a pre-tax basis (since you pay taxes at 40%), so the government tops up your pension by tax relief of £40.

For an additional rate taxpayer: You invest £55 into your pension, it corresponds to £100 on a pre-tax basis (since you pay taxes at 45%), so the government tops up your pension by tax relief of £45.

HOW DO I RECEIVE MY TAX RELIEF?

For a basic rate tax payer: If you have an employer they will deduct their pension contribution (i.e. £80) from your pay and send it to your pension provider who will add it to your account. The government will automatically top up the remaining £20 to give you to £100.

If you are self-employed: You will make the contribution to your pension provider directly and the government will automatically put in the remaining £20 to give you to £100.

For a higher rate and top-rate taxpayer: You have to ask for the additional tax relief through your Self Assessment tax return.

See pension rules overleaf.

Where to start saving into a pension?

There are a lot of different providers who offer pensions, but you have to decide what type of pension is right for you. Or maybe you already have a pension but need to consider your other options.

- **Workplace pension:** Since 2018 all employers have been legally required to enrol eligible employees into a workplace pension. One of the great benefits of a workplace pension is that your employer will also top up your contributions (this is called 'auto-enrolment') and is basically free money – or a bit like getting a raise.
- **State pension:** Once you reach pensionable age, the government will give you regular pension payments. You are eligible for the state pension if you have paid National Insurance contributions throughout your working life.
- **Personal pension:** This is independent of the contributor's employer, i.e you can have the personal pension in addition to, or instead of, the workplace pension. The personal pension is an individual contract between you and the pension provider; you choose the provider and determine the contributions. You may want to consider this option if you are self-employed, if your workplace pension isn't sufficient or if it's not flexible enough for you. There are two types of personal pensions: stakeholder pensions or self-invested personal pensions (SIPPs).

The workplace pension

No need for alarm just yet – as all employers are required by law to offer a workplace pension scheme, also known as the *workplace pension* (their names are never very inventive). This scheme is quite handy though, as it helps you save for retirement without doing *all* that much – and because workplace pensions are managed by pension providers, you don't need to be an ace at investing.

With *auto-enrolment*, you will be automatically enrolled to start saving a portion of each pay cheque (i.e. it is a 'salary sacrifice') – you only need to do something or take action if you choose not to save.

There are different types of pensions but it's likely that your money is in a *defined contribution (DC)* scheme. This means that your employer has chosen a pension provider who will invest the money that you contribute. And in the case that your employer goes bust, there's no need to worry; your pension is managed separately by your pension provider.

Contributions will be automatically deducted from your salary. Your employer will make contributions as well and you may be eligible to get tax relief from the government. Told you it was handy! It's easy to start: under auto-enrolment you are automatically signed up and avoid the hassle of paperwork/admin. It makes sense financially: your employer is contributing to it! So if you can, pay as much as you can afford to (considering your other goals and personal circumstances) and don't leave money on the table. There is a minimum amount that has to be contributed by you, your employer and the government in the form of tax relief. From April 2019 the minimum contribution increased to 5% from you (including your tax relief) and 3% from your employer, so the total minimum contribution increased to 8% of your earnings. But double-check because your emplyer could be offering a higher percentage contribution 🤩.

You are eligible if you work in the UK, are at least 22 years old and earn over £10,000 per year (for 2019/20), and you will automatically be enrolled in the scheme.

You can opt out of the workplace pension if you like and re-join later. You will not have the choice of the pension provider when you join a workplace pension. But you can still start your own pension if you are a member of a workplace pension scheme.

Workplace pensions are quite a powerful way to save money, but it depends on your personal situation: for instance, if you feel as though you don't have enough to live on or are struggling to repay debt, think about whether you should prioritize your long-term future or immediate quality of life.

HELP? With a workplace pension, your money is held by a pension provider. They manage your pension and the investments that go into your pension.

You pay them a fee for this that will have been negotiated between your employer and the pension provider. You don't have to pay for it separately; it is charged directly as a percentage of the funds in your pension each year (it is capped at the moment at 0.75% for default funds[103], unless you are using The National Employment Savings Trust/Nest, for example, which may have higher charges). Make sure you look into your pension statements and understand how your pension is managed and invested. You or your pension provider will decide on particular investments based on the level of risk you choose and the time you have to retirement. You may want to check that you have an appropriate investment option and that you understand the default option your money is put into as it may not be adapted to your goals or is too conservative. I have heard of people becoming interested in their pension only when the amount saved is higher than their base salary, but why not look into it now?

EXERCISE

Use the workplace pension contribution calculator from the Money Advice Service website to find out, based on your age, gender and salary, what workplace pension contributions are made by you and your employer[104]:

Annual Salary: £ . . . .

Qualifying earnings, as per calculator: £ . . . . (for the purpose of pension calculations we use qualifying earnings, a band of earnings that you can use to calculate contributions for auto-enrolment.)

My contribution of . . . . % is £ . . . .

My employer contribution of . . . . % is £ . . . .

= My total monthly contribution is £ . . . .

The actual amount HMRC allows you to pay into your pension in a tax year for tax relief purposes is the greater of: £2,880 a year (which would become £3,600 with tax relief), or 100% of your UK taxable earnings if greater, subject to the annual allowance.

The annual allowance for pensions contributions is the maximum amount that can be contributed into a pension per annum (from you and your employer for example) – while still receiving tax relief. This is currently £40,000. If you are a top-rate taxpayer, your annual allowance may be reduced for the tax year. This is called the tapered annual allowance.

 Don't hesitate to speak to an adviser about this.

If you are working super-hard towards putting money into your pension, bear in mind that there is a maximum you can pay into the pension and benefit from the tax relief (this is £1,055,000 for 2019/20). This is called the lifetime allowance (LTA) and is the maximum that can be put in retirement savings without being taxed. This number is scheduled to increase every year based on inflation (consumer price inflation/CPI).

If you already have a workplace pension in place: do you know how it is invested, how it has been performing and what level of fees you are paying? Do you know the level of risk on your investments?

It may come as a surprise, but you probably won't get regular statements from your pension provider, so it's worth checking with them how much you have in your pension and what the performance has been over recent years.

For workplace pensions, it may be a good idea to ask HR who your pension adviser is and set up a meeting with them.

The state pension

Another reason it's essential to start saving now for retirement is that you can't rely on the *state pension*. At the moment, the full state pension is set at £168.60 per week or £8,767.20 per year for the tax year 2019/20 and that is really not a lot to live on.

The state pension is a weekly payment from the government that you can receive once you reach state pension age. In order to qualify for the state pension, you need to make National Insurance contributions (NICs). To qualify for any pension at all you will need to have ten years of NICs. To qualify for the full new state pension, you will need to have 35 qualifying years. Previously this was 30 years.

If you are a parent who has stopped/decided to stop working and earning when you have children, don't forget to register to sign up for Child Benefit (even if you are not eligible, and for children under 12). Doing this will allow you to keep receiving National Insurance credits that will be added to your NICs and, hopefully, allow you to make the most of your state pension when you retire.

Here's a shocker: if you're under 40, you probably won't receive your state pension until you're at least 70 years old (if not later). As the population ages, the government will inevitably need to spend more on state pensions and so the retirement age will continue to rise. I don't know about you, but I don't really fancy working full time at the grand old age of 70!

Not to be alarmist, but it's important you get to grips with state pensions today in order to plan ahead with confidence. We've done the heavy lifting for you, and this is how the situation is shaping up. There will be a new flat-rate, or single-tier, state pension that came into effect for everyone retiring after 6 April 2016. The age at which you can claim the state pension rose to 65 for both sexes in 2018; 66 in 2020, 67 by 2029 and then to age 68 between 2037 and 2039. You get the drift...

EXERCISE

You can check how much state pension you can get, and when and how to increase it, by creating an account and logging on to this government website: **gov.uk/check-state-pension**

I will reach state pension age on ____________ (date) and my estimated pension will be £ . . . . a year or £ . . . . a month.

Personal pensions

A personal pension is by definition – of course – personal! You don't need to have an employer to open a personal pension. You pick a pension provider and start contributing on your own; your pension provider will claim tax relief at the basic rate and add it to your pension pot if you are a basic rate taxpayer, otherwise you will need to fill in a Self Assessment tax return to get the extra tax relief.

A personal pension is a popular choice among self-employed people and can also be used if you are not working. The drawback of being self-employed is that it's entirely up to you to make sure you're on track with your savings and pension, and you don't receive an employer contribution .

One type of personal pension that has proven to be very popular is the self-invested personal pension (SIPP). A SIPP is a DIY pension where you can choose what your money is invested in and you have full control of your pension pot. You can choose to build your own balanced portfolio with your own risk profile. You are also free to choose some more specific investments that may not be available through your workplace pension.

With SIPPs you are the one deciding your investments. This can be a big responsibility for you, so you either have to swot up or get help from an adviser.

If you already have a workplace pension but would like more flexibility managing your money, you could open a SIPP as well. A SIPP gives you greater freedom and allows *you* to manage your pension pot, including where to stash it and what to invest in, meaning you know exactly how much it'll cost (more control of the fees). One of the great tax advantages of a SIPP is that it allows you to pass on your pension to your beneficiaries on your death. Your beneficiaries can normally choose to take the pension fund as a lump sum or leave it invested in a SIPP.

FYI, there is another type of personal pension called a stakeholder pension. These pensions have specific government requirements, for example limits on charges.

How to manage an existing pension

Do you have a pension from a previous job that you have forgotten about? Or even many different pension pots? According to the Pension Dashboard (a WIP initiative by the Government that enables you to see all your pension savings at the same time) [105] the average person has 11 jobs in their lifetime. This means that today there is £400m sitting in lost pensions...

Use the pension-tracing service to track down a lost pension and check your pension statements to see how much you have and how it's invested: **gov.uk/find-pension-contact-details**

You may also want to check and validate your pension beneficiaries by completing a nomination form or what is called an 'Expression of Wish'.

Should I consolidate my pensions?

If you discover that you have some old pensions, you can transfer them and potentially put them all into one pot. You will need to decide if that makes sense for you; it could make your life easier to see all your retirement money in one place and may also reduce the fees you would have been paying on individual pots. But at the same time, there is a risk that you could lose pension benefits and get charged exit fees. It's always best to discuss consolidation with a financial adviser beforehand. After you've made your decision, either the adviser can help you to consolidate or you can do this transfer yourself by contacting your pension provider.

You can also use an app, such as PensionBee, to consolidate your pensions.

Pensions are complex and, in order to make sure you have enough saved to live well in retirement, do seek independent financial advice.

Stocks and shares ISAs and Lifetime ISAs

The other way to invest your savings for the long term, not necessarily for retirement, is to use ISAs.

The difference between the previously discussed cash ISA and the stocks & shares ISA is that the latter has to be invested in the stock market. With the cash ISA, you save so your money is available at any time; with the stocks & shares ISA, you want to invest to make your money work in the long term. Which is also much more risky! Remember that, when you want to take money out of a stocks and shares ISA, there is an additional step of selling the investments (stocks and shares) held within this ISA: you can't predict the future value (you don't want to be under pressure to do this in case the markets are not performing well).

A stocks and shares ISA is more flexible than a pension; you don't have to wait to retire to access your money, so it gives you more flexibility.

The way this type of ISA works is that you invest your money in the stock market where all income, capital gains and interest are tax-free. Of course *the value of your investments can go and up and down* and this type of investing involves risk.

Note that a Stocks & Shares Lifetime ISA also invests in the stock market (therefore it is much riskier than the Cash Lifetime ISA, so it is to be used for the long-term only).

→ Head over to Chapter 8 for a detailed explanation of investing on the stock market and choosing your Stocks & Shares ISA and Lifetime ISA.

The Innovative Finance ISA

In April 2016, the Government introduced the Innovative Finance ISA (IFISA). It allows you to invest in Peer-to-Peer (P2P) lending activities as these are now eligible for a new tax-free ISA.

General investment accounts

A general investment account (or brokerage account) is one where you can buy, hold and sell investments. While you can invest with a general account there is a huge difference in terms of tax. With a general account, any dividends you receive from your shares or any capital gain will be taxed above the allowance, unlike your ISA or a pension.

The difference between an ISA and general investment

ISAs have the big advantage of being flexible and tax-free (i.e. income, interest generated in an ISA and capital gains are free of tax). However, there are a few limitations. With ISAs, you can only open and pay into one each tax year, i.e. one cash ISA, one stocks & shares ISA. You may have multiple numbers of these open but you can only pay into *one* per year. Overall you can contribute £20,000 (for 2019/20) into ISA accounts every year. This limit will vary because of new HMRC rules each year but to invest more then you should probably use a general investment account.

EXERCISE

Based on your £££ goals, what savings account, ISA or pensions do you have in place and would like to contribute to? What accounts would best suit you? What terms can you find? Fill in the table below.

£££ goals	When do you need the money?	Type of account (current account/savings account/ ISA, pension...)	Provider

Investments (in Stocks & Shares ISAs, or held within an investment account) are also covered by the FSCS, but only up to £50,000 of investments in a firm that has gone into default. Ensure that this is the case with your current provider.

Remember that the value of investments can go down as well as up, so you might get back less than you invested.

Well Done! You have earnt  coins!

You're mastering most financial jargon around saving and investing, ISAs and pensions, and know how to navigate the financial landscape. You may or may not need some or all of the accounts and products presented in this section, but it should give you an overview of what's on offer and the financial products you may have heard of over the years.

You will see that, year after year, governments and budgets change as well as this landscape. Of course, rules and regulations are extremely important, but what's even more crucial is the way saving works. You should always take great care of your money and make sure it's in the right place.

As life becomes more complicated you may be using more of these accounts to fund yourself. Over the course of the chapter you were able to look at your financial goals and decide for each if you could save or invest, and plan what type of saving, account and tactic you will be following. If there are chunks of text that don't yet apply to you, save them for when they do; what you need to ensure is that you take responsibility for your own money education. *Small changes make a big difference over time.*

Next is...investing!

Money Talk with Jessica Skye

Job: Founder of Fat Buddha Yoga.

Fun fact: With her classes, retreats and surf trips, Jess provides a modern approach to the ancient art and science of yoga for the next generation of urban yogis. She is also a Nike ambassador and a successful DJ.

Money motto: *'Spending – when in doubt, leave it out!'*

What makes you happy?
Progress, adventure and time with loved ones.

What is your most treasured possession?
Hard to say! But losing my laptop (if not backed up) would be the most damaging.

What is the best money advice you have ever received?
You make money where you don't spend it.

What is your biggest money failure/mistake?
Not charging enough for my work in the early days of my career .

What is your greatest achievement?
Creating a lifestyle business that I love.

What is your personal mission?
To enjoy life and live it to the fullest.

What is your top money hack?
Save when you're earning well and look at ways to grow and invest money when you're feeling flush. Stop buying so many coffees!!!

Who is your go-to person to talk about money?
My dad.

Who are your inspiring heroes?
My parents.

What is your favourite book?
Bill Bryson, *A Short History of Nearly Everything*.

What is your best career advice?
Be honest with what you want and go for it. Don't get caught in a cycle of pursuing what you don't want, e.g. applying for jobs/accepting work just like the stuff you're already doing if you're unhappy doing it and looking for change. You also get out what you put in.

What inspires you?
People following their dreams.

CHAPTER 7: HOW DOES INVESTING WORK?

* *

What you will learn in this chapter:

What is the relationship between money and time?
What are some finance principles you need to understand: compound interest, inflation?
What are the risks and rewards of investing?
Why do people invest money?

* *

'DON'T JUDGE EACH DAY BY THE HARVEST YOU REAP BUT BY THE SEEDS THAT YOU PLANT'
Robert Louis Stevenson

We all know how good it feels to have a wad of cash in our purses or wallets. Or even how great it feels to check your bank balance at the end of the month and find that there's a tiny bit of money left over which you have managed not to spend. Some of us might even transfer that left-over money into a different bank account, or withdraw it and hide it from ourselves. There's even that wicked moment when you forgot you had carefully set aside money for a rainy day and you wake up and your bank balance suddenly looks all too bleak and you remember the fund you had locked away for this moment. How money kind of you 😎.

Cash savings are not just mood-boosters: they are vitally important. Regardless of how much you earn and your net worth, savings should be an integral part not only of your long-term financial plan, but also your day-to-day life.

📣 Emergency savings are a must. A shocking number of people have no real idea of what they would do financially if a crisis situation were to arise. While we all hope that no such scenario ever takes place, there's no way we can be 100% secure that adversity will not arise. That's why saving for a 'rainy day' fund is so important: should you lose your job or fall ill, you'll have a secure financial cushion to take care of all immediate needs and help you get back on your feet. It's never a good idea to leave yourself vulnerable to unexpected circumstances, so have some money squirrelled away.

What's next? You've built your financial plan and have other financial goals that also need savings, so start allocating money towards these.

As you have probably started to gather from previous chapters, if you're already got this saving habit, repaid your expensive debts, have built up your emergency funds and are saving for your short- and medium-term goals, then you can start thinking about the long term and retirement savings. For these, you want your money to grow at a rate *outpacing inflation* in order to retain your purchasing power in the future. Because interest rates are low at present, investing some of your money may be better than keeping it in cash. And this involves some risk.

But what exactly does 'investing' mean? Why is a dollar today worth more than a dollar tomorrow? And what kind of investing is right for you? In this chapter we are going to map *what happens to your money with time* and what kind of risks and rewards you can expect when investing. Honestly, once the jargon has been debunked it's really much more simple than you think. I want to provide you with a full understanding of investing, so that you will be able to decide whether it is the right thing for you now, in the future or never.

So, if you're new to the world of investing – just breathe, and read on. You can (and you will!) nail investing in a way that is right for you.

The Relationship Between Money and Time

Before we decide to invest money, there are a few concepts that are really important to understand. They are not complicated but it's key that you grasp the basic ideas behind them before starting out. It will also help you figure out whether investing is for you.

There is a good chance you did not study finance or economics but, even if you did, it was probably so theoretical that it was hard to relate to. When it comes to investing money we need to talk about *time*. Time really is your best friend when it comes to investing, because of compound interest. Simply, investing your money is doing something today that will have an impact tomorrow.

Let's do a fun exercise: What would you prefer? You can choose between receiving £100 today or £100 in a year's time.

'I would like to receive the £100 today, thanks.' But do you know why? Here are a few reasons:

1. **Money in my hand is a sure thing:** What if in a year's time someone tells me that this money is not here anymore?
2. **I can keep this money and make it grow by saving money (low risk) or investing it (higher risk):** If I wait to receive it in a year's time I won't have missed out on this opportunity.
3. **By waiting a year to receive this money, I am missing out on interest:** There is an opportunity cost: what could have I done with the extra money generated?
4. **I am worried about inflation:** I am concerned that with this £100 I will not be able to afford tomorrow what I can afford with £100 today.

This is a simplification of the fundamental principle of the time value of money (TVM): money in hand today is worth more than the same amount tomorrow. Provided money can earn interest, any amount of money is worth more the sooner it is received. And risk/return is expecting money risked today to earn more in the future. We will detail these important concepts below: *inflation* and *compound interest*. Stay with me!

Let's take a basic example. Imagine you are a football player: you are paid a base salary and also receive bonuses for each game you win at the end of the season. If you get injured or can't play certain games, you don't get your bonuses. So asking for more money today gives you certainty. It also has more value because you would be able to save or invest it today and get some interest on your savings or investment returns.

Imagine you had $299 in 2011 and decided to buy the iPhone 4 (I am using $ for simplicity here because Apple shares trade in the US). Today there is a chance your phone is outdated and you had to replace it, and maybe got $50 reselling it on eBay. If, instead of buying the phone for $299, you invested this money in Apple shares (you bought about six shares at $50), you would have about $1,000 (if you sold your 6 shares at $170, the price at the time of writing) in your account today (and $1,300 a few months ago if you had sold then because the shares were higher then!). This is called the *opportunity cost*: you decided to buy the phone so you couldn't invest in Apple stock. This is a simplified example (without fees, taxes and so on), but it shows you the power of investing. I am not recommending investing in Apple shares either – they could also have underperformed over time and shares are risky investments, but you get the idea.

Money loses value over time due to inflation

£££ today is worth more than £££ tomorrow. But £££ today does not buy as much stuff as 5, 10 or 20 years ago. And this phenomena is known as 'inflation'. Because of inflation it is always better to have £££ right now. Inflation measures the rate of increase in the price of goods and services in a country's economy. The Office for National Statistics (ONS) collects monthly prices for a basket of 700 everyday goods (so in total 180,000 prices). We're talking bread and milk, train tickets and petrol, as well as clothes and furniture. These prices then determine the Consumer Prices Index (CPI). This is the inflation measure used in the Government's inflation target (but there are other measures of inflation).

Now why is all of that relevant to you and your pocket? Imagine you have £100 today. You can buy something that costs £100. Now imagine inflation is kicking in at 2% per annum (1.9% as of February 2019); in one year's time the price of this same item will be £102. But you still have your £100 since the money you have is in cash. That means you would become poorer by £2 and you now can't afford to buy this item anymore. In this example £2 is not a lot, but imagine ten years from now, with a constant inflation rate of 2% – this item will cost £122, and so now you will be £22 worse off.

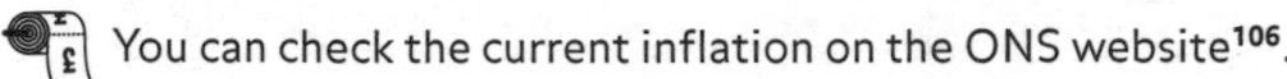

You can check the current inflation on the ONS website[106].

Your underlying goals when investing money are: #1 to maintain your purchasing power (i.e. maintain wealth); #2 to outperform inflation (i.e. increase wealth).

So, putting all your money into a cash savings account may not always be a good idea. You might think you're keeping your money safe, or feel queasy at the thought of the risk that comes with investing. In fact, experts have even coined a name for this strategy – it's called 'reckless caution'. Why? Inflation could eat away at your purchasing power, making your cash savings worth less and less over time.

The Bank of England has an inflation calculator that allows you to check how prices in the UK have changed over time, from 1209 to the present day. See the example below and visit their website[107] – it's fun (and scary)!

ROLE OF THE BANK OF ENGLAND

The Monetary Policy Committee (MPC) is a committee of the Bank of England (BoE) that votes on what the 'base rate' of interest should be in order to deliver monetary and financial stability for the people of the UK.

Hold on, what exactly is an interest rate again? An interest rate is what you earn on your money when you save it with a bank, and it's also the cost of borrowing money. It's a percentage of the total amount borrowed. For example, if you save £100 in a savings account for one year and the interest rate is 1%, you earn £1.

The base rate helps manage inflation better. Changes in the base rate will impact both your savings and loans. A higher interest rate should (in theory) mean that you earn more interest (cash) on your savings and equally it should mean that you pay more interest on your loans. But it's a bit more complicated since providers (banks, savings institutions, lenders, etc.) are not obliged to reflect the change in interest rates since their internal rates also take into account current market conditions.

The base rate as of February 2019 is 0.75%. The processes undertaken by the BoE are actually quite intriguing, since they straddle global politics and national business (and this all takes place in a particularly lovely old building in the City).

If you want to read more, check out the informative Bank of England website[108].

What is 'compound interest'?

I know it sounds like complete jargon but this term is *so* important.

You may have heard it before and labelled it as yet more opaque and mysterious terminology designed to keep mere mortals out of the financial picture. But it's one of the fundamental things to get our heads around as it is said that even Albert Einstein stated that *'Compound interest is the eighth wonder of the world. He who understands it, earns it...he who doesn't...pays it'*. However, he did make a pretty solid point: *compound interest is a key concept in personal finance*. So from now on in you're going to hear us talking about it *a lot*.

The beauty (yes, beauty) of compound interest is that interest builds on interest, making a cash deposit or an investment grow at a faster rate than simple interest. Another way to see it is that the money you generate is reinvested to earn more money. The longer you can let your money grow and *compound*, the more money you will have in the end.

Think of it like a money tree outside your back door with ten pound notes growing freely on it that you can pick whenever. The methodology behind this is simple: imagine you save or invest some money and receive some income from these investments. If you plough that profit back into your investment fund instead of cashing it in, it will grow *exponentially*, getting high on its own supply.

Here is a simple calculation to show how compound interest works:

> You save £100 today in a cash deposit at a saving rate of 2%; at the end of the year you receive £2 in interest so finish the year with £102.
> Next year you will receive interest on £102 (not £100 anymore because you are leaving your money invested, right?), i.e. £102 x 2% = £2.04, so you end the year with £104.04.
> And so on, and so on...After five years, you have £110.41.

With compound interest, your money grows over time. All by itself!

So that's why it's pretty beautiful.

On a larger scale, say a £1,000 investment, this is how it works whether you save or invest (at different annual interest rates):

		Annual interest rate				
		1%	2%	5%	10%	15%
Years	1	£1,010	£1,020	£1,050	£1,100	£1,150
	5	£1,051	£1,104	£1,276	£1,611	£2,011
	10	£1,105	£1,219	£1,629	£2,594	£4,046
	15	£1,161	£1,346	**£2,079**	£4,177	£8,137
	20	£1,220	£1,486	£2,653	£6,727	£16,367
	25	£1,282	£1,641	£3,386	£10,835	£32,919

So investing £1,000 today for a period of 15 years at an average annual rate of 5% will leave you with £2,079. Which makes compound interest much more seductive than keeping this money under your mattress.

INTEREST COMPOUNDS OVER TIME...

The graph below shows you the impact compound interest has on your savings and why starting to save now is one of the best things you can do.

In this example, Sarah and Jack both invest the same amount of money over time (£88,000). Sarah invests £2,000 per year from age 23 to 67 (£88,000 over 44 years) while Jack starts investing ten years later and saves £2,588 per year from age 33 to 67 (£88,000 over 34 years).

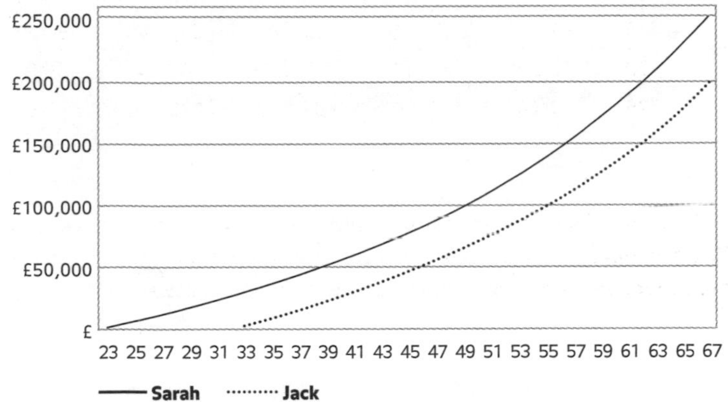

You'll note that Sarah ends up with more money (£251k) than Jack (£198k) at retirement, even though Jack invests the same amount of money, all because Sarah started investing her money 10 years earlier.

I assume here a 4% annual return (with a balanced portfolio of stocks and bonds), as per a comment from BlackRock Chairman and CEO Larry Fink.[109] Obviously, this is not a guarantee of returns.

To understand how compound interest can work for you, head over to the Monevator website: **monevator.com/compound-interest-calculator/**.

The Risks and Rewards of Investing

You should now have a better idea of the time value of money and why you may want to learn more about investing.

I also told you I was willing to take the £100 and invest it to make more money in the future. That comes down to a new relationship called 'risk and return'. When I save money in a bank account, I don't take a lot of risk, and I don't receive a very high return. If I am to take risk on my money by investing, I want to be rewarded for it. So yes, it's more risky, but let's understand what risk is and how this risk/reward relationship works.

What are the risks involved in investing?

There is *no get-rich-quick option* unfortunately and you may get back less money than you invested. I know it would be great to know the outcome of a financial decision in advance and have total certainty about the result. However, investing does not work like that. Who can predict the future? Things may not go as planned. And this is called risk. Generally, when the risk is higher, investors are expecting higher returns to compensate them for taking higher risks.

The good news is that there are different levels of risk with different asset classes and everyone will be comfortable with a different risk. And, of course, your attitude to risk may change over time: would you be as willing to take the same chances at 20, 40 and 80? Your personal barometer of risk will go up and down as life changes and you have different needs and demands on you (and, crucially, a shorter amount of time to earn money). You will also either be a natural risk-taker or more risk-averse. So, how do you know what level of risk you are comfortable with? As stated earlier, the level of risk you can swallow is basically synched to your goals and how much time you have to achieve them. The relationship between risk and reward? *The higher the potential (yes, potential!) reward, the higher the risk.*

Investing in low-risk asset classes usually comes with low returns. Let's use cash as an example: most cash savings are protected by the FSCS (see page 234), so unless you hold money under your mattress that can be physically stolen, it is very low-risk to hold cash. However, the saving rates on cash accounts are extremely low so your reward on this investment is low. Additionally, if you think keeping money in cash (even in the proverbial shoebox, piggy bank or underneath a floorboard) doesn't seem risky, think again! Because of inflation, the price of the goods you will buy when you go shopping with that saved money will increase more than the interest rate you could be getting on your money. You may effectively have less purchasing power over time.

Let's look again our £100. Let's assume we want to save it in a cash deposit account that pays 2% per annum. At the end of the year, you have £102 in your account. It's safe and you have guaranteed returns.

Now let's instead invest this £100, and your investment can increase by 3% or decrease by 3%. There is some risk involved, you are not certain to be able to preserve your capital, but you may earn more than you had initially.

If you invest £100 and your investment can increase by 10% or decrease by 10%, there is more risk involved than previously, you are not certain to be able to preserve your capital, but you may earn even more than you had initially.

With the second investment you are taking more risk, and there's an opportunity of higher returns.

You have to understand how much risk you are okay with. Time is important because if your investments decrease in value, you need more time for them to recover.

What 'risk' means is easy to understand conceptually but not so much in practice. For me, the best way to understand risk was starting to invest (start small with what you can afford to lose) and then assessing how I felt about the market fluctuations.

How can investing make your money work harder?

Economically, when we think about investing, we are purchasing something today that we hold onto because we anticipate using it in the future to add to our wealth. For example, you can invest in education, in financial markets, in property, in a car or in services.

In finance, investments are something you buy or put your money into with the aim of getting a profitable return. There are many types of investments you can make, and they all have very different characteristics and will offer different risk and return. These investments are called 'assets': do you remember the assets and liabilities in Chapter 2? *You want to grow your net worth by acquiring assets and decreasing liabilities.* When you listed your assets, you may have listed your current and savings accounts (these contain cash), your pension (contains stock market investments and bonds), your house, etc.

Assets are the things you own. An 'asset class' is a group of investments with similar risk/return characteristics. There are four main asset classes that are the most popular:

1. **Cash:** Yes, you read it right, cash is considered an investment. It's supposedly the least risky because if cash is held in a bank it's almost impossible to lose it. At the same time, the interest you receive is usually lower than that for other asset classes because of this low risk level.
2. **Bonds:** When buying a bond, you loan some money to a company in exchange for a fixed interest payment called a 'coupon'.
3. **Stocks and shares:** When you buy a share you buy a (pretty small) part of a company in exchange for potential dividends and expect an increase in share price.
4. **Property:** Buying a home or investing in real estate.

On top of these there are many other types of alternative investments available, such as cryptocurrencies, stakes in start-ups, foreign currency (FX), 'collectibles' such as wine, art, jewellery or antiques, private equity, commodities and many, many more.

→ We will be looking at investing in the stock market in Chapter 8 and investing in property in Chapter 9.

So how do these investments help you to grow your money? There are two ways of going about this:

1. **You make a profit/loss when you sell them:** You buy an asset (such as a share or a house) and it increases/decreases in value. In the future, you will sell that same asset for a better price, therefore you make a gain – if it's for less you make a loss. This is also called 'capital gain', i.e. you make a gain/loss on the capital you invested.
2. **You earn an income:** You buy an asset and it's going to provide you with some future income (i.e. you make regular money from it, such as buying a house and renting it out or receiving dividends from shares).

One or both these benefits are called a '*return*' on your investment: returns are the profits you earn from your investments. We *like* returns. Many happy returns in fact! 🤩

How to mitigate risks with diversification

Investing money is risky but there are ways you can mitigate the risks. This is called '*diversification*'.

Diversification means spreading your money across different types of investments or asset classes. Not putting all your eggs in one basket is a way of life for the canny investor, because she/he knows that if one company hits the skids, that's only going to affect a small proportion of their savings. *A diverse portfolio is a happy portfolio* 🤩! (Which is a mantra you should hold in your mind but not a tattoo you should ever think of getting.) Investing every penny you have in your best friend's new tech venture is not sensible, just as buying stock in one company is very risky. Make sure you spread your bets...

Why Invest Hard-earned Money for the Long Term?

People invest their money for as many different reasons as there are people on the planet. Investing is extremely personal and my reasons for investing money will probably be completely different from yours. While I cannot tell you why you should or should not invest money, here are some of the most common reasons for investing.

Grow your money

Investing is an opportunity to build your wealth and achieve financial independence. The money you save and invest today will be used by your future self, so make sure you start saving early. With pensions, you benefit from tax relief and, potentially, employers' contributions – all of which adds to your retirement pot. With investing you could benefit from higher returns than keeping your money in cash or in a savings account. You will give your money the opportunity to grow at a faster rate than inflation and you are also benefiting from the power of compound interest which, as described above, is when your returns are automatically reinvested again and again so your wealth keeps increasing in the long term. Investing money also means it's locked away, so there's no chance of you spending it!

Achieve your goals

In order to get to where you want to go in life, it's always useful to set some goals, as we discussed in Chapter 3. What are your personal goals? Do you want to have a family, pay for your kids' education and build a pot of money for each of them? Or perhaps you're saving for a big, one-off purchase like a house extension, a round-the-world trip or a ridiculous boat (hey, we're not here to judge...). Once you have listed your goals for the short-, medium- and long-term you may find that investing towards some of them is a way to make them happen within the timeframe you want. *Yes!* Investing money can help you make your money work harder (with the help of compound interest) and achieve your goals faster than just saving it in an ordinary bank account. Of course it is also riskier, so keep it in for the long term.

Investing in what you believe in/'putting your money where your mouth is.'

We all have strong beliefs and passion projects, and you can use investing to reflect and support the things you care about most. You may want to emphasize particular social or environmental values, so why not take a look at ethical/impact investing to see if you could combine financial returns with purpose? You can also invest in a particular venture that you are passionate about, or support a project you like (but keep in mind the risk of losing money there, so perhaps as a very small portion of your investment portfolio). Really the list is as long and rich as your imagination! Remember the concepts of diversification and risk when you make investment decisions.

Forward thinking

If you're passionate about a new kind of industry or certain trends, and you have your eyes firmly fixed on the future, then you may want to apply this way of thinking to good financial use. What about electric cars or vegan restaurants? Get clued up and analyse trends.

So while investing is not for everyone, it really *is* for anyone. You have cash saved, no expensive debts, enough to cover emergencies and achieve your short-term goals, you understand investing and the risks associated with it – you seem good to go and give it a try. It can also be fun! 🤩

Do You Want to Start Investing?

Over the next two chapters we will deep-dive into two investments categories: financial markets and property. But, before we get started, I will outline below what I see as the necessary pre-requisites to investing money.

First off, to boost the chances of your investing journey going smoothly (i.e. you making the highest return for the level of risk you are ready to accept), you need to be able to have money available to invest in the long run – anywhere between five to ten years (ideally ten years+). Which means not seeing that cash again for quite a long time. Investing is part of a comprehensive financial plan and should help you achieve your financial goals. So, if you're looking to have immediate access to your funds for an emergency (aka that flight to Lisbon or birthday present), investing is not what you need. In fact, I would recommend having at least three to six months' salary squirrelled away in a cash savings account (emergency fund) and repaying any expensive debts (such as credit cards) before you begin to invest.

Next, you need to accept that investing involves a level of risk. Nobody likes to lose their hard-earned money, but if you're depending on that investment to make a guaranteed return and can't afford to lose a penny, proceed with caution, as there are no guarantees that this will definitely accumulate.

The best way to shake off the fear of investing is to educate yourself without losing sleep. You don't have to be an expert before you start investing, but if you don't understand it, don't invest in it. Financial institutions make investment sound complicated and, sure, some aspects of it can be, but the basis of investing is pretty straightforward. Maybe starting small is the best option so you can see how it feels?

HELP? If you lack confidence about investing and would like someone to help you out, make sure you contact a financial adviser.

Here's the bottom line: you can always make excuses for not investing because it seems complex, it's laden with jargon, and if you are a woman, it's traditionally viewed as a 'man's thing' to do... Whatever your excuse, you need to shift your thinking now: it's time to change your preconceptions and negative concerns and reframe your narrative around it. Think of it is as a smart, necessary strategy for making your money work for you. Once you see it that way, you'll feel empowered to take action.

Well Done! You have earnt coins!

You're now armed with enough knowledge to understand how investing works in theory. Take your time and don't be afraid to ask questions, however silly or basic they seem (FYI no question is stupid enough). No one is born knowing what compound interest is, and we weren't taught this stuff at school either. But we hope you've come to realize that investment at a beginner's level is totally do-able for anyone who knows basic maths and has a few quid to set aside every month.

You don't have to be a high earner to start investing; you will see in the next chapters that you can start small if you don't have a lot to invest or don't want to invest a lot. All you need is a clear idea of what your goals are. You can get a real buzz from investing, and not in a stressful 'Buy! Sell! Buy! Sell!' way, but by knowing that you are part of the workings of the global economy and you become part of the conversation.

Never again will you sit quietly at drinks or dinner, bored yet anxious that someone might ask your opinion on property, interest rates or the FTSE100. Sure, you might find it boring and not feel like talking about it, but you won't be excluded. So even if you decide only to invest small in a way that works for you, you can pat yourself on the back and know that you've come out of the shadows into the world of finance. It belongs to you, too.

Money Talk
with Ambre Soubiran

Job: CEO of Kaiko, financial market data provider, and President of Féminin Pluriel UK.

Fun fact: Ambre left banking a few years ago to run Kaiko, and became one of the most influential women in the crypto industry.

Money motto: *'You can't make money without spending money.'*

What makes you happy?
Being in control of my life (financially and time-wise), great simple food, the Mediterranean Sea, candour, good wines.

What is your most treasured possession?
Family, and friends that are like family.

What is your biggest money failure/mistake?
Being too greedy/optimistic and not selling a single token at the peak of the crypto bull market.

What is your greatest achievement?
Moving to an entrepreneurial life with Kaiko.

What is your personal mission?
Create good things, share experiences, leave great descendants to this world!

What is your top money hack?
Leverage.

Who is your go-to person to talk about money?
My father and my first boss in banking.

Who is someone you admire most in life?
My ancestors.

What is your favourite book?
Harry Potter 🤩.

Investing is...
Crucial!

What do you like about cryptos/blockchain?
The fact that we managed to represent ownership of any asset in a digital, non-forgeable, auditable, transferable and decentralized way.

CHAPTER 8: INVESTING IN THE 'STOCK MARKET'

* *

What will you learn in this chapter?

Why/why not invest in the stock market?
Why is it not only for the rich (and other myths)?
How do financial markets work?
How do I build a balanced portfolio?
How do I get started?

* *

'SELL! BUY! BUY! SELL!'

I was working at Lehman Brothers – one of the largest banks on Wall Street – in 2008, the year the bank went bust. The next two months would include seven of the ten worst days on the UK stock market across the entire 2007–18 period.[110] This experience showed me firsthand that the markets – however sturdy and safe they may seem from the outside – can see stock prices going from £££ to zero in just a few days. The collapse in the market made many people worry about whether where they were keeping their savings (if they were saving anything...) was indeed safe.

Post-2008 many people were asking, 'Is my money actually safe in the financial markets?

Well, here's the secret, there's no 'one simple trick' to successful investing, just some fairly unexciting ground rules to come to terms with. And is it just for rich people? No way. It's really not. It's for anyone who wants to put away a bit of money for the future. It's not the Wild West anymore; forget those images of traders yelling, 'Buy! Sell', and frantically gesticulating at each other across trading floors. Investing is not about trying to cash in by picking the best stock – it's trying to make your money grow with a diversified portfolio over the long-term.

At the beginning, it can seem as though investing is complicated and overwhelming, but I'm here to dispel the fear: investing is not gambling. In fact, as you'll see, it can and should be delightfully, fantastically *boring*. Financial markets are unpredictable and they wax and wane constantly. So, think ups and downs rather than a big red arrow on a graph going from zero to a million. We're going to learn the rules of the game, we're going to be really patient, and we're going to invest in a smart way with a balanced portfolio. Your portfolio is an extremely powerful money tool and should help you grow your money over time...

Investing is risky. As a general rule, you should only invest what you can afford to lose. The value of investments can fall as well as rise; you may not get back what you invest.

If you're not sure about investing, seek independent advice.

Why/Why Not Invest in the Financial Markets?

There *is* obviously risk associated with investing in financial markets (the 'market') because the future is uncertain and most economic, business, political or other factors and events can cause uncertainty and can have an impact on the market. But we have also seen with inflation and compound interest that actively not investing your money can also make you 'lose' money over time, as you have less and less purchasing power.

So, before you start, begin to think about *what you can actually afford to lose*. If you *have repaid your expensive debts, have an emergency fund, savings for short-term goals on the side and have enough to live on*, do you have some money that you would not miss without losing your livelihood? Because the global markets certainly do not come with a cast-iron guarantee, and as we all know from 2008 and many other times in history (2008 wasn't a 'one-off' and big drawdowns are entirely normal – think about the 'Black Tuesday' Wall Street Crash of 1929 or the dot-com crash in 2000–02) things can change dramatically overnight. Saying, 'Don't bet what you can't afford to lose' might seem a bit redundant because, hey, who can afford to lose one hundred, one thousand or even ten grand!? But if you really think about it, could you actually survive if you did lose that money? Would you lose your home or just be very, very irritated?

Before you launch yourself onto the often stormy waters of putting your money in the stock market, it's important to understand the non-official guidelines.

When deciding to invest money, it's important to remind yourself of your goals. Are you saving for retirement 30 years away, a home, or further education? Once you have it clear in your own mind and noted down somewhere, you'll find it easier to make the right decisions about when to start moving your money, and when to leave it alone. And when to invest vs. when to save.

Time is one of the key components of investing and as I mentioned in the previous chapter, investing means thinking long term. There's no point investing in the financial markets for a year then taking your money out. This is a long game. Or at least a very mid-term game. If you're prepared to say goodbye to your money for a decade or more, you're perhaps more likely to have a nice surprise at the end of it. Or at least not a horrible surprise. But why ten years?

Well, markets are quick to react to events (think Trump or Brexit). So, if you are investing for the short term, one to maybe five years, you expose your money to ups and downs in value. If you wait longer, you have more chances for your investments to recover from these shocks.

There is always risk. You can't always get back more than you put in. Markets are risky (prices go up and down), but there are ways to mitigate this risk. You could make some money but you could also lose money. The market is liquid: you can buy or sell your investments at any time. However, the market is volatile so you may not get back the money you invested, or it could take years for the market to recover.

If you invested in the UK stock market on 12 September 2008, the Friday before Lehman went bust, it would have been bad timing[111] but your investments would have performed well in the long run. Rises and falls are painful, but they're part of life on the stock market. An investor who isn't prepared for them is ill-prepared. But of course, remember past performance isn't a guide to the future. With the 'stock market', experts often say, 'time in the market beats timing the market', meaning that actually being invested in the market is better than trying to find the best time to invest.

It's easy to start investing money with all the apps available and perhaps it's sometimes too easy, so make sure you know what you are investing in. *And just like managing money, investing is also very personal.* We are all different when it comes to risk-taking: how much can you afford to lose? How do you react when markets become bumpy: are you freaking out to see your investments losing 2%? Are you checking your Yahoo! stocks app every five minutes? You have to decide what's right for you.

Demystifying Investing

I have been running introduction to investing workshops for more than a year and, as a group, we always start the session by telling others what we have invested in so far. Most people would say that they haven't invested any money yet. And this is where I ask them, 'Do you have a workplace pension or did you have one with a previous job?' Well, if this is the case, then you are already an investor.

I want to demystify investing for you so that you find the confidence to learn more and get started with your own investments if you think it is for you. We'll start by unpicking these common myths that may be holding you back.

Myth 1: Investing = gambling

Fundamentally, gambling usually has an immediate and binary outcome, e.g. 'red' you win money or 'black' you lose money. If you invest in a single stock and the value of this stock goes to zero (i.e. Lehman bankruptcy), then you also lose all your money. But with investing you can diversify your investments by putting money across a lot of shares, bonds and/or funds so that if one does fall, it will only have a small impact on your portfolio. It is then unlikely you will lose all your money.

With investing, the outcome is rarely judged on a very short-term basis and the value of your investments can fluctuate. Which means that if the value of the market declines as soon as you have invested, you are not forced to lock in those losses but instead you have the luxury of waiting for the market to rebound – as it usually does over the long term.

Emotionally, gambling is disempowering, addictive and generally bad for the individual as it's secretive, expensive and can never do any social good. However, with investing you become an owner of something! And investing can also help you become part of your wider social consciousness. If you're an eco-warrior or a human rights activist, there's an investment package out there to help you put your money where your mouth is, i.e. you want to support something that you believe in! You may think about impact investing, where investors are looking for social and environmental impact as well as making a financial return. With investing, understand what you put your money into and always look at the potential risks and returns.

Myth 2: I have to be rich to invest

Even £50 a month can be enough to get started. Some ISAs even start at £25! As long as you follow the golden rule of not investing more than you can afford – because what's the point getting into expensive debt to fund your investment habit? Now that does sound like gambling. You can make even the smallest sums work harder. Even if, after paying off your credit cards and other expensive debts and saving for your emergency funds and goals, you are only left with a tiny amount untouched each month, set up an automatic transfer with one of the handy apps (see page 364) and squirrel away those little nuggets in a place where, unlike a current account, they will eventually grow into a fund that is bigger in the long term.

Myth 3: I need someone to invest my money for me

There's so much information available online now that advice on how, when and what to buy is just a click away.

Websites like Investor Chronicles and the Motley Fool, let alone your own high-street bank, robo-advisers and platforms will save you trawling through the Companies and Markets sections of the newspapers with a highlighter, and can hold your hand through any transactions you might want to make. Of course, you might want to undergo a session with a financial adviser if you don't feel confident enough to get started. Setting up an investment account is relatively easy and there are lots of 'basic' options that offer low-cost and diversified exposure to the financial markets.

Myth 4: It's really expensive to invest money

It doesn't have to be! Opportunities for investing are now widely available and there are many options for the newbie investor at a range of prices. Remember that investing *does* always cost money – you have to pay fees to make the transactions, pay for use of the platform and, if you work with an adviser, pay for his or her services. Online platforms and investing money into low-cost funds (a pool of money from a lot of investors) can help you keep your expenses low, which means – depending on your performance – more money in the future.

The reality: I am an investor, not a trader

The traditional image of investing in the stock market involves scanning huge columns of figures to see how individual companies are performing then grabbing the phone and shouting, 'Buy X! Sell Y!' to a broker, who then leaps around making weird hand gestures and sweating a lot.

We can think that investing is about getting rich by picking winning stocks, and selling them at exactly the right time to make the most money. This is also called 'beating the market'. I invested in a handful of single stocks in 2014 and was very excited about the prospect of making money from the stock market. Six months later, one of these went down 40% because of a profit warning (i.e. the company actually announcing bad results). I panicked and I sold my stake in the company to make a loss. Today the stock has fully recovered. That made me understand two things: investing in single stocks is extremely risky because you are exposed to the performance of one company, and secondly that it's virtually impossible to 'time' the market, i.e. to decide when to buy or sell and that allowing ourselves to hold for a long period of time is the best strategy.

Choosing individual stocks seems super-trendy, and most of the time the conversation at the pub would be, 'I invested in Tesla, or Google, Amazon', but this sounds more glamorous than it actually is. The high risk associated with single stock-picking can make you check the stock price on Yahoo! Finance more often than Instagram (not a bad thing but stressful). The second effect is that you may also be tempted to want to sell high and buy low or trying to outplay the market. Jumping in and out of the market at what may feel like the 'right' time leads to worse results than keeping calm and carrying on.

Remember – patience is a virtue, and time in the market beats timing the market.

It's hard – almost impossible – to win at single stock-picking. It seems the easy way but when investing in individual stocks it is difficult to achieve diversification and your portfolio can become very risky. It will require all your time and attention to monitor your investments. Just remember that some people are doing this as a full-time job and they don't always win. It feels like professional investors in London make tonnes of money investing in the stock market while most of us mere mortals just about manage to beat inflation. Unfortunately even for professionals beating the market is extremely difficult. A diverse portfolio is a happy portfolio! *Diversification* is key: you want to spread your money over asset classes, geographies, industries, etc. Don't pick just one horse.

Of course, you could have a tiny 'side pocket'. You could manage yourself and test how you would do vs. the returns of the market: can you outperform the market (over a number of years)? *Be warned* – the vast majority of people will not.

This is why investing should be *boring*. Not like watching paint dry – but boring as in: I am not stressed about it and don't need to check my investments every second.

So what do I need to learn?

So, what about us rookie, novice investors? How do we comprehend financial markets? What are the main traits of 'successful investors' and how do you learn about investing?

We want to be in control, at least to a certain extent, and when it comes to investing there are things we can control and others we cannot. We cannot control how markets perform, or the outcome of big global events. But we can control how we invest, what our mission and goals are, what level of risk we want to take, what fees we are willing to pay and how we diversify our investments. So, let's play the game by our own rules.

Before beginning to invest, you need to set out your *mission for investing*. This is your investment philosophy – a set of guiding principles that inform and shape your investment decision-making process. And because investing is very personal (we all have different objectives, different appetites for risk, and different personal circumstances) it's important to spend some time thinking about why we are investing. You should be able to go back to your investment philosophy at any time, e.g. when you realize your existing strategy is not delivering the expected results. Your investment philosophy should contain the following:

- Learning about how the markets work: How investors behave and why markets fluctuate.
- Defining your attitude to risk on a goal-by-goal basis: No need to be consistent for all goals. You may not want to take the same risk for all.
- Research: Spend time reasearching what you can invest in.
- Setting your values: Are you a social investor? What are your interests?
- Remember: Markets may come and go but your investment philosophy should remain the same!

Do you know why you are investing and what you want to achieve? Make sure you revisit your goals and the time horizon regularly as your personal situation may change over time.

How much risk do you want to take? It makes sense to be able to take more risk while you are young, because when you invest money, time is playing in your favour because of your capacity to absorb loss (i.e. recover lost savings with future income, which a retiree doesn't have the ability to do) and take less risk when your time horizon is shorter, when you approach retirement for example. But in the end, what matters most is how you personally feel about taking risk. Are you comfortable with the fact that you may lose money? Can you handle very volatile markets? Or would you prefer something more stable? The higher the potential return, the more risk you usually have to accept. The level of risk you will be willing to take will be represented by your *investment portfolio* and your *asset allocation, and this is a very personal decision!*

How Does the 'Market' Work?

The financial market is a place for companies to raise money. And it's also a place where investors (buyers and sellers) can sell and buy stocks and bonds. Thanks to the financial markets, companies can raise a lot of money in an organized way.

There are usually two ways for them to raise this funding in the market: they can issue new shares or they can borrow money through bonds. When a company needs money to grow (e.g. to finance an acquisition or new development), they can raise money on the stock market through an initial public offering (IPO) whereby they sell some of their stock, but they can also issue bonds. Governments can also issue bonds when they need money.

Now let's look in detail at investing in shares, bonds and funds – and what type of return and risk you can expect from them. With investing it is important to build a balanced portfolio, and in order to do that we need to know what we can put in our basket!

HELP? If there are financial products you don't understand, don't invest in them! Learn more or ask for professional advice.

What are shares?

When you invest in shares, it means you are buying a stake in a company and become a shareholder in that company – also called having equity in a company. Investing in shares is popular because historically the returns have been superior to those generated by cash and bonds. But at the same time, investing in shares is much riskier.

Please note that I am using the terms 'stocks' and 'shares' interchangeably, but 'stock' is a general term used to describe the ownership certificates of *any* company, and 'shares' refers to the ownership certificates of a *particular* company.

Shares derive their value from future profits and, therefore, *today's* price is based largely on investors' perception of what the company's future profits will be. If people think the company will do well and is undervalued at the moment, they will start buying company shares and the share price will go up, then investors may think they become 'overvalued' and so sell them.

Companies can also remunerate their shareholders in the form of dividends, i.e. part of the company's profits each year. You will probably get dividends from more established companies that are generating profit, but you might not get rapid growth. Dividends represent an income for you.

 HOW SHARES WORK

X is a company in fashion e-commerce, and they want to grow their operations to build a new warehouse. They need some funding to do this so they decide with their board of directors to increase their capital by issuing some shares. Investors will then be able to give money to X by buying the shares and become shareholders of the company. They will also get the right to vote on important decisions.

The investors become shareholders in X and in exchange for the money they are giving X, the company pays them a dividend (sometimes). The investors can also sell their shares on the stock market, hoping to recover their initial investment, but they can also make a gain or a loss.

Pros	Cons
• Possible highest return asset of the mainstream investments • Historically performing better than inflation • Very helpful to help you achieve your goals if you start early and hold for the long term	• Markets are uncertain, you can lose money and it may take years for you to recover what you invested • Investing in single shares (vs. funds) is extremely risky

What are bonds?

When you invest in bonds, you are lending money to a company (i.e. corporate bonds) or to a government (i.e. gilts in the UK) for a fixed period of time. I like to think that corporate bonds are a bit like a mix of shares and government bonds. This asset class is also called 'fixed income'. In exchange for this investment the companies or governments will pay you interest, called a 'coupon' and at the end of the fixed period you will receive your initial investment back. Investing in bonds is usually considered more risky than holding cash but less risky than investing in shares.

Gilts or government bonds are usually safer than corporate bonds if they are offered by 'safe' governments. Gilts offered by the UK government will be considered low risk because there is a low chance the UK will default on its bonds (i.e. not repay your nominal investment and interest rates) but at the same time, when the risk is lower the returns are lower!

Your investment in bonds can also be affected by inflation if the interest you receive is lower than the inflation rate (although some inflation-linked bonds or 'linkers' do exist and pay you an inflation-beating return). There is also a risk linked to the companies not being able to repay you the money you lent them; they may possibly default on the payment. This is why if you are considering bonds in your portfolio make sure they are investment grade, i.e. of good quality. Bonds are given 'ratings' that represent the likelihood of the debt being repaid, and are published by credit rating agencies such as Moody's, Standard & Poor's and Fitch. You may also have heard of the risky 'junk bonds': a high-yield or non-investment-grade bond, carrying a low rating – which means a higher default rate!

Bonds offer investors a way to diversify their portfolios away from shares because of their stable and relatively lower volatility. Also, bondholders have higher seniority than stockholders in the event that a company declares itself bankrupt.

HOW BONDS WORK

X is a company in fashion e-commerce, and they want to grow their operations to build a new warehouse. They need some funding to do this so they decide with their board of directors to borrow money and 'issue' a bond. Investors will then be able to lend money to X by buying the bond. This is simplified, but you get the mechanism of how companies can borrow money.

The investors are not shareholders in X but in exchange for the money they are lending X, the company pays them interest for a fixed period of time and at the end repays the principal, i.e. the initial amount invested.

X has issued many bonds of £100 nominal value for a term of ten years. They will pay a coupon of 5%; that means you'll get £5 a year for ten years and at the end of the term you will get your £100 back.

If you would like to sell your bond earlier because you need the money you can do so by selling it at market value on the market. This market value can be higher or lower than your initial investment, so you can make a gain or a loss.

Pros	Cons
• Historically bonds have returned more than cash but less than shares • Stable and regular income as interest rate is (usually) fixed at the beginning of the investment	• Your money could be worth less in the future because of inflation, i.e. you lose purchasing power depending on the interest paid on the bond • Returns can be lower than shares • Possible default risk by companies or certain governments

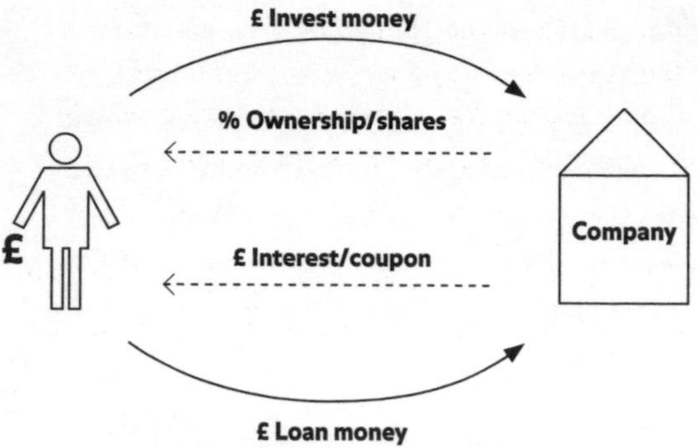

Risk and reward

You may remember from Chapter 7 that risk is a measure of uncertainty or your chances of loss on your investment, and on the opposite scale, reward is a measure of gain or loss. You may think that risk is a negative thing, but it's not necessarily – you may want to take on more risk if you are also given more chances for higher return!

When we look at shares and bonds, the risk indicator is basically how these asset classes compare in terms of price fluctuation. Shares are usually volatile, their prices move a lot which means they are risky, and they usually have a higher return in the long term. Bond prices don't move as much as shares, so they are considered less risky, and their return is usually lower.

Shares are riskier than bonds and in return they usually also offer a higher return. Bonds are less risky than shares and in return usually offer a lower return.

Once we get the concept of how shares and bonds work we can start thinking about putting them together in a *portfolio*, or a basket of investments. You remember that we talked about *diversification*, which is basically not putting all your eggs in the same basket to avoid breaking them all.

In order to diversify, you want to build a portfolio of shares and bonds that is 'balanced', meaning it contains shares and/or bonds in a proportion that you work out.

What you are trying to do with your portfolio is to limit the risk and to increase your gain. Shares and bonds have a different risk–reward profile so having both in your portfolio can help you manage risk better.

RICH AND FAMOUS INVESTORS YOU CAN FOLLOW

This is a non-exhaustive list of the best investors out there you can follow on Twitter for updates and £££ knowledge:

Warren Buffett: **If you are considering investing, you need to know about Warren Buffett – an American business magnate, investor and philanthropist as well as the CEO and largest shareholder of Berkshire Hathaway. You can read his famous golden quotes everywhere on the internet and he also draws a big audience with his annual letter to Berkshire Hathaway shareholders (online here:** berkshirehathaway.com/letters/ **or now in a book called *Berkshire Hathaway Letters to Shareholders*.)**

Ray Dalio: **Ray is the founder, co-Chief Investment Officer and co-Chairman of Bridgewater Associates, which is a global macro investment firm and the world's largest hedge fund (an investment vehicle that actively invests its sophisticated clients' money with the goal of maximizing returns and minimizing risks). In his last publication, *Principles: Life and Work*, Ray shares the principles he has developed over the years, which guide him both in business and real life, and which we can also adopt to achieve our goals. Available online on** principles.com/ **or in his book of the same name.**

Sallie Krawcheck: **Sallie is the founder of Ellevest in the US – an investment platform for women. She is a former Wall Street CEO and industry veteran and was named 'The Last Honest Analyst' by *Fortune* magazine. A super-driven 'financial feminist', she is making waves on the other side of the pond. She's written a book, too: *Own It: The Power of Women at Work*.**

RICH AND FAMOUS INVESTORS YOU CAN FOLLOW

Benjamin Graham: Benjamin was an economist and investor often referred to as the 'father of value investing' (value investing is the strategy of buying stocks that trade at a significant discount to their intrinsic value). He served as an inspiration to some of today's most successful businessmen and also mentor to the above-mentioned Warren Buffett. If you read one book on investing, make it his *The Intelligent Investor* – it's a little dense, but you'll learn a lot.

John C Bogle: John 'Jack' Bogle, founder of The Vanguard Group (one of the largest existing investment management companies) ignited the trend towards index investing by creating the first index fund in 1975, which revolutionized the way in which Americans save for their future by helping them to invest for the long term and to achieve higher returns with lower cost. He died in 2019 at the age of 89. *The Little Book of Common Sense Investing,* although US focused, is a practical guide full of his insights that will help you build a portfolio based on the investment strategy that's right for you.

Building a Diversified Investment Portfolio

Now that we've worked out what shares and bonds are, how they can work together, and how we can allocate them in our portfolio, we need to explore how we can build this portfolio.

Using funds to diversify your portfolio

Instead of investing in stocks and/or bonds, you can actually invest in *funds*! Shares and bonds are asset classes and you can invest in them directly (this is called 'direct investing' by the way). A fund is basically a pool of money that you and other investors (and it can be many thousands – you won't ever meet them) buy a specific portfolio of shares and/or bonds. Funds are not assets per se, they are a method of investing in traditional asset classes such as shares, bonds, commodities, property, etc.

Why are they great? Because funds offer something you don't get when you invest in stocks or bonds (individually)...*diversification*! There are many stocks and/or bonds in a fund and prices for some of these can go down but because you have a large portfolio, some other prices may go up at the same time, and as a result don't impact the performance of your portfolio as much as if you had just a few stocks and/or bonds. That helps spread your risk, because you are not only investing in one company share, so if something ever happens, the overall value of the portfolio should not be impacted. The diversification results in a lower risk for your portfolio.

You may think that you can also try to achieve diversification yourself by investing in a lot (and I mean *a lot*, there are thousands of companies listed on the stock exchange) of shares and bonds. Yes, you could, but there is a decent chance that the trading costs of owning lots of stocks would be quite expensive (and materially hurt your returns) and/or that you wouldn't have the time/discipline to actively manage such a large portfolio.

When you buy funds, you are diversified! Instead of having just one share in Apple or Tesla or Google for example, the fund may have shares and bonds in a lot of international companies, in a lot of different industries and locations – lowering the risk of you losing all your money compared to buying a single company's shares.

What is passive investing?

Passive investing is an investing strategy that tracks, i.e. mimics, the performance of the market, and by the market here I mean an index.

Passive investing is the opposite of active investing: when a professional is managing investments and trying to beat the market, those investments are 'actively managed'. The fund manager who 'actively' tracks every bubble, wobble and weird echo in the market on your behalf will also usually take a fee. Active investing may be exciting and glamorous, but studies have shown that it consistently underperforms passive investing, largely due to the higher fees associated with it.[112]

Note that the merits of 'active' vs. 'passive' have been debated for a while. So you might want to read more on the subject and work out which one is best for you.

Wait, so it's all done by computer? Not a shouty man in a pinstripe suit? Exactly. It's as simple as a computer program linking up your investments to the daily performance of the market. Which makes it much cheaper.

According to Barclays Smart Investor[113] you could be paying ongoing fees and charges as low as 0.07% (of your investment in the fund) with passive funds, versus around 0.65% to over 1% for active funds each year. It's interesting to note that, as per the Asset Management Survey 2017–18, the majority of assets (74%) are still actively managed, but this is lower than 10 years ago (83%).[114]

What are the different types of funds?

There are a few types of funds, namely unit trusts/OEIC (open-ended investment companies), investment trusts, index funds and Exchange Traded Fund (ETFs), which all just sound like jargon but there are big differences between them.

Unit trust/OEIC: This is a pool of money invested in shares and/or bonds and passively or actively managed – this is what investors usually call a 'fund'.

Investment trusts: These are listed companies with shares that trade on the stock market. They invest in shares and/or bonds of other companies with the money they raise. They then divide the trust portfolio into units that you could buy or sell.

Index fund (also called an index tracker): This is a type of fund or ETF that is tracking the performance of a stock market index – a series of numbers that shows changes in the average prices of shares on a particular stock market over time.[115] For example, the *Financial Times* Stock Exchange 100 Index (also called the FTSE 100 Index, FTSE 100, FTSE or, informally, the 'Footsie') is a share index of the 100 companies listed on the London Stock Exchange with the highest market capitalization. By investing in the fund, the investor gets diversification because he is not exposed to one stock but to all 100 stocks in the index. Index funds are passive, they 'just' replicate the performance of the market but are not trying to beat it! Again, the key thing about following the market rather than 'taking punts' on individual stocks is minimizing risk; while it does not guarantee against losses it should help you reduce exposure to market volatility (markets going up and down).

So, if your market of choice is the FTSE All Share, you would effectively have a small share in every single company listed on it. When the market goes up, so does your money, and vice versa. If one day a new company is added to the market, the algorithm that controls your fund would add that in to your group of stocks. If one leaves, it automatically drops off your list.

John Bogle who founded Vanguard and created the first ever index fund, says 'My ideas are very simple, in investing, you get what you don't pay for'[116]. Bogle is always telling the investor to consider basic and simple investing (a mix of shares, bonds and cash in a diversified portfolio) long term, but also low-cost investments, i.e. according to him, it is usually not worth paying the fees of active managers to try to 'beat the market'.

Warren Buffett – one of the most successful investors ever and also chairman and CEO of Berkshire Hathaway – is also a champion of passive investing. In his 2013 Berkshire Hathaway letter to shareholders[117], he is very clear about what he thinks of index funds: 'The goal of the non-professional should not be to pick winners – neither he nor his "helpers" can do that – but should rather be to own a cross-section of businesses that in aggregate are bound to do well. A low-cost S&P 500 index fund will achieve this goal.'

ETF (Exchange Traded Fund): This is a fund that is similar to unit trusts or OEICs but the difference is that ETFs are traded on a stock exchange, just like company shares. They can be actively or passively managed. Sometimes ETFs are more difficult for small investors versus unit trusts: with unit trusts, you can buy a fraction of a share – allowing small investors to invest and rebalance easily. ETFs are not divisible, except via a robo-adviser (or other model portfolio service: a selection of portfolios that you/an adviser can choose from to suit your risk profiles and investment objectives), which makes it harder for small investors to buy the appropriate amount and rebalance their portfolio. (See page 317 to learn about rebalancing.)

The first ETFs were launched in Canada in 1990 and then in the US in 1993[118] and ETFs have only been available to UK investors since 2000.

AN IMPORTANT NOTE ON FEES

Investing doesn't come free. And fees can ramp up quite quickly, especially if you are looking to invest small amounts of money. So, always be sure to compare the funds and the platform costs. Imagine you are making a return of, say, 5% on your investment, and pay 1% in fees – that sounds low – but it isn't! Your return is reduced to 4%. And, unfortunately, you will see that with a lot of platforms or advisers this will be much higher than 1%...

When looking at fees for buying and selling funds we need to talk about platform fees (the one holding your investment) and fund fees.

Platform fee: This can be a monthly subscription or a percentage of the assets under management.

If you are buying active funds: A management fee of about 0.75%.[119]

Cost to trade funds: Each time you buy or sell a unit in a fund, you have to pay anything from £5 to £25. Trading a lot means paying a lot in fees.

When you use a robo-adviser, you don't pay the above fees but pay a percentage of the money you invest with them. The basic fee is usually below 1%[120] and goes down when you increase the amount invested. It also depends on the level of service you choose!

How to decide my asset allocation?

Investing in funds is the preferred route versus investing in individual stocks and bonds. This process of choosing the percentage of shares and percentage of bonds is called the *asset allocation*. Asset allocation is based on three things: your goals, time frame and your attitude to risk. Finding your asset location is the hardest question when you want to build your portfolio and probably the biggest decision you'll make.

When you want to start building your portfolio you have to find the balance of shares and bonds in your portfolio – i.e. of funds – appropriate to the level of risk and reward you are seeking to achieve your goals. Funds can invest in stocks and bonds or both, and they have the characteristics of stocks and bonds explained above, but they also have this 'something extra' called diversification! And this is what they're called:

- **'Stock funds' (or equity funds):** When you invest in a stock fund, your money is pooled with that of other investors and primarily invested in stocks of numerous publicly listed companies as an investment strategy.
- **'Bond funds':** When you invest in a bond fund, your money is pooled with that of other investors and primarily invested in bonds.
- **'Balanced funds':** When you invest in a balanced fund, your money is pooled with that of other investors and primarily invested in a mixture of stocks and bonds.

The more time you have available, the more risk you can usually afford to take on. Each goal is different so each has its own level of risk. You want to gradually reduce your risk as you grow older, because when you retire you don't have the luxury to wait for the market to recover.

If you have a lot of time to achieve your goal(s) and you want to be exposed to more risk, you can usually take a higher proportion of shares vs. bonds in your portfolio. If you don't have that much time, want to reduce your risk and are OK with lower returns, you can take a higher portion of bonds in your portfolio.

Younger investors usually could go for a more 'aggressive' portfolio where they take more risk, i.e. more shares and less bonds, because they have time in their favour and their investments have time to go up again before they retire or need their money. More mature investors or people who need money in the next ten years or so generally chose a more 'conservative' portfolio where they take less risk, i.e. more bonds and less shares. They need more visibility (i.e. knowing their money will be available when they need it) and more predictability in their returns.

EXERCISE

This decision is personal and has to be your own *investment strategy*. Ask yourself:

Are you investing to protect your capital?
To gain additional income or grow your wealth?
How much risk are you willing to take?
How long are you investing your money?
What kind of returns are you expecting?
Do you want to manage your investments or work with an adviser?
How often will you be checking your investments and making changes?
How much will it cost you?

There is a rule of thumb in personal investing for retirement savings, the *100 Minus Age Rule*: take 100 and subtract your current age (100 – 30 years old = 70). The result in percentage is how much of your portfolio could be invested in stocks. The remainder would be invested in bonds. Based on this rule, a 30 year old would have a portfolio allocation of 70% shares and 30% bonds. According to Investopedia,[121] this rule is now outdated: we live longer so we have to save more money and have more time for our money to grow. At the same time, bonds are not paying as much as they used to, so investors may want to be exposed to a higher proportion of shares.

The 'investment pros' have updated the rule to the '110 Minus Age' or even '120 Minus Age' for the greater risk-takers.[122] That means the same 30 year old above could be invested 80%:20% shares/bonds or even 90%:10%.

This is a basic guideline for retirement savings and really just a starting point for your journey into the world of investing. No one wants to give you strict rules of thumb and the regulations make it very difficult to get to know these tricks of the trade. This rule may be an oversimplification but it helps a newbie investor. There will be so many factors that shape the way you invest your money and your investment strategy. You should really be handling the risk you are personally comfortable with, taking into consideration your age, circumstances (women live longer than men) and whether you can you afford to lose this money.

Based on this rule, you can adjust the proportions for shorter time horizons as, although the rule is for retirement, you can apply it to another time period you want to invest money for. If you need the money earlier, you could adjust the proportions for less shares and more bonds. If you want to get ideas of asset allocation you can use online platforms offering risk questionnaires, which show you examples of asset allocation you could use.

The minimum time horizon suggested by the pros is this: less than two years' horizon, you probably don't want to risk your money investing in stocks. From two to ten years, you may want to gradually increase your stock exposure and for goals of more than ten years, it starts to become appropriate to be largely in stocks (obviously depending on other circumstances like your age and savings goals, e.g. owning your house).

Based on your financial plan, you can decide to work on one goal at a time, or a few different goals and prioritize them. Remember, focus on repaying expensive debts and building your emergency savings first, and then look at your other goals. Maybe your workplace pension is where you need to start saving or you may want to start working on another long-term goal. You should review these regularly to see where to allocate your money and potential investments.

EXERCISE

Based on your goals, which ones would you like to invest money for? Can you start thinking about an asset allocation and risk profile?

Goals	Time horizon in years	Risk tolerance (low to high)	Asset allocation mix of shares/ bonds (%)

How to Start Investing

We've already discussed the accounts you can use for long-term saving and investing (see Chapter 6), namely the pensions, stocks and shares lifetime ISA, stocks & shares ISA and general investment account.

If you are in the process of deciding whether or not to invest, choosing the right accounts/products for your money or even picking investments, financial advisers are always available to help you. While some people prefer to work with a professional, others may wish to forge ahead on their own (DIY investing), often because of the fees charged by advisers. I encourage you to understand both options and make your own informed choice.

You prefer to work with an adviser or a wealth manager

If your situation is complicated or if this is all jargon and seems too overwhelming, you can always talk to a financial adviser and/or wealth manager. They will be able to assess your goals and risk and recommend what could work well for you. They can then make your investments for you, but of course this comes at a price because you will have to pay for their advice on top of what you pay for the actual investment fees, usually as an ongoing percentage of the value of your investments.

If you have a workplace pension, perhaps this would be a good place to start, as you already have an account in place with some investments in the stock market. Why don't you contact your HR department and ask to meet your pension provider? You will be able to discuss with them how you are invested and what your asset allocation actually is. Make sure you also check the fees and the performance.

The DIY approach and picking investments

If you have reached this point, congratulations! I know how it feels to buy your first investment. It's a long process. You may not have mastered all the investment concepts yet but you feel it's the right time to start.

Before starting to pick your funds, you need to open an account with an investment platform. You may have heard names such as Hargreaves Lansdown, Nutmeg, MoneyFarm, Moneybox and many more. These are all investment platforms and they are all quite different, with distinct personalities! A platform is an online service that allows you to select, buy and sell funds, and also monitor the market and receive market updates. At first it can be overwhelming to choose which one would be right for you.

It all depends on how much experience you have with investing, how DIY you want to be, what you want to invest for (pension, ISA) and the level of fees you are willing to pay for these. Remember that – like everything – the more help you get, the more fees and charges you usually pay, and the less money you'll have in your pocket.

Further, choosing an investment company is not set in stone; you may want to start with something more hands-on and, once you've learnt the tricks of the trade, move to something more autonomous which you feel you have more control over. The market has evolved a lot in recent years and the arrival of the newish robo-advisers provide a solution for complete beginners to start investing.

There are two main categories of investment platforms out there, depending on how hands-on you want to be with your investments: *fund supermarkets* and *robo-advisers* (welcome to the future!).

Fund supermarkets (also called investment platforms): These are online platforms that allow you to buy and hold a range of funds (and shares, bonds, etc.) and build your own portfolio. This is basically a DIY option for investing. It will also provide you with some research and information on the funds, as well as their performance, but ultimately you will be in charge of making your own financial decisions. These platforms are 'execution-only' – which means that they will put your money into the investments you choose, not into what they tell you to buy. Your high street bank may also provide this type of service.

In addition, lots of platforms may offer a *premium service* (model portfolio service): they will offer you some help to get you started and can provide an example portfolio or help you build your first portfolio based on your risk profile and investment objectives.

Some of the better-known UK fund supermarkets or investment platforms – some of which offer a premium service – are Hargreaves Lansdown, Interactive Investor, Fidelity Personal Investing, AJ Bell, You Invest, Barclays Smart Investor, Charles Stanley, Vanguard and PensionBee.

Fees: When you invest with a fund supermarket, you will have to pay fees for the funds but also for the platforms, either as a percentage of the investments you hold or as a fixed fee. While being execution-only, some platforms also offer regulated financial advice for an additional fee.

Supermarket pros	Supermarket cons
• You can choose all your investments and build your portfolio yourself, which is great when you are an experienced investor: it gives you freedom • Premium service is an easy way to get started • Easy to access	• You can choose all your investments and build your portfolio yourself, which is not always suitable for newbie investors as too many options often lead to headaches 

Robo-advisers: These are automated online investment services trying to bring investing to the masses. They offer investors ready-made bundles of investments. Great for the newbie investor, robo-advisers select your investments, rebalance and trade on your behalf. Lately, there's been a lot of attention surrounding robo-advisers, especially in the US and Canada.

The concept is more recent here in the UK with the first UK robo Nutmeg launching its first platform in May 2012. You may also have heard of Moneyfarm, Wealthify, Wealthsimple, Scalable, MoneyBox and evestor.

To use a robo-adviser, the usual method is to take an online questionnaire (not performed by a human financial adviser) that will assess your investment goals, financial history, attitude to risk and finances at a point in time, and risk-profile you. From this, an algorithm would make a portfolio suggestion for you.

Robo-advisers are able to make such recommendations by using the Modern Portfolio Theory.[123] This theory, which was presented by Harry Markowitz in the 1950s, and for which he received a Nobel prize in economics, is a formula that helps investors to maximize returns while minimizing risk. It is based on two main concepts: that the investor wants to maximize his return for a given level of risk, and that the risk he is taking can be reduced by diversification (i.e. building a portfolio of assets that will each behave differently in the market).

The portfolio the robo builds for you is usually composed of low-cost, passive investments that track certain indices, including ETFs. Although called 'robo-advisers', these guys don't all offer advice, but some do! As an investor, you don't have much to do – buying, selling and rebalancing is done for you by the robo. You receive information and market updates.

Robos are quite a new breed on the market and while they have been really appealing for new investors because of their ease of use, fancy websites and marketing, we still don't have a lot of information on their performance, which is also called a 'track record'.

Robo Pros	Robo Cons
• Robos are fully automated. This means there's no face-to-face interaction with an adviser and enrolment is also automated. • Your portfolio will be selected for you based on your goals and risk. • There is a chance that the robo will do the diversification better than you would do it! They will invest in a mix of funds (sometimes up to 20) that would be hard to achieve as an individual, plus they would diversify globally. • Robos rebalance your investments for you. • It's an easy way to start investing – plus you'll be exposed to different markets very quickly. • Set up is quick and easy. • Great user experience, platforms are user-friendly and usually offer an app.	• Robos don't actually personally know you like an adviser would! There are no emotional ties or considerations. For example, it won't know that you're trying to change jobs, or maybe you're thinking of starting a family or buying a house. Adapt your investment strategy based on your personal situation. Numbers don't tell your life story! • When investing, make sure you understand the market and its various fluctuations – but, most of all, how they'll affect you. A robo-adviser unfortunately won't call you to tell you of these changes! • They haven't been on the market for a long time so the track record for some is not yet available.

Choosing fund supermarkets or robo-advisers is choosing how much help you would like to manage your investments.

How do I choose my investment platform?

- Ease of use: Do you like their website? Investing can be overwhelming, so make sure you actually like the website of the provider. How easy does it seem to open an account? How easy it is to navigate their page? Can you ask questions? How is their blog? That will give you a good indication of their level of service.
- Services: Some platforms may be more suited to beginners than others and you can decide on the ones you prefer by visiting their websites

and assessing the level of information and education they provide. The robo-advisers will tend to be more jargon-free and send you more updates than some fund supermarkets. Some others may be better for more advanced investors because of the level of detail they provide on investments; they are great but can be quite daunting in the amount of information given. Also, most platforms will have apps by now, but it's an important thing to check as you may want to be able to monitor your investment and trade on the go.

- Asset allocation: Some platforms will help you build your portfolio (premium service and robo-advisers); others won't.
- Customer service: Do you want to deal with real humans or with an integrated chatbot?
- Charges and fees: Yes, you have to pay to be able to invest money and perhaps for you this is the most important thing to look into. Sometimes platforms have ongoing charges (a fixed percentage of your investments or a fixed fee per month or year), sometimes it's a fixed fee per trade. This is why it's also important to decide how often you will be trading.
- Minimum investment and size of portfolio: What is the minimum investment required by the investment platform? Some platforms just ask for a lump sum to be invested while others may ask for regular contributions to your account. Make sure you have enough to cover the minimum.
- Investment options: Not all platforms offer all investments. Would you like to hold funds and ETFs as well as shares and bonds? Do you also want to buy international funds? Do you want to be able to choose your funds (some platforms don't offer *all* the funds on the market)? If you use a robo-adviser to invest your money, you will not be able to choose the funds or stocks in your portfolio – the robo-adviser will do this for you. Ultimately, fund supermarkets are more DIY.

Always check the ratings and consumer comments on Trustpilot.

You can use websites such as Which?, Boring Money and Compare Fund Platforms to compare the platforms.

ARE WOMEN INVESTORS BETTER THAN MEN?

Do you just assume that men are better investors than women? Recently there has been a lot of research that shows the opposite: that women are great investors. Here are some of the findings:

- **According to research by Barclays Smart Investor that was carried out by Warwick Business School[124], women's returns on their investments were on average 1.2% higher than men's. Women are less likely to engage in risky trading, are more diligent in their research, make more diversified investments and are humble enough to admit mistakes, which also leads to them seeking professional advice.**
- **Another piece of research by Fidelity in the US[125] found that women save more (into both their workplace pensions and investments outside their workplace pensions) and also earn a return of 0.4% a year more than men.**
- **Terrence Odean, a professor at Berkeley who has spent his career studying investor trends, found that men traded 45% more than women in the 1990s, which he blames on overconfidence[126]. However, all that extra trading caused men to have average returns that were lower than those for women.**

To conclude, a calm, steady and longer-term approach is key to successful investing, and women seem to be perfecting the art.

EXERCISE

List of selected platforms, fund supermarkets and/or robo-advisers: why have I selected them? What are their services and fees?

....

....

....

How much £££ do I need to get started?

You don't need a lot of money to start investing and actually it's better to start small. Why? Because you're not trying to time the market by investing a big lump sum at the best time (which is a bit like jumping on a moving carousel) you will learn more by actually doing it yourself.

The key for me is to get some 'skin in the game', as per the excellent book of the same name by Nassim Nicholas Taleb. The expression means that when you have incurred risk (monetary or otherwise) by being involved in achieving a goal (putting money in the stock market and taking some risk) you will learn a huge amount. This is how I got started, investing small amounts and understanding I could lose it all, not for the sake of losing it but because by losing I would have a better understanding of how it all works. You should experience the feeling for yourself: it's very different to using fake £££ or playing Monopoly. It's there! It's happening! It's real! And this feeling of having skin in the game is not just something for newbies – everyone over time understands it more and feels more empowered.

To get started investing these days, you don't need much money, either a regular investment of £25 per month with some platforms or £50/£100 one-off for the lowest entry platforms, usually the robo-advisers for the ISAs. (£25 is what? Four OK lunches?) Pensions usually have a higher minimum investment threshold of about £1,000. Apps such as MoneyBox also invest your spare change and they are very easy to use (micro-investing), and while what you invest may not be enough for retirement, it will help you to get started.

However, it's important to bear in mind the *cost* of investing that I've explained above. Especially when you invest small, because you don't want the costs to be higher than your potential gains.

REGULAR INVESTMENT VS. ONE-OFF INVESTMENTS

Knowing *when* to invest is another million dollar question. Investors try to time the market, i.e. invest at the right time when markets are low and investments seem cheaper, and sell when markets are high, or when investments are high. Unfortunately, timing the market is near enough an impossible mission. That way madness lies...and losing money.

When you start investing, you have two options:

- **Invest a lump sum immediately: You may want to 'be in the market' sooner rather than later because of the power of compound interest and the positive effect of time but, at the same time, you may end up buying when markets are high...**
- **Drip-feed into the market: This is the best of all the jargon terms, and means to invest smaller amounts regularly (also called 'dollar cost averaging'). This is sometimes advocated because it's less risky. This way, you invest something when the market is sometimes high, sometimes low.**

Some investors also keep some cash in their investment portfolios (we are not talking about emergency or other savings but what you were considering investing). Why? Because they may want to invest opportunistically when the market is low, sometimes to reduce volatility (the markets are going down, but holding a portion of cash provides peace of mind...).

How do I choose funds?

Now that you have a better idea of how asset allocation works and how much you would be willing to invest, you can start looking for investments. The bad news is that there are thousands and thousands of funds out there to choose from. The important rule of investing is *never to put money into something you don't understand*. We've all made that mistake, and frankly it becomes more like gambling than investing. If you work with an investment professional make sure you also question them on the funds they are investing your money into. If you do it yourself, it's all about spending a bit of time on it, researching, asking questions and taking the plunge. Professionals are always there if you're not sure.

Many DIY platforms have a lot of online content (articles, videos about how to invest, what to invest in, market updates, etc.) as well as lists of best buys and favourite funds. This is a good place to start, at least with your own research. Check how they selected the funds, what methodology they adopted. And some platforms even have filters to help you choose your funds.

I personally enjoy *ready-made portfolios* (the premium service offered by some investment platforms) and this is how I invested initially: AJ Bell, Hargreaves, Vanguard, etc. offer this service. If you are just getting started and lack a little bit of confidence, and also to save you the hassle of asset allocation, a lot of the platforms give you the option of choosing ready-made portfolios. Based on a risk questionnaire they ask you to fill in, the platforms suggest a portfolio of funds. You don't have to decide your initial allocation yourself – the funds are selected for you. Once your portfolio is built you also have the flexibility to change it and add/remove some investments. I start from a suggested portfolio and then read up about it and as I discover more I adjust and sell some funds and buy others to create my own portfolio. Take your time to look into each suggested portfolio and really question everything (see below). All this is done online, you won't talk to anyone and have no pressure whatsoever to act fast; try to enjoy it and feel that you're in the driving seat.

What's in there? Usually different types of funds, some equity funds, some bond funds and a bit of cash. Depending on your risk you will see more of one vs. the other. The ready-made portfolio could suggest 5 to 15 funds you could buy, that have names such as FTSE100 MSCI, S&P500, EM Bonds; these are the *tickers* of the funds (a ticker is a symbol or abbreviation used to identify a fund or a stock). By clicking on these you can see a full description of what they are. The first part is usually what the fund is, e.g. 'FTSE 100', and the second part is the provider, e.g. MSCI, Vanguard, Barclays, Blackrock, etc. Each one is unique. There are many funds tracking the FTSE 100 so you could choose the best/cheapest provider for you.

Once you decide it's time for you to invest, you can transfer money to your brokerage account (be it an ISA or SIPP, for example) then buy the funds suggested in the portfolio. Once you have bought them (it may take a few hours or days depending on what you buy) you receive confirmation and see the funds appear in your account. You can now just hold the funds until you decide to sell them in the long term.

With robo-advisers, this process is slightly different. You won't have to choose your investments – the robo-advisers invest your money for you in a lot of different funds: it's even more diversified. The more you buy the more it costs usually, so working with a robo can give you this diversification at a lower cost. They are pretty inflexible: you have to leave your money invested the way they decide and cannot add your own investments.

You need to ascertain types of investments you would most like to take. To help you find and understand how to look at them in even more detail:

- Read financial news websites. Go to Interactive Investor, Morningstar, Motley Fool, Citywire or your investment platforms (AJ Bell, Vanguard, Hargreaves, etc.) or get yourself a subscription to the *Financial Times*.
- Spend some time browsing websites.
- Enter the ticker symbol of the fund or share you want to look into: you can then discover all the characteristics of the fund, as well as some articles, ratings, etc.

- Check the fees and the minimum investment: how much will you have to pay to invest with them, is there a minimum?
- Look at what the fund is made of: funds are also diversified by geography and asset classes ('holdings'). A fund will have a prospectus you can look at to understand what it is made up of and what its investment strategy is.
- Websites will also show you the past performance of funds, but remember that these are not an indicator of the future – the future is not predictable!

Rebalance your portfolio

Maybe you had a specific asset allocation based on your risk profile per goal on Day One, but the markets are moving all the time, so your asset allocation is also moving. Prices of stocks tend to grow faster than bonds, so you could well end up with a higher proportion of stocks vs. bonds in your portfolio. You may also have had major life changes or decided on new investment goals. Perhaps it's time to rebalance your asset allocation? Check your portfolio at set intervals (e.g. every year) to make sure it's not going off piste...this process is called 'rebalancing', and it's just meant to be restorative.

For example: you had an original portfolio of 80% stocks and 20% bonds. As the years pass the value of your stocks hopefully gradually increases. In five to seven years your asset allocation is way off your initial target (90% stocks and 10% bonds), and with more stocks you are exposed to a lot more risk than you had initially planned (remember 80%:20%). You may want to correct the balance to come back to the original level by lowering your stock exposure (selling some stocks and buying some bonds) or investing more and buying bonds.

You may think that rebalancing is too much work! So, you can always ask for help from financial advisers or look at the robo-advisers or other model portfolio services that will be able to do it for you.

Ten Rules of Investing

1. **We cannot predict the future:** Your investments can go up, but they can also go down and you could lose money. Don't overreact! Only invest money you can afford to lose, based on your goals and risk appetite. You need to have an emergency fund in place, some money for short-term goals, and have repaid your expensive debts otherwise investing does not make sense.
2. **Invest for the long run:** This means thinking in terms of ten years or more. Time is your friend.
3. **Make sure you invest as tax-efficiently as possible:** Understand your options: ISAs vs. pensions.
4. **Don't put all your eggs in the same basket:** You don't want to lose it all. *Diversify* your investments to reduce risk. A diversified, low-cost portfolio invested for the long-term is a happy portfolio.
5. **The more time you have, the more risk you could possibly take:** If you don't need the money for a very long time, you can usually take more risks. However, if you need the money sooner, you should definitely avoid this course of action.
6. **Invest in a low-cost way:** Always check the fees. Compound interest is fab but fee cost compounding not so much.
7. **Review and rebalance your portfolio:** Your life as well as the markets change all the time.
8. **Think about who can help you:** Don't hesitate to shout out for help and never, ever invest in something you don't understand.
9. **Start small and invest regularly**.
10. **Have fun but be boring in the way you invest**: you are not a trader !

Well Done! You have earnt  coins!

As you may have gathered, I like investing, but it may not be for you! Only you will know how you want to manage your money and your attitude to risk.

I hope this chapter is detailed enough to give you a basic understanding of how the markets work and how you could get started. *Knowledge is power!*

This kind of pro-active, independent, grown-up thinking about your future financial health is important to being and feeling involved in the world. I promise you it will make the grass look a little greener! 🤓

If you have even £25 a month to spare (and you know that's just a couple of weeks of Starbucks), there's no time like the present to get started in investing. It does not have to be perfect the first time, or the second or the third for that matter. But you'll get better at it and you will find what works for you. And you'll feel like a boss while you're doing it!

Finally, I suggest you now pay it forward and get other people you know to talk about investing. It is one of those singularly life-changing activities we should all engage in. Educating yourselves, sharing experiences and boosting others' confidence will help you build insight and gain valuable knowledge – and confidence – into how to do it.

If the somewhat theoretical wizardry of stock markets is not exactly your thing, we'll talk about something more tangible in the next chapter: investing in bricks and mortar.

Money Talk
with Dame Helena Morrissey

Job: Head of Personal Investing at Legal and General, Founder of the 30% Club diversity project and author.

Fun fact: After being the CEO of Newton for 15 years, Dame Helena is now on a mission to encourage the nation to save and invest more. One of the best-known women in the City, she is inspiring, empowering and human.

Money motto: *'Think big, start small, start now.'*

What makes you happy?
Time just hanging out with my family; sitting in the garden in the sunshine; Buddy (our dog) running to greet me when I get home from work – with the younger children right behind him! And women getting in touch to tell me how they have taken control of their own destiny after reading *A Good Time to be a Girl* or listening to one of my talks – that means so much more than any accolades or awards.

What is your most treasured possession?
I'm not really materialistic – it's the emotional attachment that means something. Our home in Berkshire is full of happy memories, photos of the children as babies and is a place everyone keeps returning to, so has to be our most treasured family 'possession'.

What is the best money advice you have ever received?
Ask if you don't understand. We all worry about seeming ignorant or foolish but we need to ask the questions that are on our mind – otherwise we might not get started at all.

What is your top career advice?
Women are bombarded with career advice but a lot of it is very convoluted and negative – don't do this, don't do that. Instead, sometimes we need to go for it! Take things one step at a time, build your confidence and self-esteem – and learn how to make the most of whatever makes you different. If you need help (and most of us do) get a mentor!

What is your biggest money failure/mistake and success?
Early in our married life, Richard and I had real money issues – we had negative equity in our tiny flat and were struggling with astronomical mortgage and childcare costs. It was very stressful. But that point of failure turned out to be the motivation for success – the experience made us determined to do better financially, and ultimately led to me looking for a better paid job, developing my career and making better investments.

What is your greatest achievement in life?
My family.

How can we boost our confidence managing our money?
Through knowledge. If we don't know, we won't ever feel on top of things. I encourage everyone who doesn't feel confident to go on a course, sign up to a financial education seminar, or even just read a book on money basics. In all areas that might seem daunting, I have learned to think big, start small, but to start now.

Who is your go-to person to talk about money?
My husband and I talk about our finances – I am the professional but he has strong views and great 'antennae' when it comes to both risks and reward. Obviously all our important financial decisions have to be taken together. And I talk to our children about money!

Who are your inspiring heroes?

I admire people who are kind and generous and who work to genuinely make things better. My late grandmothers inspired me personally to work on gender equality. They were both fabulously clever although neither had great opportunities – and they showered me with unconditional love. Today, I greatly admire Liz Dimmock who leads the 30% Club's mentoring scheme (now the biggest cross-company scheme in the world), Andy Haldane at the Bank of England for his thoughtfulness on diversity, Nimco Ali who works to prevent FGM, Mary Goudie who does so much to prevent child trafficking...the list goes on and that's the point – today we have a patchwork quilt of amazing work that together adds up to the solution.

What is your favourite book?

Tender is the Night by F. Scott Fitzgerald. I just love the writing style – and the poignant storyline.

Investing should be...

A regular habit, not for special occasions. I think we need to invest in our financial well-being like we take exercise – little and often will yield results.

What is your personal mission?

To engage the nation, especially women and young people, to save and invest. At the moment too many see investing as only for the wealthy or something that's complicated or boring! If we don't take control of our financial destiny, it's hard to be empowered in other areas of our life. I am on a mission to do what I can to help.

* *

CHAPTER 9: WANT TO BUY A HOUSE?

* *

What you will learn in this chapter:
How do you develop a home-buying strategy?
What is the real cost of buying a house?
How do mortgages work?
What is the process of buying a house?

* *

QUICK GOOGLE NEWS SEARCH ON 'MILLENNIAL HOUSING':

'ONE IN THREE UK MILLENNIALS WILL NEVER OWN A HOME'

Encouraging? Certainly not. 

I started investing in real estate when I was 10 years old. I was extremely lucky to be able to afford to buy a property on Park Lane and another in Mayfair, whilst earning a good salary, paying my bills and taxes, avoiding going to jail and managing my cash flow.

I was extremely competitive when it came to playing Monopoly. 20 years later, Monopoly has just released a new game for millennials and the box says: 'Forget real estate. You can't afford it anyway.' Apparently, the point of the new game is to enjoy experiences rather than buying real estate.

Monopoly taught us the property game and killed it 20 years later. 

What has happened to us?

'One in three UK millennials will never own a home'
'Millennial housing crisis engulfs Britain'
'UK millennials are getting priced out of the housing market'

In fact, home ownership among 25 to 34-year-olds has plummeted in the UK over the past few years. It's hardly surprising, given the insane rise in house prices, coupled with the fatalistic 'Why even bother?' attitude that many young people have now adopted in the face of these huge increases. But let's remain positive – after all, buying a home isn't just a financial decision, but an emotional one too.

Before you start, consider whether it is right for you. As with any other investment, there are risks involved and property prices go up and down, so always make sure you have repaid your expensive debts and have some emergency savings before investing your money in a diversified way. Ready? Let's look beyond the socio-economic factors of home ownership and assess real estate as an asset.

Generation Rent...Getting on the Ladder

For our parents and grandparents, owning a home was the norm. A three-bedroom Victorian terraced house with a back-facing garden was what a typical family could expect to buy. Nowadays, for first time buyers (FTBs), a one-bed flat is more likely. Rising house prices have not only left fewer young people able to buy a home, they have also divided them into property 'haves' and 'have-nots' with a '*clear economic difference*' between older and younger generations, and homeownership among 25 to 34-year-olds falling from 55% in 1997 to 35% in 2017.[127]

Is it even worth trying to buy? Whilst the housing market has performed well in some parts of the country, with the average property price going up by 173%[128] since 1997, the average income for 25 to 34-year-olds has only gone up by a mere 19%. Prices go up and down unpredictably, but recently the situation has become even more disorienting due to political and economic changes like Brexit. If you're prepared to ride out a few fluctuations and stay in the game for the long haul, you should be fine. Ultimately, the decision to buy is up to the individual, but if you *do* want to, this chapter is for you.

Is it stressful buying a place? Yes. Does it continue to be stressful owning a property and taking full responsibility for its maintenance (not to mention taxes)? Yes. The choice is yours: stay cosy in the rental market where you have the flexibility to move whenever and wherever you want, or try to get on the property ladder. You can do it if you really want!

Property ownership is a wonderful thing, and so is hindsight. If you're new to home buying in the UK, start by taking off those rose-tinted glasses and researching the drawbacks, loopholes and hidden nasties of buying before diving in headfirst. It can be a lengthy and overwhelming process with plenty of ups and downs, but it's all about preparation (and a little bit of luck). From setting yourself realistic expectations to understanding the importance of lenders' timings, what follows is the definitive checklist to buying a home in the UK (and will hopefully reduce your homebuyer anxiety!)

In order to buy your home, you will need to save for a deposit and also borrow some money to cover the full cost of the house and buying fees. Unless you've won the lottery or have financially secure parents, the likely option is that you will need a mortgage in order to purchase your first home.

So, what *is* a mortgage? In basic terms, it is a loan you take out to buy a property. The loan is secured, which means that, until you pay it all off, the lender has an asset he will be able to rely upon, some sort of security in the value of your property (he does not own a share of the property). Worst-case scenario, if you can't repay the loan, the lender can take back ('repossess') the house to sell it and get his money back (mortgage lenders don't lend 100% to cover themselves for this possibility, but recently, in some cases, you could obtain 90–95% of the price of the property).

Where do you even start? Getting your finances in order

Buying a home is a big decision so you want to be prepared, do your homework and get organized. I started looking at houses a year before actually buying, contacting agents and doing visits just to get clued up about the market (plus it's actually pretty fun because there's no pressure!).

- Build up your credit score! Remember from Chapter 2 that it isn't just about having no bad debts – potential borrowers need to build up a digital footprint by being registered at their address for bills, bank statements, council tax and, very importantly, the electoral register (or roll). Do make sure you're on the register; don't be tempted to leave bank statements going to your parents' address; if you're in a shared house make sure you're named on the bills rather than leaving them in someone else's name. A clean *credit score* can affect a bank giving you a mortgage, so check it and work on improving it if necessary.
- Register on a website such as Zoopla, Rightmove or PrimeLocation to get property alerts. This will give you an idea of how fast-moving the market is in your preferred area. If only one house in your price range

is coming onto the market every six months, you'll know you'd better pounce as soon as you're ready.

- HELP? Find an agent you trust and keep in regular contact with them. Shop around until you find one you get along with, because you're going to be seeing a lot of them.
- Start visiting places to get an idea of what you like and what you can buy within your value range. Talk to neighbours, and check out planning permission posters on trees in the vicinity and on your council website to really get a sense of the area.
- Check the prices of houses that have recently been sold in the area. You can find this on the same sorts of websites listed above.
- Enjoy the process! Try out the local pubs, parks and cafés! Remember, this is a positive and exciting move – one of life's big adventures.
- Prepare for your mortgage application by making sure all your documents are in order. Lenders like to see three years of business accounts (and may ask who your accountant is), three months of bank statements and details of any loans and credit cards you may have.
- It's also a good idea to know the maximum deposit you're able to put down on a home.
- Start saving – you usually get the best rates with a greater deposit!
- Start paying off your debts. Credit cards and expensive loans should be top of your list when clearing your financial decks.
- Register on the electoral register at your current address, as many mortgage companies use this to verify your identity.
- As stated above, you don't want to be inflexible, so you should know what your trade-offs will be. For instance, you need to be open to discovering new neighbourhoods. I didn't buy where I looked initially and I recommend trying to see as many properties as you can stomach or fit into your diary, so you have a full sense of the property landscape and greater confidence of your convictions when you finally make a decision.
- Leasehold vs. freehold: mind the lease length. If you're looking to buy in London, chances are the property will be 'leasehold'. Leasehold is an ancient form of tenure unique to England and Wales, which essentially means you have a lease from the freeholder (aka the landlord) to use the home for a number of years. The leases are usually long term, but lately there's been an increase in short-term leases of 20 to 25 years. It may

seem like a technicality, but the truth is that lease length is important, and it's worth seeking professional advice on what is best suited to your financial situation before taking a decision.

Find a really good mortgage broker

A mortgage broker, i.e. a financial adviser who specialises in mortgages, can be a great help. In order to select your mortgage and find the best deal you could apply directly to a bank and also use comparison websites to find the best deals. But you needn't do this on your own. I have used mortgage brokers and think it's really worth it, as they ease the strain of the arduous home-buying process.

A mortgage broker will give you their expert opinion on the best mortgage for you in terms of the interest rate and likelihood of your application being accepted. Mortgage brokers also have a view of market conditions and can definitely add value to the process. They will provide you with an understanding of how much the bank can lend you, what costs will be involved and who can actually lend you the money.

Brokers could also have access to deals only offered to intermediaries (themselves) and not the public. They may smooth the mortgage process for you and buy you time: a good broker will also help manage the whole house-buying process, liaising with you, the estate agent and solicitor right through to successful completion of your purchase. Many brokers say they start a mortgage process as a financial adviser and end it as their client's home-buying agony aunt!

Mortgages can be complicated, so brokers are a great support, offer you peace of mind and save you time during the sometimes long process of finding the right mortgage. They will also chase the lender on your behalf and send your missing documents .

So how do you find one of the *good* ones? As with many things, family and friends can give great recommendations. However, be aware of how up-to-date the information is, e.g. your boss who got a mortgage for £1,000 in 1960 may not be the ideal adviser. Having said that, it's smart to go for a brokerage firm with a long record of business in your area of the market because it means they've been good enough for their company to thrive.

Another place to look is the Financial Conduct Authority (FCA, **fca.org.uk**) which has a register of approved firms. Seeking out an independent one rather than one attached to an estate agent is usually a wise move. You should carefully vet these people both by checking on the FCA records and also by having a good old-fashioned chat with them to see if they seem sensible, calm and easy to work with and talk to.

How much does it cost to have a broker? Again, adding services can cost you money. A mortgage broker would cost on average £500 or charge you a commission (according to MSE, this 'procuration fee' is about 0.35% of the value of the mortgage, i.e. £350 for a loan of £100,000[129]).

There are also online brokers now! These new disrupters on the market, the digital mortgage brokers, do the legwork of finding a mortgage for you for free, offer you online education and search all mortgages deals to find the most suitable one for you. The websites receive a fee when you complete your mortgage. You can check Habito and Trussle or search for 'free online broker' on the Internet. Always make sure they are FCA authorized and regulated. After the selection process, there are still 'human' brokers to make sure your application is correct.

You can also use comparison sites to compare the various advisers.

It's your call: human or robot!

How much can I afford to buy?

In a nutshell, you need a deposit of *at least* 5% to buy a property, ideally more than that – because with a mortgage you are taking on a loan and borrowing money has a cost. The more you can save to put towards your deposit, the less you borrow, and the less you borrow, the less you'll pay in interest. At the same time, what you should always keep in mind is that *you don't have to put down the highest possible deposit* because it's really important to retain a financial buffer...

You can save for a deposit by putting money away each month and this will involve curating a leaner lifestyle. It might mean walking to work and not visiting Pret for a while, but it's only temporary. When borrowing, it pays to show banks that you're good at controlling your spending and understand the importance of frugality, as they will want to see whether you can swallow unexpected costs if interest rates increase.

What the mortgage lender will look at

Mortgages are based on how much you earn per month minus your expenses and any other debt repayments. Basically, your income minus your needs and debt repayments. The lenders will ask you how much debt you have and this will include any loans or credit card debt because these affect your ability to repay a loan. Lenders want to make sure that if they lend you money you will be able to repay them – and also pay the interest on your mortgage. Measures of affordability are becoming increasingly sophisticated these days but as a rule of thumb, income multiples are a better guide than anything else (a maximum loan of four to five times gross income) according to mortgage brokers.

If you have a deposit, remember that the bigger it is, the cheaper your mortgage should be. The more you borrow, the more expensive it will be for you. There is an important metric called Loan-To-Value (LTV) that indicates the percentage of the value of the property that is covered by the mortgage. Subtract your deposit as a percentage of the property value from 100%. So, if you have a £40,000 deposit on a £200,000 home, that's a 20% deposit. This means you owe 80% – so the LTV is 80%.

Based on the houses you have seen and what you want to buy, can you afford it?

The Money Advice Service has a super-handy Mortgage Affordability Calculator that helps you understand how much you can afford to borrow by looking at your monthly income and your outgoings. Mortgage lenders will look at these figures very closely to work out how they'll offer you.

EXERCISE

Use the Money Advice Service calculator to find out how much you might be allowed to borrow: **moneyadviceservice.org.uk/en/tools/house-buying/mortgage-affordability-calculator**.

Based on numbers in Chapter 4, can you find out the following data to plug into the mortgage affordability calculator?

Income/salary:

Gross: £ .... and Net £ ....

Essential costs from your budget:

£ ....

Lifestyle costs from your budget:

£ ....

Based on the calculator, I could borrow £ .... over a term of .... years with an interest rate of .... %. My estimated monthly costs would be £ .... compared to my current rent or mortgage payment of £ ....

'I don't have a deposit but I still want to buy'

This is the case for most people. According to a report by the Resolution Foundation, it would take just under 20 years for first-time buyers in their late twenties to save for a deposit without asking for money from family (or friends). Twenty years ago it took the same demographic three years to get there...[130]

The good news is that there are some government schemes available for first-time buyers (from help-to-buy to shared equity) that allow you to put together a smaller deposit than normally required – so you may be closer to home ownership than you think. Regardless of whether or not you *could* benefit from these schemes, the first step is to start saving for a deposit. If this is one of your goals, you may already be working towards it. You can adjust your goals based on the information in this chapter. One of the reasons it's nigh impossible to save enough money for a deposit is because the price of renting, especially in city centres, is painfully high. Figure out a way to reduce your rent (downsize, move out to the commuter belt) and you'll be able to save more in the long run. Another solution people have been pursuing is moving back to their parents' house for a *determined* period of time, but this is obviously not for everyone.

Saving For a Deposit: Options and Schemes Available

Here are a few schemes that are available and will help you to buy your first home.

Help to buy scheme

The Help to Buy scheme (**helptobuy.gov.uk/**) allows first-time buyers to purchase a property with a 5% deposit. The scheme has different parts: one to help you save (the Help to Buy ISA), and one to help you get a mortgage (the Equity Loan).

First, you can save money into a *Help to Buy ISA*. The scheme is available until 30 November 2019. After this date you will no longer be able to open a Help to Buy ISA but, if you already have one in place, you can keep saving into it until November 2029.[131]

When you save into this ISA the government is encouraging you by giving you a bonus: you save £200 and you receive £50 – a 25% top-up – to a maximum of £3,000 overall (which means you would have saved £12,000 into your ISA). The minimum you can save to get the bonus is £1,600 for a £400 top-up. You will be able to open this type of ISA with most banks. If you want to buy property with someone else you could each have a help to buy ISA and double the amounts previously mentioned.

You will need to instruct your solicitor or conveyancer – a person whose job is to manage the legal process of moving land or property from one owner to another – to apply for your government bonus, when you are close to buying your first home. It is advisable to use a lawyer or other qualified conveyancer – see box overleaf.

CONVEYANCING

'Conveyancing' is transferring a property from one person to another. For this step find a solicitor, because you never want to sign any legal document without some help, but also because he/she will have some additional work to do to transfer the property into your name.

Property law is not something you want to take on yourself, so ask friends and family to recommend a good solicitor who will help you with the paperwork. Someone friendly, open and trustworthy.

The solicitor will help you get answers from the seller on everything related to the property (disputes, fixtures, etc.) that has been raised by the lender, and check the guarantees, planning permissions and building regulations. The solicitor will also check that the seller really owns the property and he/she will prepare an exhaustive report showing the history of ownership of the property called a Report on Title.

You can apply for a government-backed *Equity Loan* to get an extra 20% of the cost of your newly built home (40% for London), so you'll only need a 5% cash deposit and a 75% mortgage to make up the rest (55% in London). This loan is free for five years and you then have to pay an interest rate of 1.75% – cheaper than most mortgages – and you won't be charged loan fees on the 20% loan for the first five years of owning your home. The home you want to buy must be newly built with a price tag of up to £600,000.

For example:

Emma is a first-time buyer outside London. She found a new-build flat worth £200,000. She is eligible for the Help to Buy scheme, so she will need to save for a 5% deposit of £10,000. She also gets an Equity Loan from the government of 20% of the cost of the new home (£40,000). So, she will need a mortgage of £200,000 – £10,000 – £40,000 = £150,000 (75% of £200,000).

Olivia is a first-time buyer. She wants to buy a new-build apartment in London worth £500,000. She is eligible for the Help to Buy scheme, so she will need to save for a 5% deposit of £25,000. She also gets an Equity Loan from the government of 40% of the cost of the new home (£200,000). So, she will need a mortgage of £500,000 – £25,000 – £200,000 = £275,000 (55% of £500,000).

Help to buy shared ownership

If you can't afford the mortgage on 100% of a home or love where you live and it's impossible to buy, the government has another scheme called Help to Buy Shared Ownership. Under this scheme, you purchase a 25–75% share of a new build or existing property leasehold and pay rent on the remaining share. You can increase your share in the future to own a larger part of the property. This offers you the chance to buy a share of your home and pay rent on the remaining share. In England, you need to be a first-time buyer (or to have owned a home before but you cannot afford to buy again) and have a combined household income of less than £80,000 (£90,000 in London). You can then pay the deposit with the money you save or take a mortgage for the share of the property you are buying. [132]

Lifetime ISA

There is another way to save for a deposit on the market and it's called the Lifetime ISA. We talked about it in Chapter 6, and it allows first-time buyers to save up to £4,000 a year, with the government adding 25% on top up to a maximum per year of £1,000 – that means a bigger bonus than the Help to Buy ISA. With this ISA, you decide to use the savings to buy your first home or you can keep it open and save for retirement.

You can use the money you saved into a Lifetime ISA to buy your first home with the following conditions: you have to buy a residential property valued under £450,000 in the UK with a mortgage at least 12 months after opening the Lifetime ISA account. You must be aged 18 or over but under 40 when you open a Lifetime ISA, and once you're over 40, you can continue to save into it until the day before your 50th birthday.

It's worth noting that if you need to withdraw the money for other reasons than buying your first home or retirement (unless you become terminally ill or pass away) there will be a 25% penalty. If you had £4,000 in the account and got a 25% bonus of £1,000 and then withdraw the £5,000, you would have to pay back the government 25% of £5,000 = £1,250, so you would get back £3,750 or, in the end, *be paying* 6.25%...

BANK OF MUM AND DAD

Yup, the Bank of Mum and Dad (formerly known as BOMAD; no joke...) plays a big role in the UK housing market for new young buyers. In 2018 it was estimated that a total of 27% of buyers would be receiving money for their deposit from family members (or friends); this was up from 25% in 2017.[133] Parents lent £5.7bn (£6.5bn in 2017), providing deposits for over 316,600 mortgages (298,300 in 2017) purchasing homes worth £81.7bn. And, while such gestures are indeed testaments of parental generosity, it is a symptom of how broken the housing market is. First-time buyers that get a 'boost' from their parents, whether in the form of a deposit or a loan, can buy 2.6 times earlier than those who get no such help.[134]

Getting a Mortgage

How do mortgages work?

When you take on a mortgage, you borrow some money (the capital) to buy a property. In exchange, the lender charges you interest until you repay them in full. The *interest* you pay on your mortgage is the cost of borrowing the money; it defines how much you will be paying each month and over the course of the mortgage. Different mortgage providers also charge different interest rates.

You can choose to pay monthly interest *and* capital (called a '*repayment mortgage*') or only to pay interest on your loan (called an '*interest-only mortgage*'). With repayment mortgages, because you have been paying some interest *but also a portion of the loan* each month, your balance decreases with time, and at the end of the term you would actually own the property – which is not the case with an interest-only mortgage. Your monthly repayments with repayment mortgages will almost certainly be higher than with interest-only mortgages but at the end of the day (the day in 25 years!) you will actually own the place. Since you are repaying a portion of the capital every month, the interest you are paying will gradually decrease.

It's worth noting that since the credit crunch it has been harder (especially for first-time buyers) to get an interest-only mortgage and this is understandable. There is a max pressure at the end of the 25-year period to be able to repay the bank the capital still owing – which by the way doesn't have to be 25 years! Lenders might (I say *might*) give you an interest-only mortgage if you can show them a great plan to prove that you will have enough money to repay them in 25 years, based on your level of savings and a consistent income over that period.

EXERCISE

Use a calculator to determine how much you will have to pay every month on your mortgage:
moneyadviceservice.org.uk/en/tools/mortgage-calculator

Price of the property: £ . . . .

Your deposit: £ . . . .

Mortgage term: . . . . years

If you have a repayment mortgage, monthly mortgage cost:
£ . . . .

If you have an interest-only mortgage, monthly mortgage cost:
£ . . . .

The calculator will also give you the updated monthly payment in case your interest rate goes up by 3% repayment £ . . . . or interest-only £ . . . .

Whichever mortgage you have in place (interest-only or repayment) you can choose how your monthly payments are calculated by choosing between a fixed rate, a variable rate mortgage and a tracker mortgage.

- **Fixed rate mortgage:** With this type of mortgage you have the certainty of paying the same amount of money each month for a period of time, between two and ten years, regardless of how interest rates are moving in the meantime. This type of mortgage is obviously helpful for your budget because you will know how much you have to pay monthly. Of course there is always a trick, and rates on fixed rate mortgages tend to be higher than with variable rate mortgages because of this guarantee of how much you will pay: this usually has a cost for the lender and if rates go down you would still be paying the same. At the end of the period you will be put on a *standard variable rate* (SVR – see below) which can be much higher, so then it may be time to look for a new mortgage.

- **Variable rate mortgage:** With this the interest rate can change at any time, so your mortgage payments can go up if and when interest rates increase and go down when interest rates decrease.

- **Tracker mortgages:** These move directly in line with the Bank of England's base rate. They have become quite popular because interest rates are low. So it will cost you less when the base rate is low but your repayments can also go up if this increases. There is a lot more uncertainty than with the fixed rate regarding future payments. As of February 2019, the base rate is 0.75% and banks add a few percentage points above the tracker to determine your cost of borrowing.

You can check the current base rate on the Bank of England website: **bankofengland.co.uk/boeapps/database/Bank-Rate.asp**

- **SVR mortgages:** SVR or standard variable rate is the rate lenders charge you for the loan. With this sort of mortgage they can decide to move the rate over time, usually following the BoE's base rate. That's not very helpful for budgeting. It can also be quite risky for you in case interest rates go up a lot and you are in a position where you can't afford your monthly repayments.

  There are, however, three other types of variable rate mortgages: **discount mortgages** offer a discount on the lender's SVR – although not to the base rate. Remember that banks fix their SVR for two to three years. **Capped rate mortgages** move in line with the lender's SVR up to a cap, so the rate can't rise above a certain level. **Offset mortgages** link your savings to your mortgage, so you only pay interest on the balance between mortgage and interest.

Visit the Money Advice Service website for more details on all these mortgages: **moneyadviceservice.org.uk/en/articles/mortgage-interest-rate-options**

How do I choose one mortgage over another?

There is no right or wrong answer. Choosing a variable over a fixed rate mortgage is a difficult choice and a very personal one (unless you have a crystal ball that can predict the interest rates for the next 25 years, in which case, please share it with all of us). Fixed rates can be more expensive but they give you this amazing visibility of how much you will be paying over the years. Variable rates can cost less (for now...or never) but they can put you in a very difficult situation if interest rates go through the roof as you will become exposed to potentially very high monthly payments. You need to consider whether you will you be able to service such a debt. Do you have the spare cash?

With mortgages there is again this relation of risk and return. With fixed rates, you choose more certainty so less risk, but potentially a lower return. However with variable rates, you choose a higher return but this has a higher risk. How much are you ready to swallow? Take an informed decision and live with it!

This is a really crucial area where advice from a mortgage broker is invaluable. The same goes for the mortgage term.

COUPLES AND MORTGAGES

Obviously you can get a bigger mortgage, and usually deposit, if you buy a home with your partner or someone else (friends, family... from two to four people). Both your names will be on the mortgage agreement (this is called a Joint Mortgage) and you are both responsible for making repayments. If the other party can't make the repayment, you are also liable and will have to come up with the money. This could also have an impact on your credit score, as you become associated financially with someone who has bad credit . You don't have to own the same percentage of the house, and that also affects how much you will need to pay off.

In order to decide how much you will be able to borrow, lenders will look at your combined income. So, if you earn £35,000 and your partner £50,000, it's £85,000 combined and the lender could lend you about *up to* five times this amount, or £425,000 (vs. £175,000 on your own, on very rough calculations).

Of course buying with a partner can often seem sensible, but there are disadvantages as well as advantages. Pros: sharing a mortgage can help you get on the property ladder and make the purchase cheaper because you would be sharing the mortgage costs, and also maintenance and bills. Cons: You are both responsible for making the payments and if one can't or doesn't want to pay anymore (for example, they lost their job or want to purchase another property), this can affect both your credit history. The golden rule is: you need to trust the person you are taking a mortgage with.

Remember that you are *both* responsible for your mortgage payments and you *both* have to decide to either keep or sell the property (at a certain price), so you need to be on the same page...

Shop around

Do you know how much time we spend trying to find a mortgage versus other purchases? According to a recent study by Noodle,[135] while a mortgage is usually our biggest purchase ever we research our options for just 3.6 days (compared to 6 days for a new car and 5 days for a holiday)! Are we missing out on the best deals just because the research bores us? The research also highlighted that one in four mortgage holders didn't shop around *at all*, which probably means we're likely to miss out on getting the mortgage that's best for us.

Now that you have a better idea of how mortgages work and how much you would need to borrow, you can start the hard work of convincing the lender to actually give you the money you need on the best terms.

1 . Prepare your paperwork and build a strong case

Don't worry about asking for money – a lenders role is to lend money so you should not feel uncomfortable. The money you borrow will not even touch your account – it will go directly to the seller, so it has a definite purpose.

Depending on your personal situation (an employee or self-employed?) you will need to build up a case to show exactly why you can afford to borrow. Lenders will want full details of your employment/self-employment, your existing loans or credit card debts, bank account details and, of course, full details of the property you want to buy.

This is usually the information you will need to have handy: payslips, P60, bank statements. If you are working part time you may be earning less than someone full time and that can affect how much you can borrow, but you will be asked for the same documents as full-time employees.

For the self-employed securing a mortgage was traditionally a headache-and-a-half. Thankfully, the market is responding to the shift in work patterns and self-employed people nowadays have more mortgage options than ever before. You will need to get that paperwork prepped – you'll need to have two or three years' worth of accounts, as well as any associated tax calculations at the ready, as well as your Self Assessment tax return. Some lenders will consider your application if you are able to provide evidence of regular work, or that you have work lined up for the future. Unfortunately, banks may be more hesitant to lend to people who are self-employed because it's a bigger risk than lending money to those who can show they are full-time employees.

Lenders will also check personal details: they will want to verify who you are and where you have lived for the past three years, so be prepared to show valid ID and official paperwork (council tax, utility bills, bank statements).

Lenders will review all the documentation you send and they will also have additional questions that you will need to answer. You will usually have a meeting with the lender (or your mortgage broker if you have one) and they will ask about your understanding of the mortgage, and your capacity to borrow based on the documentation you provided. The goal of the meeting is to really understand if you can afford the money you are about to borrow. You should feel confident that you can and use the opportunity to ask all the questions you have.

2. Submit your application

Mortgage agreements are really finicky legal documents, so try to fill in all the forms as carefully and comprehensively as you would a passport application. When asked to enter your name, include middle names. When asked for previous addresses with the dates you lived there, be precise and give as much detail as possible. Get all your paperwork together – the payslips and details of employment. You must check and re-check everything *yourself* to be sure there are no mistakes. If you are working with a mortgage broker, he or she won't generally send borrowers a copy of the application; he or she has to check it for you. Finally, once you've started an application don't start tinkering with the figures if, e.g., you suddenly decide you want to borrow more. This can cause unnecessary hold-ups, so be sure of what you want before you set the process in motion.

3. The lender also needs to value your property

This is usually a formality to enable them to compare the amount you've requested with the price of the property. Hopefully all will be well, but do be aware that mortgage lenders are often less willing to lend against properties that might prove difficult to re-sell, should you default on your repayments; these can include flats above commercial premises or old buildings. Allow plenty of time for this process to take place. This transaction can take up to a few weeks.

4. The lender has accepted...or not

If all is well, the lender will write to you and your solicitor (and your mortgage adviser, if you have one) confirming how much money they are prepared to give you and under what conditions. You will see on this letter all the details of the loan, and the monthly payments from now and for the term of the loan. Read that small print!

If your application is turned down, you will naturally want to know why: it could be that you don't have enough money saved as yet or that you're not on the electoral register. Whatever the reason, don't be too disheartened. It's just a bump in the road. You can change all these contributing factors and try again in a little while.

5. The lender will issue a formal Mortgage Offer

Big moment! Copies will be issued to the borrower, their solicitor and, if relevant, their mortgage broker.

6. Ready to move in? Conveyancing

Your offer has been accepted: that's awesome but there is still some work to do and more parties have to get involved. You can now start the legal process of *'conveyancing'*: transferring a property from one person to another (see page 334).

The solicitor will also look at local authority searches. These are important because they include all the information relating to the area surrounding the property (for example, large developments nearby, road maintenance, planned new train tracks) collected and researched by the local authority. He or she can then send the Report on Title to the lender and arrange for the property to be placed under your name. This process can take four to six weeks.

GAZUMPING, GAZUNDERING AND GAZANGING: FUN WORDS, NOT FUN PROCESSES

Imagine you've put in an offer for a property, done *all* the paperwork and started the searches and...the seller pulls out for some reason, usually because of a higher offer! You've just been 'gazumped'. This is legal as no contract has been signed yet but it is extremely frustrating and infuriating.

Now imagine you are the seller, and you are in the quite advanced stages of negotiation with the buyers but they drop their offer just before exchanging contracts. You are usually left with no offer or something lower, and the sale may never happen. This is called 'gazundering'.

'Gazanging' happens when a seller decides against selling the property at all and leaves the buyer 'hanging'.

7. The exchange

This is the last step of the process. All parties are happy with the sale and you can fix exchange and completion dates. At this point you need to be 100% sure of your wish to purchase otherwise you will lose your deposit and legal costs incurred. You have to pay a deposit (usually 5% to 10% of the property price) before you exchange contracts. Things are serious – you've just made your biggest transfer of money. Cheers! 😎

8. Completion

You receive a completion statement from the solicitor that also lists all the money you still need to pay: outstanding deposit, stamp duty (within 30 days of completion, through your conveyancer or directly), and legal fees (see below). These will have to be paid on completion date which is also the day you finally receive the keys!

Well done, the place is yours!

The 'Hidden' Costs of Buying

Keep in mind the *cost* of buying a home: fees can run into the thousands and you'll probably have to pay stamp duty too. The actual cost is not only the price you've seen in the real estate leaflet but a lot of other upfront fees (which we've mentioned as part of the buying process):

- *Stamp duty*: Most people will have to pay this tax on the purchase, if your property is valued at over £125,000. Make sure you check the current rules but at the moment, first time buyers are entitled to tax relief for the first £300,000 of stamp duty on properties up to a value of £500,000 (no relief if the property you buy is worth more than £500,000). For properties above £500,000 you have to pay stamp duty.

- *The deposit*: This is not really a fee because it is part of the purchase price, but you will have to pay it upfront. It is normally at least 5% of the purchase price.

- *Legal fees*: The whole buying process costs money and you will need some help from a solicitor. This can total about £750–£1,500.

- *Council searches*: These are required for information such as planning applications and road information. This can be about £200–£300.

- *Surveys*: Once you have found the property, you need to arrange surveys. There are three types: basic/valuation (usually the minimum as carried out by the lender), homebuyers' (for example, checking for things like damp and subsidence) and full structural. Full structural surveys are generally recommended for houses, with homebuyers' surveys perhaps more suitable for flats.

- *Fees on mortgage*: According to MoneySupermarket[136] you will sometimes need to pay a booking fee (£50–300) but not always, an arrangement fee (a fixed sum of £2,000–3,000 or a percentage of the mortgage value) and a mortgage valuation fee (that is dependent on the price of the property).

- *Broker's fees*: Depending on the agreement you have with your broker you may have to pay him/her a fixed fee of £300–£500 or a percentage of the loan.

- *Land registry fee*: This fee is in order to register the property under your name (up to £500).

- *Moving costs*: Have you thought about this one? If this is your first home there is a chance you won't have a lot to move. Even if you are a Marie Kondo decluttering addict, there is a cost to rent a van to move your stuff or hire people to do it for you (this will range from a few hundred to a few thousand pounds!).

EXERCISE

Check the stamp duty calculator from the Money Advice Service: **moneyadviceservice.org.uk/en/tools/house-buying/stamp-duty-calculator**

For a property valued at £ ....

I will pay a stamp duty of £ ....

I will pay a deposit of £ ....

Other fees £ ....

Other fees £ ....

Other fees £ ....

Taking Care of Your New Home

Home sweet home...almost!

Once the property is yours, it is very important that you consider whether you will be able to keep it should anything unfortunate happen. You are responsible for your home from now on. Life cover should be considered (sometimes it is required by the mortgage) as well as buildings insurance (especially for freehold property).

If you don't have any savings left by the time you move in – because, yes, we get trapped in additional costs and buying a new sofa for the house – don't forget to *start saving* again to replenish your emergency fund. Because it's *your* home, any potential repairs and incidents (such as replacing the boiler, fixing a leaking roof 😢) are now coming out of *your* pocket.

How will you pay your mortgage?

It's a fact of life that interest rates fluctuate. They are set by the Bank of England and there's nothing you can do to escape these tricky figures. However, there are a few things you can do to buffer yourself against the worst impact of rising rates:

1. Make sure you know exactly what type of mortgage you have as this will affect your exposure to changing interest rates.
2. When your mortgage term comes to its end, you're going to have to get a new one, and one thing that will really help future-proof your life is *having and maintaining a healthy credit score*, so keep in mind what it looks like to be a healthy and responsible credit card user! Pay as much into your mortgage as you can before the rates change, even if it's more than your monthly plan. This is one area where overpaying is good!
3. If the worst happens and you find your mortgage payments going up a lot, don't be complacent. Take an honest look at your budget. Consult a debt adviser (refer to Chapter 2 or our Little Black Book of Finances on

page 362 for advice on getting help with debt). Talk to your family and partner about what's going on. *Whatever you do, don't ignore your worry* because it'll only escalate. I know it's hard to face financial insecurity but if you confront it now, it will feel so much more manageable (albeit still a pain in the neck) this time next year.

 REMORTGAGING?

You may have heard this term since one third of mortgages in the UK are remortgages[137]. A remortgage is a new mortgage on an existing property you own. It's not a second mortgage! It is used because you want to replace the existing mortgage or take a new mortgage against your property.

You may want to remortgage for a few reasons: you have an old deal and you think you could get better terms and save money, or maybe you've been paying interest only and now want to start repaying the capital, or you want to borrow more to build a new extension, for example.

When remortgaging, always make sure you do the maths and understand all the fees associated with repaying an old mortgage and getting a new one. You will almost certainly be charged an exit fee or early repayment fee on one hand, but you also have to pay the fees associated with your new mortgage. Also make sure you can afford the new terms of the mortgage.

Should I overpay my mortgage?

This is a question I am often asked: 'Should I use my spare cash to pay back more of my mortgage?' I can't tell you if this is what you should be doing, but the positives are that it helps to remove some money from your bank account so you can't spend it, and you could significantly reduce your future payments.

Check the terms of your mortgage, but usually you can overpay up to 10% of your mortgage balance each year, without paying a penalty (check the small print on your contract for further conditions), helping reduce your monthly interest bill. It's not always possible and you may have to pay a penalty to do so. At the moment interest rates are low, so you have to ask yourself if this is the best option or if you could do something better with your money (like contributing more into your pension or investing money).

If you want to use a calculator, go to MoneySavingExpert.com: **moneysavingexpert.com/mortgages/mortgages-vs-savings/**.

What About Buy-to-let?

Buy-to-let is, surprise surprise, buying a property to rent it out to tenants. It is a long-term investment that you hope will pay you some income over time. Just as with buying a home, there is some risk involved: property prices can go up and down and there are risks associated with renting too (i.e. tenants not paying their rent or damaging the property) and you must also consider the costs linked to managing the property.

You can pay for a residential property with your savings or get a buy-to-let mortgage with a deposit. As stated above, taking a mortgage involves some risk and you want to make sure the value of the property will be more than the outstanding balance on the mortgage at the end of the term. There is also an additional risk of not finding tenants for a period of time, in which case you would have to pay for your monthly mortgage payments, but receive no income from the property.

This is how you hope to make money from a buy-to-let: your tenants pay you a rent and you pay all the maintenance and running costs, repairs, etc. And just like buying a house you hope that the price of the property will increase in the future and you will make a profit.

Remember that, when there is money earned, there are taxes to be paid! Since April 2017, the legislation changed regarding how landlords account for and pay taxes for their buy-to-let investments. They used to be able to deduct their mortgage payments from the rent they were receiving and pay taxes on the balance, but today they have to pay taxes on the rental income (fully implemented from April 2020).[138] The landlord is then given a new tax credit, helping to reduce this tax bill, but less generously than the previous regime (always check the new tax rules on the gov.uk website.[139]

Buy-to-let mortgages

Beware! Mortgages designed for landlords (buy-to-let mortgages) are not the same as mortgages designed for homeowners (residential mortgages). These are the main differences according to MAS:[140] the fees as well as the interest rates with buy-to-let are much higher. Most buy-to-let mortgages are interest-only. This means you only pay interest each month, but at the end of the mortgage term, you repay the capital in full.

Please visit **gov.uk/browse/housing-local-services/owning-renting-property** to help decide if this is for you.

Well Done! You have earnt coins!

We've negotiated the famously murky waters of estate agents, mortgage brokers and sellers without being gazumped! Whether you're seeking to buy a property to live in forever or to flip, or, as with most of us, just as a place to call home for as long as life stays the way it is now (which is goodness knows how long), you're now well equipped to start the journey.

It's never going to be plain sailing – there's a good reason why people always say that buying and selling houses is one of life's mega stress-inducers. There can be so many false starts and disappointments along the way, then, when you do finally have a place to call your own, it's only human nature to start wondering whether you made a good decision.

Whatever property you buy, celebrate your achievement. Now you just have to learn how to assemble those flat-pack wardrobes...

Money Talk
with Claer Barrett

Job: Personal Finance Editor at the *Financial Times* and editor of 'FT Money', Claer broadcasts daily on LBC radio.

Fun fact: Claer writes excellent, personal and relatable pieces about money for the *Financial Times*. A financial literacy advocate, she regularly comes up with radical ideas for the investment industry to encourage people to make better financial decisions.

Money motto: *'We need to talk about money.'*

What makes you happy?
Spending as little as possible on the things that don't matter, so I have as much as possible to spend on the things that do, like holidays with my extended family.

What is your most treasured possession?
Happy memories of a life (hopefully) well spent. I spend a lot of time turning our digital pics into photo albums, and writing little stories about all the things we've done together.

What is the best money advice you have ever received?
We need to talk about money much more. It is slowly becoming less of a taboo, but much of the financial world's profit margin boils down to consumer ignorance. Few of us can afford a financial adviser – especially younger people – but there is a wealth of information out there. Don't be afraid of asking questions .

What is your biggest money failure/mistake?
Not starting a workplace pension in my first 'proper' job. I thought I'd only be there for a year or two – I ended up staying for seven years.

What is your greatest money achievement?
Buying a flat in a deeply unfashionable part of east London 15 years ago, which has now more than trebled in value. Although this 'achievement' has more to do with the financial crisis and the effects of quantitative easing than any great genius on my part.

What is your greatest money regret or fear?
I am the main breadwinner in my household, and I do all the family money. So if I get hit by a bus, they're all doomed! I do spend a lot of time educating my stepchildren about money matters, and I have a huge life insurance policy (but please don't tell my husband in case he gets any ideas).

What is your top money hack?
Never buy anything from an online retailer without looking up the name of the shop and 'discount code' in a separate window. Saves me money every time. And make your packed lunch the night before to save time in the morning!

Who is your go-to person to talk about money?
Paul Lewis and Martin Lewis [financial commentators] do a brilliant job of explaining the basics, and the industry's many failings, but Merryn Somerset Webb is one of the few people who can do this well on the topic of investment.

Who are your inspiring heroes?
It can only be my parents. Growing up, we had hardly any money, but they taught me to use it well – and not be a slave to it.

What is your favourite book?
Anything that involves a grisly murder, a dogged detective and some unexpected plot twists.

What is your best property-buying tip?
People say you should 'buy the worst house on the best street' but unless you are seriously into DIY, don't do it. A friend did this, and has been stressed, miserable and skint, living in a building site for three years. Don't rush to 'get on the ladder' with an unsuitable property in a place you don't want to live. Save a little longer. Aim to buy once, and buy well – with stamp duty, moving house costs a huge amount of money.

What do you wish you had done earlier in terms of financial planning?
Everything! But nobody has life figured out at the age of 21. I feel lucky that I managed to get reasonably on top of things at the age of 30, rather than 50. Financial planning is a dangerous thing to ignore the longer you leave it. Getting into the savings habit as early as you can is the key.

Let's Continue Our £££ Conversation

I hope *You're Not Broke You're Pre-Rich* will help you to overcome any fear of looking money in the eye and make you excited about starting to write your own £££ story.

Remember that rules change all of the time. The *UK Budget* set by HM Treasury takes place every year (usually in Autumn) with an important announcement for the following year in terms of taxes, personal allowances, and so on. Keep an eye out on the Government website: **gov.uk/money/personal-tax**

The Vestpod community and I will always be here for you, so if you have a question and want to continue our money conversation, you can follow me on Instagram **@vestpod** and register on **vestpod.com** for events, workshops, updated information and additional content.

I wish you well on your money journey. You really *are* in control of your financial future 🤩.

With love,
Emilie xx

Vestpod Jargon Buster

This mini money jargon buster in plain English will help you navigate the world of finance. I will revise this list regularly on vestpod.com.

Active investing: When a professional is picking investments and trying to beat the market (opposite of *passive investing*).

Annual allowance: The maximum savings you can pay into a pension – in a year – that qualifies for *tax relief*.

Annuity: A type of retirement product that will provide a regular income for the rest of your retirement/life.

AER/APR: AER (Annual Equivalent Rate) is the percentage of interest earned on savings or investments whereas APR (Annual Percentage Rate) is the percentage of interest and fees you pay on a loan (e.g. credit cards).

Assets: What you own (opposite of *liabilities*).

Asset classes: Things you can invest in, such as property, *shares*, *bonds*, cash, etc.

Asset allocation: The way you decide to spread your money over different *asset classes*.

Automatic enrolment: The obligation for employers to automatically enrol their eligible workers in a pension scheme.

Bond: A loan to a company or a government.

Capital Gains (Tax): When you sell an asset for more than you paid for it. If this is a positive number you usually have to pay tax on it, called the Capital Gains Tax.

Contributions: What you and/or your employer actually put into your pension.

Compound interest: Interest on interest.

Credit score: The result of a credit report. It gives financial institutions an indication of your financial health and the likelihood that you will default on (not be able to repay) a loan.

Crowdfunding: Process by which projects or start-ups raise funding from a lot of people investing small amounts of money.

Debt: The amount of money you owe. When you borrow money, you have to repay it with interest (credit card debt, loan, *mortgage*, etc.).

Defined contribution pension: A pension pot that is built up using your *contributions* and your employer's contributions (if applicable) plus investment returns and *tax relief*.

Dividend: Payments made by companies to their shareholders (i.e. the ones who hold *shares*).

Emergency fund: A pot of cash savings that is always available and will literally save you in case you need to pay for something urgently.

ETF (Exchange Traded Fund): A fund that is similar to *unit trusts or OEICs* but the difference is that ETFs are traded on a stock exchange, just like company *shares*.

FCA (Financial Conduct Authority): The regulator of financial services in the UK.

Financial plan: Your very personal ongoing plan/process that you develop on your own or with a financial adviser to help you achieve your financial goals.

Fund: A pool of money invested in a wide range of *assets*.

Fund manager: Someone who manages investments on behalf of others (like you).

Gilts: A type of *bond* issued by the government to raise money.

Index fund (also called an index tracker): A type of fund or *ETF* that tracks the performance of a stock market index. Index funds are passive.

IFA (Independent Financial Adviser): A person who gives you advice on your finances. They are regulated and approved by the FCA.

Inflation: The measurement of how the prices of goods and services in the economy are moving over time.

Interest rate: A percentage of a loan (the cost of what you borrow) or deposits (the gain on what you save).

Investing: Putting your money to work with the expectation of increasing your capital, usually by taking some risk.

Investment trusts: Listed companies with *shares* that trade on the stock market. They invest in shares and/or *bonds* of other companies with the money they raise.

ISAs (Individual Savings Accounts): A tax-free way to save money.

Liabilities: What you owe, your *debts* and other unpaid bills.

Life insurance: A type of insurance that pays money when you die to your beneficiary.

Mis-selling: When bad advice is given to you and you buy a financial product on that basis.

Mortgage: The money you borrow when you buy a property, in exchange for which you pay the bank an amount every month in the form of interest and repay the money borrowed at the end of the term.

Net worth: The difference between what you own and what you owe (*assets* minus *liabilities*).

Payday loan: A short-term, expensive loan – usually repaid at the next payday.

Passive investing: Investing strategy that tracks, i.e. mimics, the performance of the market (opposite of *active investing*).

Personal allowance: How much of your income you don't pay tax on.

Portfolio: A mix of investments in different *asset classes*, much better when diversified!

PPI (Payment Protection Insurance): A product designed to cover repayments on, e.g., mortgages or credit cards, if something goes wrong and you become unable to meet your financial obligations. These products have been mis-sold to millions of consumers (see *mis-selling*).

Principal: The amount you still have to repay on a debt or loan.

Premium bonds: Issued by National Savings and Investment (NS&I), these are bonds that don't pay regular, fixed interest but interest on the bonds is distributed in monthly cash prizes.

Rebalancing: Bringing back your portfolio to its initial *asset allocation* of *bonds* and *shares*.

Return: The profit you make on an investment (it can be positive or negative i.e. loss).

Risk (or rather, risk tolerance): Investing is risky. Risk is the chance of you losing the money that you invested. When you want higher potential returns, you usually have to take more risks.

Remortgaging: Taking a new mortgage (with new terms and usually a higher *principal*) on a property you already own, which can allow you to pay off some of your existing *mortgage* and in some cases release equity (take some cash out).

Robo-adviser: Online platform that will help you invest your money or will do it for you. Some of them also provide financial advice.

SIPP (Self-Invested Personal Pension): A type of personal pension. It is an individual contract between you and the pension provider. This type of pension lets you invest anywhere you like and choose your own investments.

Stamp duty (for Stamp Duty Land Tax or SDLT): The taxes you have to pay to the UK government when you purchase a property (that costs more than a certain amount).

Shares: See *Stocks and shares*.

State pension: The pension you recieve from the government when you reach state pension age.

Stocks and shares (also known as equities): When you buy stocks or *shares* you are buying a piece of a company and become a shareholder of it.

Tax code: A personal code provided by HMRC that tells your employer how much tax you should pay.

Tax relief: When you pay less tax on, e.g., pension contributions or self-employed business expenses.

Unit trust (also called OEICs/Open-Ended Investment Companies): A pool of money invested in *shares* and/or *bonds* – this is what investors usually call a *fund*.

Vestpod: Your 'inVESTment POD'. Good vibes only. **vestpod.com**

Volatility: How prices of *assets* move over time: when prices move a lot or very quickly the market is said to be volatile.

Vestpod Little Black Book of Finances

Wow, you've done it 🤑! Hopefully you want to learn more, so I have put together this Little Black Book which is a careful curation of my personal finance universe. You will find tools, sites, resources, books and apps but also the inspiration to go further and build your own financial world. I will be keeping this list live and updated on **vestpod.com**, so please don't hesitate to send me your suggestions. This is a fast-moving world, so stay tuned!

Pre-Rich Websites

- Go-to website for everything you want to know about money: Money and Pensions Service (**moneyadviceservice.org.uk**) and MoneySavingExpert by Martin Lewis (**moneysavingexpert.com**)
- Regulation and pensions: Money and Pensions Service (**pensionsadvisoryservice.org.uk**), UK government website (**gov.uk**)
- Price comparison websites: Compare the Market (**comparethemarket.com**), MoneySupermarket (**moneysupermarket.com**), Go Compare (**gocompare.com**)
- Financial news: *Financial Times*, *New York Times* money, Bloomberg, Morningstar, Monevator, MoneyWise, Boring Money, investment platforms and robo-advisers' websites, personal finance blogs

Finding an adviser: Personal recommendations, but also Unbiased (**unbiased.co.uk**) and VouchedFor (**vouchedfor.co.uk**)

Dealing with debt: Citizens Advice (**citizensadvice.org.uk**), StepChange Debt Charity (**stepchange.org**), National Debtline (**nationaldebtline.org**), PayPlan (**payplan.com**), and Mental Health & Money Advice (**mentalhealthandmoneyadvice.org**)

Pre-Rich Books

Money

The 100-Year Life: Living and Working in an Age of Longevity, Lynda Gratton and Andrew Scott

Money Master the Game: 7 Simple Steps to Financial Freedom, Tony Robbins

Your Money or Your Life, Vicki Robin and Joe Dominguez

Rich Dad Poor Dad, Robert T. Kiyosaki

You Are a Badass at Making Money: Master the Mindset of Wealth, Jen Sincero

Career/Negotiation/Entrepreneurship

Getting to Yes, Roger Fisher and William Ury

Becoming, Michelle Obama

The Business Romantic, Tim Leberecht

Shoe Dog, Phil Knight

Mindset: Changing The Way You think To Fulfil Your Potential, Dr Carol Dweck

A Good Time to Be a Girl by Helena Morrissey

Never Split the Difference by Chris Voss

Investing

The Essays of Warren Buffett, Warren Buffett, also available online: **berkshirehathaway.com/letters/letters.html**

The Little Book of Common Sense Investing, John C. Bogle

The Intelligent Investor, Benjamin Graham (advanced)

Pre-Rich TED Talks

Tammy Lally, Let's get honest about our money problems

Adam Carroll, When money isn't real: the $10,000 experiment

Bill and Melinda Gates, Why giving away our wealth has been the most satisfying thing we've done

Pre-Rich Apps

- Neo-banks: Starling, Monzo, Revolut, N26
- Budgeting: YNAB, Money Dashboard, Yolt, Moneyhub, Bud, Cleo, Bean, Emma, Spendee, Mint (US)
- Pay-off debt: Pariti
- Automated saving only: Squirrel, Chip, Plum
- Investing by auto-saving small amounts: MoneyBox, Oval Money, Plum
- Robo-advisers: Nutmeg, Scalable Capital, Moneyfarm, WealthSimple, Wealthify, PensionBee, Moola
- Investing platforms: AJ Bell YouInvest, Vanguard, Fidelity, Hargreaves Lansdown
- Exchange money into other currencies: Transferwise, Revolut
- Send and receive money easily: PayPal, Revolut

Pre-Rich Podcasts

- Money: *FT Money* podcast, *Secrets of Wealthy Women* (WSJ), *Planet Money* (NPR)
- Entrepreneurship/Inspo: *Ctrl Alt Delete*, Emma Gannon; *Boss Files*, Poppy Harlow (CNN); *How I Built This*, Guy Raz; *The Entrepreneurs*, Monocle; Tony Robbins podcast; *The 20 Minute VC*, Harry Stebbings; *Super Soul Conversations,* Oprah

Pre-Rich Calculators

Pension: **moneyadviceservice.org.uk/en/tools/pension-calculator**

Inflation:
bankofengland.co.uk/monetary-policy/inflation/inflation-calculator

Compound interest: **monevator.com/compound-interest-calculator/**

Overpaying your mortgage or saving money:
moneysavingexpert.com/mortgages/mortgages-vs-savings/

Pre-Rich Events and Workshops

See **Vestpod.com** for upcoming events and workshops.

Bonus Resource

We have a little bonus gift for you, so go to the website and enter your email address to subrscribe to our newsletter. We will then send you an additional chapter on Alternative investing: cryptocurrencies and angel investing. Get it here: **Vestpod.com/secretbonus**

Index

E

F

N

O

P

Endnotes

Chapter 1:

1 https://www.psychologytoday.com/files/attachments/34772/money-beliefs-and-financial-behaviors-development-the-klontz-money-script-inventory-jft-2011.pdf

2 https://www.moneyadviceservice.org.uk/en

3 'Habit Formation and Learning in Young Children', authored by behaviour experts at Cambridge University

4 Dweck, Dr Carol (2012) *Mindset: Changing The Way You think To Fulfil Your Potential*, Robinson.

5 https://www.cambridge.org/us/academic/subjects/psychology/social-psychology/employment-and-unemployment-social-psychological-analysis?format=PB&isbn=9780521285865

6 https://hbr.org/2016/09/how-to-talk-to-your-kids-about-money-when-you-have-a-lot-of-it

7 https://www.nih.gov/news-events/news-releases/human-brain-appears-hard-wired-hierarchy

8 http://www.natsal.ac.uk/natsal-3.aspx

9 https://www.independent.co.uk/news/science/talking-about-money-is-britains-last-taboo-10508902.html

10 https://www.moneyadviceservice.org.uk/en/corporate/uk-couples-financial-secrets-revealed

11 http://www.stateofourunions.org/2009/bank_on_it.php#_ftn9

12 https://www.fidelity.com/bin-public/060_www_fidelity_com/documents/couples-retirement-fact-sheet.pdf

13 https://www.payscale.com/about/press-releases/new-payscale-study-reveals-employees-perceptions-pay-fairness-transparency-five-times-impactful-engagement-actual-compensation

14 http://psychclassics.yorku.ca/Maslow/motivation.htm

15 The Notorious B.I.G, Artista (released 15 July 1997).

16 http://www.pnas.org/content/107/52/22463/tab-article-info

17 http://worldhappiness.report/ed/2018/ (UN Sustainable Development Solutions Network)

18 https://www.ncbi.nlm.nih.gov/pmc/articles/PMC2824994/#CIT1

19 https://www.psychologytoday.com/gb/basics/dopamine

20 https://www.elle.com/fashion/shopping/a41845/shopping-dopamine/

21 https://www.cam.ac.uk/research/news/spending-for-smiles-money-can-buy-happiness-after-all

22 https://research.cornell.edu/news-features/intriguing-human-behavior

23 https://news.sfsu.edu/contrary-expectations-life-experiences-better-use-money-material-items

24 https://www.princeton.edu/~deaton/downloads/deaton_kahneman_high_income_improves_evaluation_August2010.pdf

25 https://yourmoneyoryourlife.com/book-summary/

26 Anik, L., L. B. Aknin, M. I. Norton, and E. W. Dunn. 'Feeling Good about Giving: The Benefits (and Costs) of Self-interested Charitable Behavior.' In *The Science of Giving: Experimental Approaches to the Study of Charity*, edited by D. M. Oppenheimer and C. Y. Olivola. Psychology Press, 2010. [Accessed 14 January 2019: https://www.hbs.edu/faculty/Pages/item.aspx?num=36778]

27 https://greatergood.berkeley.edu/images/uploads/Simpson-AltruismReciprocity.pdf

Chapter 2:

28 https://directory.rockstarfinance.com/personal-finance-blogs/

29 https://www.ons.gov.uk/peoplepopulationandcommunity/personalandhouseholdfinances/incomeandwealth/bulletins/wealthingreatbritainwave5/2014to2016

30 Allen, Lily, *My Thoughts Exactly* (Blink Publishing, 2018)

31 Available with Noddle and CrealScore

32 https://www.nao.org.uk/wp-content/uploads/2018/09/Tackling-problem-debt-Report.pdf

33 https://themoneycharity.org.uk/media/August-2018-Money-Statistics.pdf

34 https://www.rsph.org.uk/uploads/assets/uploaded/75b46b96-10e8-48a3-bc597f3d65d91566.pdf

35 In the UK, two excellent sources of advice are: Citizens Advice: https://www.citizensadvice.org.uk and StepChange https://www.stepchange.org/, formerly known as the Consumer Debt Counselling Service.

36 https://www.ifs.org.uk/publications/9334

37 If your undergraduate degree course started before 1 September 2012, you will have a Plan 1 loan that you will start to pay back when you earn more than £18,330. Plan 2 Loans are paid back once you start to earn £25,000 or over.

38 https://www.citizensadvice.org.uk/debt-and-money/help-with-debt/get-help-with-your-debts/get-help-with-your-debts/

39 According to TransferWise.

40 FCA: https://www.fca.org.uk/consumers/finding-adviser. The FCA register: https://register.fca.org.uk

41 https://www.ft.com/content/bd99a084-9c84-11e8-9702-5946bae86e6d

42 https://www.fca.org.uk/publication/corporate/famr-final-report.pdf

43 https://www.fca.org.uk/publication/data/data-bulletin-issue-13.pdf

44 https://www.moneyadviceservice.org.uk/en/articles/Guide-to-financial-adviser-fees

45 https://www.unbiased.co.uk/cost-of-financial-advice

46 https://register.fca.org.uk/

47 https://www.actionfraud.police.uk

Chapter 3:

48 http://images.mscomm.morningstar.com/Web/MorningstarInc/%7bb87a29d4-9264-4e6f-a5d7-5e65f8714f92%7d_US_ADV_MoreLess_Whitepaper_Final.pdf

49 The acronym first appeared in George T. Doran's article, 'There's a S.M.A.R.T. way to write management goals and objectives', *Management Review* (November 1981)

50 https://link.springer.com/article/10.1007/s13524-018-0651-1

51 http://news.cornell.edu/stories/2018/04/enough-income-and-wealth-cohabiting-couples-say-i-do

52 https://bridebook.co.uk/article/bridebook-wedding-report-2018

53 https://www.ifs.org.uk/publications/10506

54 http://www.100yearlife.com/

55 https://www.biba.org.uk/

56 https://www.moneywise.co.uk/insurance/life-insurance/mind-the-life-insurance-gap

57 https://www.citizensadvice.org.uk/family/death-and-wills/who-can-inherit-if-there-is-no-will-the-rules-of-intestacy/

58 https://www.gov.uk/government/publications/make-a-lasting-power-of-attorney

59 https://www.gov.uk/power-of-attorney/register

Chapter 4:

60 https://stories.usbank.com/dam/possibilityindex/USBankPossibilityIndex.pdf

61 https://news.gallup.com/poll/162872/one-three-americans-prepare-detailed-household-budget.aspx

62 https://www.psychologicalscience.org/news/releases/can-gratitude-reduce-costly-impatience.html and https://www.today.com/money/be-thankful-save-more-study-says-gratitude-helps-us-reach-1D79801892

63 Warren, Elizabeth and Warren Tyagi, Amelia, *All Your Worth: The Ultimate Lifetime Money Plan* (Free Press, 2006)

64 Try this one for starters: https://www.thesalarycalculator.co.uk/salary.php

65 Student loans repayment would have been taken out of your take home pay if you are fully employed.

66 https://www.daveramsey.com

67 Suggested by Kristin Wong: https://thegetmoneybook.com/save-money-and-time-with-the-1010-rule/

68 https://www.mrmoneymustache.com/about/

69 https://www.endsleigh.co.uk/press-releases/2nd-february-2018/

70 https://www.which.co.uk/news/2018/08/british-gas-pays-out-2-65-million-for-overcharging-customers/

71 https://www.moneyadviceservice.org.uk/blog/how-much-is-the-average-water-bill-per-month

72 http://www.energysavingtrust.org.uk/home-energy-efficiency/boiler-replacement

73 https://www.cse.org.uk/advice/advice-and-support/upgrading-your-boiler

74 https://www.ofcom.org.uk/__data/assets/pdf_file/0030/113898/pricing-report-2018.pdf

75 https://www.ofcom.org.uk/about-ofcom/latest/media/media-releases/2018/streaming-overtakes-pay-tv

76 https://motherboard.vice.com/en_us/article/3daaj5/how-much-money-do-people-spend-on-uber

77 https://www.npdgroup.co.uk/wps/portal/npd/uk/news/press-releases/the-unstoppable-rise-of-the-takeaway-delivery-phenomenon-means-the-market-is-now-worth-4-2-billion-up-73-in-a-decade/

78 https://www.npdgroup.co.uk/wps/portal/npd/uk/news/press-releases/the-unstoppable-rise-of-the-takeaway-delivery-phenomenon-means-the-market-is-now-worth-4-2-billion-up-73-in-a-decade/

79 https://www.home.barclaycard/media-centre/press-releases/longer-nights-tv-shows-and-rise-of-on-demand-services-fuel-vampire-economy.html

80 http://files.constantcontact.com/150f9af2201/1ade4980-7297-467a-86b5-d6a4b93371e4.pdf

81 https://www.zuora.com/resource/a-nation-subscribed-2017-state-of-the-uk-subscription-economy/

82 According to the British Coffee Association (Research conducted by the Centre for Economics and Business Research (CEBR)): https://cebr.com/reports/the-independent-brits-now-drinking-95-million-cups-of-coffee-per-day/

83 https://www.moneysavingexpert.com/reclaim/council-tax-bands-change/

Chapter 5:

84 https://hiring.careerbuilder.co.uk/news/almost-one-third-of-british-workers-live-paycheck-to-paycheck-careerbuilder.co.uk-survey-finds

85 https://www.lendingtree.com/finance/survey-44-of-100-149k-earners-live-paycheck-to-paycheck/

86 https://www.ons.gov.uk/peoplepopulationandcommunity/personalandhouseholdfinances/incomeandwealth/bulletins/theeffectsoftaxesandbenefitsonhouseholdincome/financialyearending2017

87 https://www.ifs.org.uk/publications/8429

88 https://www.glassdoor.com/research/new-study-best-countries-in-europe-for-workplace-gender-equality/

89 https://hbr.org/2018/06/research-women-ask-for-raises-as-often-as-men-but-are-less-likely-to-get-them

90 https://www.cii.co.uk/media/10120355/moments-that-matter-pensions-life-journey-for-women.pdf

91 https://hbr.org/2005/03/off-ramps-and-on-ramps-keeping-talented-women-on-the-road-to-success

92 https://hbr.org/2014/06/why-women-dont-negotiate-their-job-offers

93 https://hbr.org/2018/09/research-simple-prompts-can-get-women-to-negotiate-more-like-men-and-vice-versa

94 https://www.tandfonline.com/doi/pdf/10.1080/23743603.2017.1309876

95 https://www.gov.uk/tax-employee-share-schemes

96 http://time.com/5312483/how-to-deal-with-impostor-syndrome/

97 https://www.ons.gov.uk/employmentandlabourmarket/peopleinwork/employmentandemployeetypes/articles/trendsinselfemploymentintheuk/2018-02-07

98 https://hbr.org/2012/03/choosing-between-making-money

99 https://www.reed.co.uk/career-advice/part-time-pastimes-earn-brits-249-million-per-month/

Chapter 6:

100 https://www.gov.uk/apply-tax-free-interest-on-savings

101 At the moment, but look out for potential changes to legislation in the future.

102 It is important to note that there has been some speculation that due to their current unpopularity the lifetime ISAs may be scrapped.

103 https://www.ftadviser.com/auto-enrolment/2017/11/16/pension-default-fund-charge-cap-sticks-at-0-75/

104 https://www.moneyadviceservice.org.uk/en/tools/workplace-pension-contribution-calculator

105 https://pensionsdashboardproject.uk/

Chapter 7:

106 https://www.ons.gov.uk/economy/inflationandpriceindices

107 https://www.bankofengland.co.uk/monetary-policy/inflation/inflation-calculator

108 https://www.bankofengland.co.uk

109 https://www.cnbc.com/2017/10/24/blackrock-chair-larry-fink-tells-investors-to-only-expect-a-4-percent-investment-return-with-a-balanced-portfolio.html

Chapter 8:

110 https://www.hl.co.uk/news/articles/10-years-on-a-lesson-from-lehman

111 https://www.hl.co.uk/news/articles/10-years-on-a-lesson-from-lehman

112 'By and large, the findings of the empirical literature accord with recent experience; after fees and expenses, the average active equity fund underperforms the market portfolio over long horizons (eg Jenson (1968), Carhart (1997), Fama and French (2010), Busse et al. (2014))', https://www.bis.org/publ/qtrpdf/r_qt1803j.htm

113 https://www.barclays.co.uk/smart-investor/investments-explained/funds-etfs-and-investment-trusts/active-or-passive-funds/

114 https://www.theinvestmentassociation.org/assets/files/research/2018/20180913-fullsummary.pdf.pdf

115 Cambridge Dictionary.

116 https://www.nytimes.com/2012/08/12/business/john-bogle-vanguards-founder-is-too-worried-to-rest.html?module=inline

117 http://www.berkshirehathaway.com/letters/2013ltr.pdf

118 https://advisors.vanguard.com/VGApp/iip/site/advisor/etfcenter/article/ETF_HistoryOfETFs

119 https://www.which.co.uk/money/investing/types-of-investment/unit-trusts-and-oeics/are-fund-charges-eating-into-your-returns-as43q0j6wsrq

120 https://www.boringmoney.co.uk/learn/investing-guides/product-guides/robo-adviser/

121 https://www.investopedia.com/articles/investing/062714/100-minus-your-age-outdated.asp#ixzz5Yc5e5otB

122 https://www.investopedia.com/articles/investing/062714/100-minus-your-age-outdated.asp

123 https://www.investopedia.com/terms/m/modernportfoliotheory.asp

124 https://www.barclays.co.uk/smart-investor/news-and-research/investing-for-beginners/are-women-the-better-investors/

125 https://www.fidelity.com/about-fidelity/individual-investing/better-investor-men-or-women

126 https://faculty.haas.berkeley.edu/odean/papers%20current%20versions/behavior%20of%20individual%20investors.pdf

Chapter 9:

127 https://www.ifs.org.uk/publications/13268

128 https://www.ftadviser.com/mortgages/2018/10/08/younger-generations-suffer-from-173-rise-in-house-prices/

129 https://www.moneysavingexpert.com/mortgages/best-mortgages-cashback/

130 https://www.resolutionfoundation.org/publications/house-of-the-rising-son-or-daughter/

131 https://www.helptobuy.gov.uk/help-to-buy-isa/faq/

132 https://www.helptobuy.gov.uk/shared-ownership/

133 https://www.legalandgeneralgroup.com/media-centre/press-releases/bank-of-mum-and-dad-lending-needed-for-1-in-4-uk-housing-transactions-in-2018/

134 https://www.gov.uk/government/publications/home-ownership-access-to-first-time-buyers-in-the-uk

135 https://www.blog.noddle.co.uk/finance/mortgages/brits-spend-more-time-looking-for-a-holiday-than-a-mortgage/

136 https://www.moneysupermarket.com/mortgages/first-time-buyers/cost-of-buying-your-first-home/

137 https://www.moneysavingexpert.com/mortgages/why-remortgage/

138 https://www.which.co.uk/money/tax/income-tax/tax-on-property-and-rental-income/buy-to-let-mortgage-tax-relief-changes-explained-atnsv0j6j782

139 https://www.gov.uk/guidance/income-tax-when-you-rent-out-a-property-working-out-your-rental-income

140 https://www.moneyadviceservice.org.uk/en/articles/buy-to-let-mortgages

Thank You

It takes a village...to bring a book and a vision to life!

It all started with an email from journalist and author Tabi Jackson Gee who introduced me to Romilly Morgan, thanks Tabi!

I am so grateful to have found in Romilly the most brilliant sparring partner you could wish for. Romilly has been the best ambassador for this book and definitely understood the vision behind Vestpod. She pitched and commissioned the book, and we now share the mission to help us all get better with money. Thank you for challenging me, motivating me and giving this book all the care it deserves.

I am also very lucky to be surrounded by a team of fantastic women at Octopus: Leanne Bryan who spent days polishing and editing this book before going on maternity leave and Louise McKeever for taking over, Juliette Norsworthy who worked with Jeremy Tilson designing all these beautiful pages, Harriet Walker and Caro Parodi who are making sure this book is read and lands in the right hands, and Mireille Cassandra Harper who helped us with the editing.

You will have certainly bought this book because you loved the genius bright yellow neon cover, right? It could only have been designed by the extremely talented Juliette Norsworthy, with the assistance of Claire Huntley. Summarizing a book in a single visual requires a touch of magic. We can also all thank the brilliant Alix d'Anselme for making finance more fun by making these little smileys and creating a kick-ass visual identity for Vestpod.

Melissa Katsoulis is the passionate writer who gives me a hand with our weekly Vestpod newsletter and she also helped me to put some of my ideas on paper. Thank you for your positive attitude, good mood and perfect words. Veronica Morozova was also behind Vestpod in the early days, writing beautifully and finding ways to make money more visual on social media.

Thank you to my friend Claire Trachet, you have been here from the beginning, bouncing ideas and supporting me from chapter to chapter. Amanda Green, Ambre Soubiran, Aurélie Jaclot, Lottie Leefe, Hemant Bedarkar, Olivia Sibony, Rob Gill, Janet Knapton, Samantha Seaton, Scott Tindle and Vivien Adeosun, you dedicated hours to reading one or more chapters of this book, commented and shared your knowledge on those key topics. You are the experts in your fields and you also strive to make the world of finance a better place. Thank you for helping me make this book a million times better than the first draft.

THANK YOU

Thank you to my nine interviewees who agreed to share their £££ stories to empower others, you are an inspiration for all of us! Alice, Ambre, Bonnie, Claer, Helena, Jessica, Louise, Sarah and Romilly. A special thank you to Helena Morrissey who gave me a beautiful quote for the cover of this book: you are leading the way for so many of us.

Anji Clarke taught me more about publishing contracts and copyrights than I could have dreamt of. Pragmatic, open-minded and super knowledgeable, a massive thank you for getting us where we are today. A perfect early introduction by book lovers Justine Solomons and Hermione Ireland from Byte The Book. Christopher Dearie also gave me some very valuable advice.

There is a very special thank you for The Family, especially Alice Zagury, Oussama Ammar and Nicolas Colin who are helping me bring Vestpod to life and gave me the courage to transform a vision into a brand that keeps making more and more impact. Entrepreneurship is tough but it's amazing. That's also why I want to thank my tribe of start-up friends who I love and respect so much. Thank you to Google Campus for Mums program and NatWest Fintech Accelerator and the team at TeamSpirit for your support, and my friend Daniel Jung for sharing your office for months!

All this would not have been possible without YOU my dear Vestpod-ers. You come or speak at our events, read our newsletters and/or follow us on social media. And to those of you who have invited me to speak to your staff, community or have supported and encouraged Vestpod in any way. You are the reason Vestpod and this book exist! I am very lucky to be surrounded by supportive friends in London, Paris and beyond. To my Vestpod 'crew' (Amanda, Charlotte, Christina, Claire, Enrica and the team at Huckletree, Lottie, Nadia, Sarah, Victoria and Vivien), thank you for always giving me your time and energy whenever it is needed. I am so proud of what we are building together!

To my parents and my brother, you have supported me every step of the way and have encouraged me in everything that I do. Thank you for your unconditional love. A big thank you also to the rest of my family, especially the Morins, Victoria and Claire for your everlasting support and loving kindness.

Octave and Archibald my two baby boys, you are everything! Thank you Charly, you are my greatest supporter and champion and at times...my best critic :)

I am sure I am forgetting some of you, but you are definitely all a part of it... So a big thank you! This is book is all yours.

About the Author

Emilie Bellet is the founder and CEO of Vestpod. Having previously worked in private equity and at Lehman Brothers, she launched Vestpod as a way of empowering women financially and in order to start breaking the taboo around money. Vestpod is a digital platform with a popular weekly newsletter as well as personal finance workshops and networking events.

Emilie's writing has appeared in the *Financial Times* and Vestpod has been featured on TV and in publications such as *BBC News*, *Financial Times*, *Vogue*, *Stylist*, *Sheerluxe*, *Monocle* and *Courier Magazine*.

Emilie is a public speaker and co-authored *The WealthTech Book*. She has been included in the Women In FinTech Powerlist 2018 ('Rising Stars') and is a finalist in the 2018 Women in Finance Awards ('Disruptor of the year').

Emilie lives in London with her husband and two sons.

Join me: **vestpod.com**